King of the Sideshow!
WARD HALL

The Official Biography

by

Tim O'Brien

Casa Flamingo Literary Arts LLC
Nashville, TN

*"If I have told you once, I have told you a million times,
I Do Not Exaggerate."*

– Ward Hall

Ward Hall – King of the Sideshow!
Copyright 2014 © by Casa Flamingo Literary Arts, LLC. Printed and bound in Nashville, TN, U.S.A. All rights reserved. No part of this book may be reproduced or transmitted in any form or by any means, electronic or mechanical, without prior written permission from Tim O'Brien, CEO, Casa Flamingo Literary Arts, LLC at casabooks@casaflamingo.com. Reviewers may quote brief passages in a review to be printed in a magazine, newspaper or on the web, without written permission.

Paperback first printing, May 2014
ISBN: 978-0-9743324-2-0
Library of Congress Control Number (LCCN): 2014905690

Cover Photo and Design: Andrew Brusso
Page and Text Design: Jennifer Wright
Production Director: Jennifer Wright
Distribution: Ingram Global Publisher Services

For additional copies of *Ward Hall – King of the Sideshow!*, ask your local bookseller to order or visit www.casaflamingo.com or www.amazon.com. Distributed by Ingram and available throughout the U.S., Canada, Australia, United Kingdom, European Union and Russia.

"Prepare to be amazed! Within this fascinating history of one of the greatest entertainers alive, author Tim O'Brien artfully captures the spectacle of the great Ward Hall's sideshows over the course of two centuries. Told with all the substance of a scholarly text delightfully written for all audiences, readers will find themselves swept away like Dorothy Gale on a whirlwind tour of countless carnivals and circuses across an America filled with all the colors, marvels and oddities you'd expect of L. Frank Baum's Oz."
– Jacopo della Quercia, author of
The Great Abraham Lincoln Pocket Watch Conspiracy

"With a keen eye for the telling detail Tim O'Brien does a masterful job bringing to light one of the last great characters in sideshow history. The advance men may have brought in the crowds, but it was the intoxicating banter from men like Ward Hall that sold them the tickets!"
– Jamie MacVicar, author of
The Advance Man: A Journey Into the World of the Circus

"Many observers have tried to capture in words and pictures the fleeting, magnetic image of impresario Ward Hall. Few, if any, have gained greater insight to the highly unorthodox life and times of the King of the Sideshow than Tim O'Brien, a veteran scribe of the carnival and circus industry. To paraphrase Ward's clarion call to the would-be patrons of his kingdom of freaks and illusions, don't miss this big book!"
– Lane Talburt, Circus historian

"The United States of America gave the world Rock and Roll and The American Sideshow. Rock and Roll is Elvis Presley; The American Sideshow is Ward Hall. You know a lot about Elvis; You need to know more about Ward. This book is a great start."
– Penn Gillete (of Penn & Teller)

"I can think of no better person to chronicle the life and times of the last great sideshow impresario than Tim O'Brien. Besides being a magnificent writer, Tim has a deep understanding and appreciation of the world of the American sideshow. I truly enjoyed reading this book."
– Todd Robbins, Showman

"As an experienced writer of entertainment and amusement history, Tim O'Brien's direct path to the heart and soul of Ward Hall allows us to be exposed to the daily trials, tragedies and achievements of the showman that we have not seen or read before."
– Ralph D. Pierce, Robert L. Parkinson Library & Research Center, Circus World Museum

"Ward Hall: Once heard, never forgotten!"
– Johnny Meah, banner painter, veteran showman

"All right, roll up here. This is the one! You've heard about him and seen him on television, now's your chance to get the real story, right here, right now. He's Ward Hall, King of the Sideshow. He is real, live and on the inside. It's a story that will make you laugh, will make you smile and will fill you with wonder, surprise and astonishment. His is the world of freaks, geeks and human curiosity. You'll hear about the ups and downs of the greatest showman of our time.

"From humble beginnings he has risen to the top of his industry. He is the torchbearer of a magnificent corner of American popular entertainment. And now's your opportunity to take it all in, right here, right now. Just turn the page and away you go.

"But first a word of warning. Once you enter his world, you will never be the same. You are about to take a remarkable journey, and when finished you will look at reality through a new pair of eyes. Now's the time to go. Meet Ward Hall, King of the Sideshow, right here, right now.

"It's show time on the inside!"

– Todd Robbins

Table of Contents

For Ward: *Ward Hall – King of the Sideshow!* 1

Step Up a Little Closer: Meet Ward Hall 3

Why a Book on Ward Hall? 5

Sideshows: A Brief and Basic History 7

Chapter 1 1938: Prelude to Greatness 9
2 1930: The Show Begins.. 11
3 1946: Permission to Leave 17
4 Ventriloquism: Ward and His Dummies 21
5 Partnership: When Harry Met Ward 23
6 Fooling the Public: Blusters, Buncombes and Bombasts 29
7 Selling the Show: The Art of the Bally................................. 33
8 Visualizing the Show: Value of the Banner Line 39
9 Hitting the Boards: Ward Gets Theatrical Experience 43
10 Creative Showmanship: Ward Makes a Baby...................... 49
11 Ward Meets Pete: How a Dwarf Won the Heart of a King....... 63
12 House Guests: A Poem to Ward and Pete 69
13 A Society Circus: The Froman Brothers are Born 71
14 April 1960: First Time on Broadway 81
15 11/24/1964: Ward Suffers Tragic Loss in New York........... 97
16 Big Screen Action: Ward as a Celluloid Hero.................... 101
17 Act Needed: Knife Thrower, Please Apply 109
18 The Kudos: Awards, Prizes and Honors 127
19 Gibsonton: The Utopian Society of Carnies..................... 131
20 Landmark Cases: Oddities Vs. State of Florida................ 137
21 1971: Off to St. Thomas 141
22 Ringling is Calling: Ward and Chris Build a Super Show 149
23 Trouble in Mexico: Magic Show Goes South.................... 157
24 Punk Problems: Dead Babies Vs. State of Illinois.............. 163
25 Adding Oddities: A Small Woman and a Fat Man Sign Up... 167
26 The Smithsonian: Being Saluted as True Americana......... 171
27 Wondercade 1981: Big and Costly Show Premieres 181

28	So Few: Why have all the Sideshows Disappeared?	185
29	Focus for 1982: An Even Bigger Wondercade	193
30	1985: The Bankruptcy	199
31	The Musical is Alive: *Saigon Doll* Premieres in Florida	209
32	A Hallowed Venue: Ward Sings in Carnegie Hall	211
33	9/11/2001: "We Were Way too Close"	215
34	NYC 2011: To Lincoln Center and Beyond	223
35	Taboo Talk: Sexuality on the Midway	225
36	Here Come the Kids: New Generation Makes Its Move	229
37	Doing All Right, Thanks: Enjoying Life; Working a Little	233

The Blow-Off: Additional Stories for Only a Quarter 238

Say What? Jargon, Lingo, Definitions and Acronyms 240

Bibliography: Where it all Came From 243

Acknowledgements: Credits, Thanks and Kudos 246

About the Author 249

Index 250

For Ward:
Ward Hall - King of the Sideshow!

I first met Ward Hall and his partner Chris Christ in the late 1980s when I was senior editor of *Amusement Business,* a weekly publication of the outdoor entertainment industry. It was the successor of *Billboard* magazine, considered a bible of the industry by showmen dating back to 1894. As you read this chronicle of Ward and his associates, you'll see how important *Billboard* was to the development of the entire industry and how much all showmen, scattered throughout the country, used the magazine to keep abreast of the entire industry.

Through the years as I wrote about Ward and Chris and their sideshow operations I pestered him to let me write his biography. He always said, "Not yet." In 2013 at the age of 83 he consented. I spent many hours with them over the past 15 months, conducted many, many interviews and countless hours perusing just about everything ever written about them.

"But I digress" is one expression I heard a thousand times (oops, sorry, his aptitude for exaggeration rubbed off on me) during the year-long series of interviews. This man has so many stories that one reminds him of another and that one of another. One day, I got him on the phone and he started talking. I turned the recorder on, went out and mowed the lawn and came back and he was still talking.

When reading this tome and laughing at its anecdotes and marveling at the history of the industry, it's important to remember that most of this was told to me by Ward and other veteran show guys who have made their livings by exaggerating, telling small lies, and humbugging the public. Before you get upset or ecstatic with anything in this book – please remember the source!

Maybe he warned you himself when he told a reporter for the *St. Petersburg Times* in 2011 that, "One advantage of being so old is you can tell stories and write things and you're able to embellish things a little because the other people who were there are all dead. There's nobody to dispute what you say."

He promised to tell me the truth. The truth as he remembered it. It was a fun year.

Tim O'Brien
Author
April 2014

Step Up a Little Closer:
Meet Ward Hall

Ward Hall's title of King of the Sideshow! is not a new or recent act of coronation, and as the ruler of his own little world of misfits and human anomalies, Ward's title isn't self-awarded, but rather a judgment rendered by his peers. The year 2014 is the King's 70th year anniversary in show business.

Ward Hall ran across town and joined the circus for a part time gig in 1944 when he was a kid living in Colorado. A year later, as a 15-year-old 10th grade dropout, he ran away for good, joining the Dailey Bros. Circus. He never looked back. By 16 he was performing in a sideshow and by age 21, he owned a sideshow!

Today, 70 years later and countless circus and sideshow, vaudeville and burlesque house performances under his belt, Ward Hall is still in the business. He plans to retire when he reaches 100 so he can "see the world." Now 84, he is the undisputed King of the Sideshow.

"Ladies and gentlemen, boys and girls of all ages,
the man you are about to meet will astound and amaze you.
Welcome to the stage now Ward Hall, King of the Sideshow!"

Every king has to receive his crown from someone, and it appears Ward's title came from sideshow historian James Taylor, who in his first volume of *Shocked and Amazed! – On & Off the Midway* in 1995, called Ward the King of Sideshows. "I had never seen it before I did the story on Ward and I have never seen it used prior to 1995, so yes, I guess I am the one who came up with calling him king of the sideshows." No one refutes that moniker.

Ward has worked with monkey girls, several half-lady/half man attractions, numerous fat men, countless sword swallowers, fire eaters, several giants, huge snakes, immense rats and diminutive horses. He has mastered juggling, ventriloquism and the art of enticing thousands of curious onlookers to part with their money and go inside the tent of his world-famous sideshows.

Ward and Harry Leonard were partners for 19 years until Harry's death in 1964. During those years, they trekked the midways, the vaudeville houses and the variety theaters – any place that would book their acts. They owned their first sideshow together and had their first financial successes together.

In 1966, C.M. "Chris" Christ joined Ward's show full time, and by 1967, they were full partners and shared ownership of a respected 10-in-one sideshow. For nearly 50 years, Ward and Chris have owned and operated sideshows, animal shows, magic shows, and illusion shows with such fashionable names as Magic on Parade; Wondercade: Aquarama water circus; Gladiators vs. Mankillers wild animal show; World Attractions; Sky High Circus; the Wonder Circus; the Pygmy Village; and the World of Wonders. Ward has exhibited the world's smallest woman, the world's tallest giant, and employed Pete Terhurne, the mighty fire-eating dwarf for 55 years.

In addition to owning or co-owning sideshows and circuses, Ward has written four books, four musical stage productions, has appeared in seven movies and more than 100 videos and television specials, performed at Madison Square Garden and the Lincoln Center in New York City and has sung at Carnegie Hall. He is in the Hall of Fame of both the Outdoor Amusement Business Assoc. and the International Independent Showmen's Assoc. and is a member of the prestigious Circus Ring of Fame in Sarasota, Fla. Ward is the only person in all three of those esteemed halls of honor.

Ward has operated the sideshow for many big time big tops, including: Ringling Bros. and Barnum & Bailey Circus, the Toby Tyler Circus, the Al G. Kelly & Miller Bros. Circus, Circus Vargas (where he was part owner), Clyde Beatty-Cole Bros., and the E.K. Fernandez Circus.

In a *Chicago Tribune* story in 1994, reporter Ron Grossman drew a vivid word picture of the vagabond showman. "Ward Hall's traveling companions tend to be astoundingly short or hugely tall, mountainously fat or exquisitely thin. Some have lacked an extremity or two. A few have been missing all four." That pretty well sums up the long and strange life of Ward Hall.

Ward has the memory of an elephant, the exaggerative dialogue of a Ginsu Knife salesman and a sequined wardrobe that would have made Liberace turn his head. In this colossal world of thousands of showmen, none have proven themselves over the long term to be more successful, long-lasting or more popular than Ward Hall. He is the undisputed grand ole man of all showmen.

Why a Book on Ward Hall?
"Because he is an American Treasure"

When composer Jerome Kern was asked what he thought Irving Berlin's place in American music was, Kern replied, "Irving Berlin has no place in American music – he *is* American music." And that's how I feel about Ward Hall and the American sideshow. Ward Hall *is* the American sideshow.

Here is a man who truly is the world of the strange and the unusual, the bizarre and the unconventionally beautiful. He is the last of his breed. He is our link to a grand and glorious show business tradition that goes back 150 years to the days of P.T. Barnum. Ward has traveled thousands of miles and has literally talked millions of people into buying a ticket to see his shows. He has made and lost fortunes, but his real wealth is the love and respect he has earned during his many years on the road. He is the best of the best, and possibly the best that ever was.

Todd Robbins is flanked by Chris Christ, left, and Ward Hall, 2008.

I met Ward back in the 1980s and immediately became a devoted fan. I asked Ward if I could buy a copy of his two books. He grabbed a copy of each, autographed them and handed them to me and refused to take my money. "These are a small reward for the good work you have done out in Coney Island," was his comment. How could you not love a guy like that?

On another occasion Ward's sly humor came through. I had just met Penn & Teller. They had just seen a performance of mine, liked the cut of my jib and we became friends. Though I really didn't know them that well, they invited me to come with them to the Meadowlands Fair in New Jersey. One of the highlights we were all looking forward to was seeing Ward's World of Wonders sideshow.

As we rolled up to the bally stage, there was Ward in full bloom mesmerizing the tip. He spotted us, and without missing a beat he said, "One of the joys of traveling the country is seeing our wonderful friends. And it is even a greater pleasure when we our honored by the presence of friends that are well known and well respected. Ladies and gentlemen, it is my privilege to introduce to you – Mr. Todd Robbins!" Penn & Teller were rather startled by this, thinking they were the ones to be introduced. They turned slowly and shot me looks that seemed to say, "Who the hell are you?" How could you not love a guy like that?

Many memorable hours have been spent with Ward cutting up jackpots. Many happy minutes have been spent talking with him on the phone. In short, I am glad to have him as part of my life. I am a better man for having known him. And now, with the book you hold in your hands, you will have the pleasure of knowing him too.

Todd Robbins
Showman, Sideshow Entertainer, Playwright
March 2014

Sideshows:
A Brief and Basic History

Sideshow, as a term, originated in the circus where customers would walk the midway between the entrance to the circus lot and the "big top" tent (the main show) and pass all the shows located along the sides of that midway.

Sideshows truly exploded in popularity with the dawning of traveling carnivals in the decades spanning the 19th and 20th centuries. Carnivals were originally, with the exception of the handful of rides, food and games, grand showcases for shows of all kinds. A carnival that presented more shows than rides was the rule rather than the exception. Technically all shows on a circus or carnival outside of the big top and mechanical rides are considered sideshows and there have been a variety of offerings through the years. A partial list consists of:

- **Girl shows:** from reviews (high-end burlesque) to hootchie kootchies (low-end burlesque) to posing shows (performers posing in tights and appearing naked, recreating "great art") to nudist camps. The latter were in world's fairs more than carnivals.
- **10-in-ones** (10 acts in one show). Also called freak shows because of the human oddities they exhibited
- **AT shows** (athletic shows, usually wrestling)
- **Motordromes** (motorcycles racing around a vertical wooden drum)
- **Illusion and magic shows**
- **Wax shows** (wax museums under canvas)
- **Torture and crime shows** (with attractions just as you'd imagine)
- **Midget villages**

James Taylor hams it up with his hero, Ward Hall.

- **Baby shows** (usually pickled punks of both real fetuses and rubber dolls passed off as real)
- **Freak animal shows** (both live and taxidermied)
- **The world's smallest shows** (horse, woman, married couple, etc.)
- **And of course, the world's largest shows** (horse, pig, rat, man, etc.)

If it could gather a paying audience, it would become a show. By its golden age between the World Wars, 1917 to 1939, there were hundreds of sideshows in the numerous carnivals in addition to the sideshows on circuses traversing the United States. Additionally, variety talent worked the novelty end of the dying vaudeville era, the assorted resort locations/amusements parks (the most prominent – but not the only one – being Coney Island); the last of the dime museums, including the one-off "store shows" (store fronts rented for short-term shows between other engagements) and any other venues where performers could make the money.

It's from this era that we get the vast majority of the sideshow performers remembered today, including: the conjoined twin Hilton Sisters; half-people Johnny Eck and Jeanie Tomaini; monkey girl Percilla Bejano; Eko & Iko, the Men from Mars; Sealo the Sealboy (Stanley Barent); Viking giant Johann Petursson; the midget Doll Family: and mule-faced woman Grace McDaniel; among many others. You will come to know many of them during your journey through this book.

Interest in the weird, the strange, the bizarre, the odd and the unusual – being, at core, what makes us human – has never flagged. Meaning that the sideshow hasn't lessened in importance at all: It's part of all of us. And it's everywhere, whether it's acknowledged as such or not.

James Taylor
Sideshow Historian
Publisher of *Shocked & Amazed!*
March 2014

Editor's Note:
This book contains many strange and somewhat mysterious words and phrases not commonly known outside of the circus, carnival and sideshow industries. Many of them are totally strange words. Some of them are just strange uses of words we already know. To help our readers along, we have created a special chapter starting on page 240, "Jargon, Lingo, Definitions and Acronyms," that will help you follow along and better understand this journey.

1938:
Prelude to Greatness

CHAPTER 1

The circus had come to town.

The little boy tugged at his mother's sleeve as they walked toward the big top of the Lewis Bros. Circus, in Kankakee, Ill. His mother, Opal, held free passes to the circus and, unbeknownst to the little 8-year-old, he was on his way to see a sight that would set him on course for the rest of his life.

A booming voice caught his attention and as he drew closer, not only could he hear the man on the small stage much clearer, he was awed by the colorful and somewhat bizarre paintings on the canvas banners at the front of the tent. It was the first sideshow he had ever seen.

Totally mesmerized by the sounds and color, he pulled away from his mother, ran ahead, stopped, watched, and witnessed his first bally, a free show presented outside a paid sideshow to attract a crowd of potential customers. It was at that moment he first became fascinated by the sights and sounds that both blessed and cursed him through the years.

As his soul filled with inspiration and wonderment for what he was seeing, the history of the sideshow industry was set in motion, although no one could have possibly realized it at that time. It was an epochal moment for the young man.

A stranger standing in front of the outdoor platform looked down on him and asked, "Do you want to see the sideshow?" The boy responded that he had no money and the man handed him a dime, remarking that he should, "Go take a look."

Thanks to the kindness of that stranger in Kankakee that warm summer's eve, Ward Hall's fate was changed and a showman was born. He was destined to become one of the most dominant nomadic entertainment entrepreneurs in the history of outdoor entertainment in America.

Six years after seeing his first sideshow, Ward had dropped out of school, joined a circus and was eating fire, juggling and serving as a sideshow magician. A year after that, he was managing a circus sideshow. Within 20 years he would be called the best talker ever in sideshow history. Fifty years later he would be tagged as a sideshow impresario, and 70 years later, he would be known as "Ward Hall – King of the Sideshow."

The path to this acclaim was not an easy one, especially during his youth. Ward had little in common with other kids, made few childhood friends and felt like a loner. Instead of normal childhood activities he preferred visiting theaters and live performances by himself. Then at home, he would spend hours honing the skills of the entertainers he had just seen perform.

His parents' separation when he was seven created an unstable family environment and not something in which he trusted. He moved several times and when he was in one place among others his own age, he never felt like he was one of them.

In 1946, just before his 16th birthday, he found his first true home where he reveled – the circus. It felt good, and much like the diverse group of workers and performers he would employ and care for later in life, Ward had found his new home and a new family on the road. It was the first time he fitted in and he flourished.

This is his story.

1930:
The Show Begins

CHAPTER 2

The first time the world heard Ward Hall's harmonious and vociferous voice was just after 10 p.m. on June 21, 1930. It was a dark, hot and steamy night in Trenton, Neb., when Ward was born to Glen and Opal Hall in a little white frame house halfway up the hill on Main Street. Four years earlier, Opal had given birth to Glenna, and tonight, when the village physician, Dr. Prest, reported with a smile that the newborn was a boy, the family rejoiced. Opal and Glen had married five years earlier in Trenton.

In late summer 1935, six-year old Ward was first introduced to the outdoor amusement industry when he attended the annual Indian Pow Wow in Trenton. Elite Exposition Shows provided the entertainment that included a small carnival of five or six rides and a large variety show. Ward's father was on the committee sponsoring the event, and that provided Ward with an endless number of free tickets for all the rides and attractions.

At age 6, his first ever spin on a carnival ride was on a small merry-go-round. He said the only feeling he can remember from that first night on a midway is happiness. "I was very gleeful," he recalls. Ward said he remembers one of the most fascinating things about that night was that it was the first time he had ever seen a black man, a carnival employee who became ingrained in Ward's mind for two reasons. He had a wooden peg leg AND he was black. He had seen neither before.

Glen, who had mobility problems due to childhood

Ward's father, Glen Hall, 1907.

polio, spent a great deal of time on the midway and in the cookhouse when the carnival came to town, enjoying a friendship he had with its owners, Ma and Pa Frear, who several years later would own a complete carnival on which Ward would book his first independent sideshow. The black man Ward saw that night was the first of many diverse and "different" individuals he would see and work with in the future. It became his human nature to not only accept but to seek out and embrace those who were different.

Ward also grew to respect and somewhat fear water at a young age while living in Trenton. When he was five, the nearby Republican River overflowed and flooded the lower parts of town. Luckily when his grandfather built the house in which Ward was born, he chose a location high on the hill for that very reason: to avoid flood waters. Ward's great-grandfather had drowned in a flood and the family was vigilant of rising waters. Ward would nearly drown at one point in his life because that fear kept him from taking swimming lessons.

Ward's sister, Glenna.

"That flood is one of my first memories," said Ward. "I recall standing on the porch and looking down the hill at the water in the streets and the people trying to get out of it. My mother said we had 109 people staying with us until they could get into their own homes again." A baby was born in Ward's room that night, his mother told him years later.

Three major floods, this being the first, would visit Ward through the years, costing him thousands of dollars in repair and replacement costs to his sideshow equipment. He would find that floods, mud, wind and fire were the bane of every traveling circus, carnival and sideshow.

His parents separated in the spring of 1938 and Ward moved to Kankakee, Ill., with his mother and his sister. It was there he saw the Barnett Bros. Circus that featured Lee Powell as The Lone Ranger. More importantly, it was on that show that he saw his first sideshow.

In 1940, his father took Ward (who often refers to this particular move as an abduction) back to Trenton where he lived with his aunt, Alda Adams. It was there he was exposed to a wide variety of art and live entertainment. She was a piano teacher and introduced Ward to the

1930: The Show Begins

Ward at age 12 in 1942.

pleasures and creativity of music, passions he would use in many ways as an adult when he wrote his stage musicals and scored his big variety shows. Ward likes to say he comes from cultured folk. His mother sang and played organ in the church and his father appreciated good music and enjoyed reading the classics. His grandmother was a musician and his grandfather was a successful miner who went to Colorado and owned several mines, only to lose his fortune during the Depression.

In 1943 Ward and his father left Trenton and moved to Denver, Colo., where he was exposed to yet another form of show business, musical tab shows, which played as many as eight shows a day at the Orpheum

Theater. Tab shows, short for tabloid musical revues, are musical and variety presentations less than 60 minutes in length. Ward explains: "If a show lasted 60 minutes or more, it was required to carry union stagehands, so to save money, these shows would make sure they never lasted more than 60 minutes, but they would perform many shows each day."

It was in Denver where he discovered the requisite tool used by the world's best showmen, the *Billboard*, a weekly magazine that by then covered all facets of entertainment. He would save his allowance and spend 25-cents for the magazine each week. If he didn't have the money, he would read it at the library. It was on those pages he learned of the vast expanse of entertainment and excitement that awaited him in the "real" world.

On weekends while in junior high, he would pack his lunch and tuck the latest edition of *Billboard* under his arm and head to the Orpheum where one ticket would allow him to stay as long as he wished. He would usually stay the entire day and it wasn't uncommon for him to see eight shows, reading his magazine between performances. It was at the Orpheum he saw the famous comedy magician, Carl Ballentine. After watching him all day, Ward was able to learn the show's narrative by heart. He took notes and observed, went home and practiced and then went back for another full day of observation later that week. By the end of that year, he was able to duplicate Ballantine's act.

Ward's aunt Alda, 1940.

"Unfortunately, I never met Carl Ballantine to thank him for many hours of happiness in a rather sad and uncomfortable school year," said Ward. One of the mandatory courses he took while at Morey Junior High School was the Basics of Printing, where one of his assignments was to create and print a business card. He created one for himself.

"The Great Hall, Circus Preformer," the card read. "I flunked the assignment because I misspelled performer," he laughs. "I had no need for a card, except to fulfill my ego, which it did."

While other young lads of his age were roughing it up on the streets, playing baseball or other sports, Ward remained a loner and discovered vaudeville at the Tabor Theater and stock variety entertainment at the Isis Theater. He saw the Cole Bros. Circus and about a month later, the Russell Bros. Circus as each came

1930: The Show Begins

through town. "All this, plus Lakeside and Elitch Gardens amusement parks, and Denver was a heaven on earth for a 13-year-old boy," Ward said. During those formative years Ward had been bitten badly by the show bizz bug.

His first, albeit short, step into the show business realm was in 1944 when he worked for a few days as a prop man when the Cole Bros. Circus played Denver. It was a strenuous job for a 14-year-old but he loved it, made $2 a day and got to eat with everyone else in the cookhouse. When the circus left town, Ward went back to his first year at East High School but dropped out after one month.

In April 1945 he landed another short-time job, this time as a clown with the short-lived Larry Sunbrock's Super Colossal Wild West Show and Hollywood Thrill Show. Sunbrock had listed some of the biggest names in the business as performers when, in actuality, none of them were booked. He was arrested for false advertising and the show folded. Ward's clown career lasted less than a week. "The show's performance was pretty bad and I was the worst clown ever to put on make-up. I was atrocious," he admits.

Ward's tenacity prevailed! After seeing an advertisement in *Billboard* in spring 1945, he wrote to the Al G. Kelly & Miller Bros. Circus applying for a position as a clown and was sent back a contract to join the show. An excited Ward was shut down quickly by his father who refused to let him go and Ward had to be content for a little bit longer staying away from the life for which he felt destined. There were no circuses booked for Denver that summer on which to work, so he took a summer job as a bingo caller at the city's Lakeside Amusement Park for 40-cents an hour.

After he completed his bingo gig each night, around 10, he would walk over to the open ballroom and camp out on a bench for several hours listening to the big bands of the era. To this day, music of that era dominates the soundtrack of Ward's life. That same summer, the Dailey Bros. Circus played Boulder. Ward asked for the day off from his bingo job and, when they wouldn't give it to him, he quit and rode the Greyhound bus the 26 miles to Boulder.

When he arrived on the lot, Bill Curtis, the show's lot man,

Dailey Bros. Circus oddities museum entrance, 1946.

asked Ward if he would like to get in free in exchange for helping put up the sideshow tent. He did, and afterward Ward informed Curtis that he wanted to stay with the show, help tear down later that night, and join them on the road. They shook on it and Curtis showed Ward the way to the cookhouse, where he enjoyed a hearty meal. After enjoying the afternoon show and part of the evening performance, he slipped quietly into the night to catch the 9 p.m. bus back to Denver.

Another person he met that day was Milt Robbins, who was to become Ward's lifetime friend and the man who would, the following year, give Ward his first big break in the business. Meeting Robbins, and witnessing the excitement that day, made Ward more determined than ever to become a circus performer.

In addition to his father, one major barrier stood in his way of a life in the circus. He knew nothing about the circus arts. He started schooling himself as soon as he got home that night from Boulder. "With some pain by trial and error, and with the aid of library books, I tried to teach myself how to eat fire and do magic tricks," he said, noting that he was much better learning magic than eating fire. He doesn't remember the details of quitting school except, "One day I just didn't go back." He rationalized that he might as well quit because the teachers weren't teaching him what he needed – circus knowledge. Always a loner, he had no friends to confide in or to talk about quitting. He just did.

His father didn't mind that Ward wasn't in school. His son could now get a full time job and forget that crazy circus crap and start earning money to help the family. Looking back, Ward doesn't remember school officials ever following up on his absence. "That was during the war and many of the child labor laws were abolished if the job was essential to the war effort. I guess they felt whatever job I had was essential because it freed up another man to go fight in the war."

His father was by then working on the Denver & Salt Lake Railroad and was able to get Ward a job washing the exterior of passenger train cars. That was okay during the summer, but as fall and winter approached, that water got colder and colder. He ended up getting sick and never returned to that job. By the time he got well, his father had moved over to the Colorado and Southern Railroad as the commissary chief and secured Ward a job as a waiter in the employee mess hall. His father "took control" of his wages but Ward was given enough to keep buying *Billboard* and attend live variety shows in Denver.

Glen lost his job on the railroad, and ironically, if he had not been laid off, Ward may never have received "permission" to run away and join the circus.

1946:
Permission to Leave

CHAPTER 3

"My job was still okay, but he had me quit because he was mad at the railroad for laying him off," Ward recalls. "With both of us out of work, he reluctantly agreed to let me find a job with a circus." It was spring 1946, Ward was 15, and he was prepared, or at least he thought he was, when a *Billboard* ad caught his attention. Dailey Bros. Circus, the same show he had visited in Boulder the prior summer, was looking for a magician and fire eater. He didn't know how to do either very well. He didn't tell them he was only 15, and he didn't have a plan. He just knew he had to join the show at that time. Ward responded to Milt Robbins asking for the job, and soon a telegram arrived that read:

Salary OK.
Show opens April 1. Join anytime.
Winter Quarters, Gonzales, Texas.
– Milt Robbins, Show Manager

Ward daringly told his father that he was going to leave and take the job with the circus. His father didn't argue, telling Ward that he would get the circus out of his system and be "back in two weeks." Ward laughs. "They are still waiting for me."

Using what he had left of his last paycheck from the railroad to buy a $51.50 bus ticket, he caught up with Dailey Bros., still at its winter quarters in Central Texas. He borrowed his uncle's steamer trunk, packed it with his one suit, a few other pieces of clothing and a small collection of homemade magic tricks. The day he climbed off the bus in Gonzales, Ward recalls thinking that at that point, he "was beginning the second part of my life. On that momentous day, my childhood ended." It was March 27, 1946 – 116 days before his 16th birthday.

Anxious to get on with his life, he arrived in Gonzales more than two weeks early. Instead of the circus bosses sending him home, he was put to task on several small projects. He slept in a small shed along with sideshow equipment that would be traveling with the show that year. Ward's pay was $30 a week with cookhouse privileges, which meant he could eat at the official circus cookhouse and share a berth on Car 79 of the circus train when the show hit the road. While new to the circus itself, he had a pretty good idea of what to expect before he stepped off that bus, having been reading news and stories about the big top in *Billboard* for years.

There were 21 other teens working on Dailey Bros. when he joined. "We were all very close in age and we were all ready to learn and grow up on the circus," he said. One of those 22 teens was a 14-year-old African-American boy named Richard Penniman who wanted to sing and dance in the jig-show band. But he wanted to play a new type of music, rock and roll, and the band leader would not hear of it. Instead, the kid, who all the other kids called "tootie fruity" because of his effeminate and flamboyant ways, went to work in the big top. He left mid-way through the season and went to King Bros. Circus, then on to a couple different shows before Ward lost track of him. Forty years later, the same kid, who had risen to stardom using the stage name Little Richard, was inducted into the Rock and Roll Hall of Fame. His first hit, which he co-wrote and which charted in 1956, was Tutti-Frutti.

Milt Robbins on the left, and Ward on the right on the Dailey Bros. bally stage, 1946.

It didn't take Ward long to be noticed on the lot, but not necessarily in an endearing way. On his second day, he decided to further educate himself on fire eating, having never truly learned the skill. In his letter to Robbins, Ward claimed he could eat fire, so he thought he had better learn as soon as possible. On his first attempt he badly scorched his lips, turned around in pain, kicked over the fuel can and caught the shed on fire. Needless to say, a good eye was kept on this aggressive but polite newcomer to the business from that point on.

Ward moved into the men's dormitory where he spent only a few nights. "Having been a loner all my life, I was not knowledgeable on how men act after drinking large quantities of alcohol, so I discovered an abandoned circus wagon which became my living quarters until we moved onto the train." Charlie Ali, the sideshow boss canvas man on Dailey Bros. took a liking to the new kid during those first several weeks and taught him the proper way to eat fire, a skill he would use the rest of his life.

1946: Permission to Leave

Milt Robbins, son of Frank A. Robbins who had toured the Frank A. Robbins Circus in the late 1800s and early 1900s, obviously had seen the potential in the young Ward and didn't fire him for causing the shed fire or for exaggerating how much magic and fire eating he already knew. In fact, Robbins, a magician himself, in addition to being the sideshow's manager, loaned Ward his personal magic props and taught him how to use them. "Milt had a nice way about him and I am sure he realized immediately that I was not a performer, just a punk kid who lied to get the job," said Ward, noting that Robbins was the "greatest influence" during his early development.

Ward would later repay Robbins' early kindness. In the mid-1970s, when Ward had the contract to produce the sideshow at Ringling Bros. and Barnum & Bailey Circus World theme park in Florida, it was Milt Robbins who Ward chose to manage it. After leaving Circus World, Robbins went on the road for Ward and his partner Chris, running various shows, including a baby show, a pickled tiger shark show and a wax museum. "By this time, my friend and mentor Milt was getting old, but he was still good and I totally trusted him."

During his later years, Robbins gave Ward a box with 52 items inside, including a lifetime pass to Barnum & Bailey Circus, letters from James Bailey and correspondence with all five Ringling brothers. "I treasured that box and had copies made of each of the items," he said. "When Milt died, I sold the contents to a circus fan for $1,300 and gave the money to Milt's wife Ena. "She carried his cremains around in her purse and when she felt the time was right, she sprinkled them in a center ring of a circus, of course unbeknownst to the show's owner."

One afternoon that first summer, Ward was helping out as part of the bally show next to Robbins when he was handed the microphone and told to take over talking, something that he had never done before. "I didn't know what to say, so I looked over at Norma (Davenport, the daughter of circus owners Ben and Eve Davenport) who was selling tickets and she hollered at me, 'Tell 'em about the painted-face mandrill.' Well I did that and then I looked back at Norma and she would tell me what to say next," Ward laughed. "That's how I made my first official opening bally of my career."

It was with Dailey Bros. that Ward first became aware of the importance of advance men and press agents. Advance men post the advertising posters weeks before scheduled performances letting everyone know the circus is on its way, and once the circus is in town, press agents create publicity stunts and activities that let everyone know the circus has arrived.

He remembers in 1948 that the Native American Sugar Brown family joined the show. When the train arrived in town, all members of the family would put on their feathered bonnets and full Indian garb and be taken downtown where they all went their separate ways. Each one would go to a different restaurant for breakfast and then would walk around and shop, talk to people and go in and out of the various stores. "It didn't take long for the entire town to realize that the circus had arrived," Ward said. "It was brilliant."

The sideshow became Ward's passion, but he never lost the desire to "perform in the big top." With no athletic talent and unable to learn the type of skills needed to perform in the circus he soon realized that being a center ring performer was probably never going to happen. However, being in the sideshow allowed him to be close to the big top, and occasionally it allowed him to be in the big top.

Sideshows turned out to be the best fit for him. "What kept me interested in sideshows in the very beginning were the people. They were so kind and so nice to me," Ward said. "Sideshows didn't have the jealousies, dissatisfaction or the dissention that I saw among the performers in the big top."

"Join the Circus Like You Wanted to When You Were a Kid"

Ward calls that first year on the road with the Dailey Bros. Circus the "happiest year of my life." He still looks fondly back at that year. "I've been very happy at times in my life and have had loads of great opportunities, but I still look back at that initial feeling of freedom, as the happiest time of my life," Ward said, noting that he wasn't scared or concerned about his future for a minute. "I was finally able to escape my father's domination and meet people who I liked and who I identified with. I felt at home."

The three-and-a-half years he spent with Dailey Bros. were the ultimate in on-the-job training. Nary a day went by that he didn't learn something new from his colleagues. Milt Robbins taught Ward sideshow banter and guided him in his magic training.

Dave Curtis, the supervisor of ushers for the big top as well as the featured magician, who had shown Ward around when he visited Boulder the year before, taught Ward how to make sales pitches during his magic presentations. Ward was able to make extra money right from the start by selling magic tricks that he created himself. Also, Robbins' wife Ena, "helped straighten out my wardrobe and consoled me through some tough times."

Charlie Ali, who had taught him to eat fire, "taught me how to handle the various pieces of equipment while his wife Martha got me over a fear of snakes." Millie Curtis taught him to "lecture" and Floyd Arnold taught him to play music on old bottles. He learned the art of laying out a lot, of driving stakes and the importance of good canvas.

Millie Curtis was also Ward's personal banker. She made sure he learned the necessity of saving money during the short summer season because when the season ended, there would be no income the following season. Ward trusted her with his savings while he was with Dailey Bros.

Ventriloquism:
Ward and His Dummies

CHAPTER 4

Ventriloquism, as most know, is an act in which a person changes his or her voice so that it appears it is coming from elsewhere, usually from a "dummy" character. Within the industry, it is known as a vent act. The act of "throwing one's voice," was once thought of as a sort of witchcraft. It emerged as a form of entertainment in the mid-18th century and reached its peak in the U.S. as a popular featured act in vaudeville. Edgar Bergen popularized comedic ventriloquism and along with his figures, Charlie McCarthy and Mortimer Snerd, hosted a very popular radio program from 1937 to 1956.

Listening to Bergen on the radio and watching other ventriloquists perform on stage solidified Ward's interest in the art, and once he got his first dummy, he became proficient quite quickly.

18-year-old Ward with his first Perky Perkins, 1948.

Ward saw the opportunity to learn the art when he spotted an ad in *Billboard* for a ventriloquist dummy for $35, more than a week's pay at that time. He ordered it and when it arrived about three weeks later, he took it to show Gene Mercer, the ventriloquist on the show. Mercer liked it and offered Ward $35 for it. As part of the deal, Mercer would work with Ward and teach him the act, plus, Ward could have Mercer's old figure.

Several weeks later Mercer decided to leave the show, vowing that he would never do ventriloquism again. He sold the dummy back to Ward for $35 and left. Ward now had two dummies and a skill base on which to grow. He would soon perfect the act and would perform it hundreds of times during his career – the most recent being the Seminar of the Sideshow Arts, a symposium he and his partner Chris presented in Tampa, on Feb. 2, 2014.

He always treated what he calls his "Two-headed Dummy Boys" well and purchased several more as he developed his act. In March 2013, he sent two of his 12 figures, Perky and Homo the Brave – The Queer Indian Boy, off to the vent hospital for a total refurbishment with the hopes that he would be able to perform more shows in the future. By the amount of applause he received in Tampa during his 2014 outing, he still "has it."

"Vent acts, if done properly, could still be very popular today," Ward believes. "There needs to be a fun interaction between the dummy and the ventriloquist, and of course, there can't be any visible mouth movement."

Ward said he always liked the vent act because all you have to do is "pick up the dummy and start working" without all the prep work that is involved in magic acts. A vent act also offers flexibility. "With just a couple of figures, you can play any type of spot and fit into any show."

Ward's long time dummy character, Perky Perkins, has been with him since the late 1940s and is still his favorite. "He is a smart-ass little boy who talks back to me in the family show we do. For the sideshow, we get a little more edgy with more of an adult angle to it, but we don't use dirty language." The physical character of Perky has been updated over the years, but the personality and the shtick have remained the same.

35-year-old Ward with his updated Perky Perkins, 1965.

Today, the act that gets the biggest response is when he dusts off Homo the Brave - the Queer Indian Boy. The act is old time burlesque comedy at its best with a large dose of double entendre. "The edgy humor in the act is what is not said," Ward noted. "We don't cuss, we don't use sexual language and we don't talk dirty. But it is a very sexual, somewhat dirty comedic exchange."

By the way, the fear of ventriloquist's dummies is called automatonophobia.

Partnership:
When Harry Met Ward

CHAPTER 5

Dailey Bros. was a 20-car railroad circus in 1946, Ward's first year on the road. He looks back and remembers that "most everyone had a great time that year," including himself, even though sleeping berths were a bit crowded. Since he was the new kid, he got the top-level berth, the one with no window, and he had to share it with several others during that first year with the show. His first berth mate was Rex "Americo" Carson, an 82-year old anatomical wonder who could collapse his stomach so you could see the front side of his back bone. The last of several bunk mates that year was a 15-year-old novice clown. Only department heads had single berths, he discovered.

During September of that first year on the road with Dailey Bros., Ward met a congenial knife thrower named Harry Leonard, a veteran showman 27 years his senior. When the show on which Harry had worked closed for the season, he came over to spend the rest of the tour with the Dailey Bros. show.

Ward and Harry hit it off, became partners and were inseparable for the next 19 years, until Harry's death on Nov. 24, 1964. Harry was not ambitious nor did he aspire to greatness, said Ward. He was a good sideshow man, but he wasn't interested in owning or managing a sideshow. Ward had enough ambition for the two. Shortly after arriving on the Dailey Bros. lot, Harry asked Ward to be the target for his knife-throwing act for a couple shows. That couple of shows turned into a 17-year stint as Harry's target.

When that first season came to a close and the train came to a stop back in Gonzales, at winter quarters, Ward was dismayed to see his father standing there waiting for the train. "He no doubt thought I would have some money saved that would help him through the winter and I had no intention of giving him a penny or of going back to Denver with him," Ward said.

Instead, Ward and Harry spent six weeks in San Antonio with Ray Marsh Brydon's "Believe It or Not" store-front sideshow where Ward performed a vent act and served as a target for Harry's knife-throwing act.

Born Harry Leonard Gottsacker in 1903 in Sheboygan, Wisc., Harry was a slender, mild-mannered performer. During his career, he performed as a knife thrower, trapeze artist, a dramatic player, a comedian and

Harry Leonard and Ward Hall, 1957.

a character actor in several films. His Punch and Judy puppet act was second to none at the time.

During his life, Harry played both the sideshow stage and the big top, spending the 10 years before joining up with Dailey Bros. working within the Johnny Bejano sideshow operation. He also appeared as a member of several touring stage companies and, with Ward, he appeared for 17 years during the off-season in numerous touring revues, most notably their own Broadway Varieties, in which they re-packaged their sideshow skills into theatrical presentations.

By 1947, his second summer on the road, Ward had expanded his performance capacity by perfecting his juggling and once the circus closed for the season in the fall, he and Harry joined Woods Famous Show in Texas. There they shared the spotlight with Bryan and Billie Woods, 40 trained monkeys, and numerous dogs and ponies.

Ward remained busy on stage performing his vent act, performing magic, eating fire, and playing water-filled musical whiskey bottles. Harry performed a magic show, a Punch and Judy, and finished up the set with his knife throwing act. For years, *Punch and Judy,* a classic puppet act with Mr. Punch as the central figure, was considered a top draw throughout the world and hundreds of puppeteers advertised that they performed the act.

With the Wood's family, Ward and Harry played three-night stands in villages and small towns not large enough for a movie theater, so each night a different movie was offered under the big top. Then when the movie was over, the audience was ushered out to buy another ticket to return to watch the live show, which was different on each of the three nights. Harry and Ward were also required to help set up the tent and then tear it down, load it and get it to the next town. In February 1948, growing tired of the small crowds that came with those small towns and not having seen a payday yet, he and Harry jumped to the Rogers Bros. Circus.

As a "proud" 17-year-old, Ward talked the front and then quickly assumed the sideshow manager's position when the show's regular manager was fired due to excessive drinking. By all rights, Harry should have gotten the job because of his age and experience, but he wanted nothing to do with management, so it was given to Ward. The arrangement worked for a short time until the others on the show started to resent the "kid" for running the show and things started to get tense. Ward turned once again to *Billboard.* Thanks to the information gleaned from the magazine, the two decided to leave the circus environs and try their luck on their first carnival gig, Frear's United Shows, as sideshow managers and performers. Ma and Pa Frear, owners of the carnival, had been friends of Ward's father when they ran the cookhouse at the Trenton's Massacre Canyon Indian Pow Wow, the first show Ward attended, in the early 1930s.

The Frear family had built a beautiful new sideshow and was in search for someone to operate it. Ward and Harry took over the new equipment and had the responsibility to create and present a profitable show. An ad in *Billboard* recruited several acts, including "Diane the Human Hermaphrodite Double-sexed Wonder." While some midway hermaphrodites were the real thing, most were total gaffs, humans dressed up to look like they were of both sexes.

When not performing, Diane De Elgar was actually drag queen George Searles. She became good friends with Harry and Ward and was a great attraction for the sideshow. She remained with them off and on through the early 1960s. As any sideshow operator of the times will acknowledge, sexual bizarreness sells tickets. A totally exaggerated bally helped:

> "What you are about to see is not a half-man/half-woman. Because Diane is all woman and Diane is all man. Diane could dress legally as a man or as a woman. Diane could be the mother or the father of children. Diane is a true living hermaphrodite, a person who possesses the sexual organs of a male and a female. She prefers the female part of her life the most. She is married with two children, a perfectly normal boy and a girl.
>
> "Today, you are invited to come into our show and once in there you will be invited into Diane's own private theater where, away from the eyes of the children, the adults will see Diane as she exposes to you that she has the organs of both male and female on her body. If you do not see Diane as I tell you, I will apologize to you for taking up your time, give you your money back, plus a crisp $100 bill."

Standing next to Ward on the bally was Diane, who would then take the microphone:

> "In a clean, moral, refined manner I will expose my body to you and you will see for yourself."

Diane always wore beautiful gowns and would carry a fan. Ward notes that the cost to enter Diane's "private theater" was usually priced twice, sometimes more, than what the sideshow entrance fee was. "We were getting 50-cents admission at that time and in certain areas, we were able to charge an additional $1 to $1.50 more for Diane's private show." Those extra shows inside the sideshow tent were called the "blow-off" attraction, or the "annex" attraction and the star of those attractions usually received the highest percentage of the additional fee.

Hermaphrodite shows, also known as half-and-half shows, appeared on most sideshows up to the mid to late 1950s. By 1960, they were illegal in most states. Ward employed a number of them through the years. Francis Doran, a half-and-half who went by the name of The Original Maxine, joined Ward but only stayed a few weeks in the early 1950s, and in 1959 in Valdosta, Ga., Bertie Lupage walked up to Ward asking for a job, Ward dressed him up and presented him as a half-and-half, calling him "my mother" in the bally.

As a twist on the theme in 1955, Charlie Hunter was the blow-off, performing as Charlotte the Gorilla Girl. She was one-third man, one-third woman, one-third gorilla. Ward recalls that Hunter, out of drag, "looked like a lawyer."

When states started closing down the hermaphrodite shows, Searles became magician George Val George. While not performing the half-and-half act anymore, he was still working as a talker and lecturer with Ward and Harry. "One day I asked George why he never stayed at the same hotels the rest of us did," Ward recalls. "He told me that he needed to be alone because he spent his off time practicing magic. It turns out he had 20 doves that he was using in the act he was preparing and they made so much noise cooing, he had to find a cheaper motel that didn't care if he had all those birds." At the end of the 1961 season, George Val George moved to Las Vegas where he had a successful magic show for many years.

Hall and Leonard Show, 1954. From left, Ward, Jan Del Rio, Diane De Elgar, Frank Donnell, Pete Terhurne, and Harry Leonard.

STRANGEST SHOW ON EARTH

Fooling the Public:
Blusters, Buncombes and Bombasts

CHAPTER 6

It was probably P.T. Barnum who nationalized the art of hokum, bluster, bombasts and buncombes. But with all of the showmen throughout history trying to separate a penny from a patron, it is hard to trace back who the first was to exaggerate the importance of what they were selling! The showmen could justify, as Ward has, that exaggerating is not really cheating – it's just stretching the truth and perhaps not being totally honest. The fat girls were never as fat and the giant was never as tall as the colorful bally promised.

> "This is the world's largest fairground show where you are going to see the strangest people in the world alive – created by magic, illusion and legerdemain."

Such is the beginning of nearly every bally Ward has ever made, boasting the superlatives while creating a sly disclaimer. He told them it was magic, that it was illusion and that it was legerdemain. But how many midway patrons really understand what legerdemain is?

"I didn't when I first started," admits Ward. People only hear the superlatives and very rarely the disclaimer. When a magician waves his hand over a hat and pulls out a rabbit, he is performing an act of legerdemain, the skillful use of his hands as trickery.

> "Inside, you are going to see the strangest anthropomorphic human freaks that the world has ever known."

Anthropomorphic? In loose terms, it means "manufactured to resemble humans." Ward loves the word. "When I first heard it and learned what it meant, I remember thinking that it was the greatest word ever created – especially for the sideshow business."

Ward has found that if you use those four words – anthropomorphic, legerdemain, magic, and illusion in a bally, few can legitimately call you out on it. "I'm telling the people up front but they don't listen to the fine print," Ward said. "You humbug people and tell them what they want to hear, but you word it in a way that you aren't telling them something that makes them not want to see it."

The claim that a woman with two heads, or a headless woman, is "alive" on the inside is an outrageous claim, but a good talker, using the disclaimer about the "created by magic illusion" can goad the crowd to come in and see for themselves. "It comes to a point where they know they can't believe you but they want to see how the claims I make might be true," Ward adds.

> *"You are going to see here today, from Hamburg, Germany, Vena Hess – a woman who is alive, 26 years of age, who had a horrific automobile accident and was completely decapitated. Through the miracle of modern medicine, the doctors were able to keep her body alive. Today, you will see a girl alive who has no head – a living body. When you come in, you will be invited to walk right up to the headless girl, extend your hand out to her and she will reach out to you. She has no eyes, no nose, and no ears. She can't see you. She can't hear you. She can't smell you. But somehow she will perceive that someone's there. She will reach out and if you wish, she will grasp your hand and you will feel her warm flesh. You will then know that beyond the shadow of any doubt that Vena Hess is a real, live girl – without a head."*

Legitimate two-headed and disfigured baby fetuses floating inside large jars of preservative were once the rage on the midway. They were called pickled punks because they were small babies (punks) in a preservative solution (pickled). After showing the real fetuses became illegal in most states, the real babies were substituted with baby dolls manipulated to look like the real thing. The babies changed, but the pitch promoting them as real was never altered. The new ones were called bouncers because they were often made of rubber, but few people complained even though they knew the faked pickled punks had been passed off as real.

"P.T. Barnum discovered that, in a way, people liked to be humbugged and throughout my career, I can say he was right," Ward said. "People would laugh and leave and few if any ever wanted their money back."

In 2010, Jamie MacVicar, a former advance man for Ringling Bros. and Barnum & Bailey Circus, published *The Advance Man: A Journey Into the World of the Circus*, the real life story about his years on the road with the circus. He observed the buncombe and noted that it seemed to him that the admission paid to see a sideshow is more about witnessing "the disparity between reality and the advertising than it was to see the freak of nature itself."

When Ward needed an extra act, he would often take a man and paint his upper body with a mixture of Casco Adhesive and green food dye. Once dry, the man would flex his muscles and move around, crack the glue making it look like a skin condition. With that man, now being pitched as the Alligator Man, Ward had an extra act. Is it buncombe and humbug or just lying? Everyone agrees there is a fine line between the three.

You bally to sell tickets and in the process, you exaggerate because if you told the truth no one would come in. "If you tell them that what we have inside is a tall statue of an ordinary man that we call a giant, not too many tickets would be sold. In reality, you have to exaggerate," said Ward, who proudly calls himself a professional liar.

"Ward's hyperbole is so lyrical and rhythmically punctuated that you want to believe everything he's saying is real and you don't really care if it's not," wrote Lynn Waddell in her book *Fringe Florida*. Did all this "theatrical exaggeration" ever get him in trouble? "Not really," notes Ward. "A couple times we were warned that a consumer advocate group was coming out to the midway to make sure we were not deceiving their town people, but to my knowledge, we were never challenged by a group," although he noted "maybe a dozen or so people as individuals" each season would complain and want their money back.

"If you go to any dinner buffet in town, you will see dozens of women or men fatter than the ones we have in the show. If you told the truth about their weight and showed an actual picture, you couldn't sell a ticket. It's all in the salesmanship," Ward said.

Sideshow veteran Johnny Meah, who has worked with Ward and many other operators, agrees with the need for exaggeration but in the end, the buncombe provides us "with the very vital ability to laugh at ourselves and our fears and foibles."

Meah writes in his book, *Freaks, Geeks & Strange Girls,* that people who come into a sideshow don't always expect what was promised outside. "Did you really expect Freddy the Frog Boy to be perched in a Disney-like swamp setting, sloshing his amphibian feet and peering at you through bulging green eyes? Well no, not really, but you didn't imagine him as a bored little gnome of a man in a dirty t-shirt either."

The Frear's United Shows was a typical small carnival operation of the era. In addition to its six basic rides, which included a Ferris wheel, Tilt-A-Whirl, carousel, and several kiddie rides, the show also carried six shows, also typical of the time. The shows consisted of a snake show, an athletic show in which show wrestlers would challenge the local athletes, a girl show, the 10-in-one, and the simple but popular Mickey Mouse Circus, which showcased 50 white mice running around on a caged table top playing on wheels, teeter boards and a little carousel. "I'm sure Mr. Disney would not have approved of the name if he had known about it," Ward surmises.

Living arrangements on Frear's were also typical of the times. Usually, the women who worked in the girl show were married to either one of the wrestlers or someone else on the show. These women most often slept on mattresses shared with their husbands under the girl show stage. The unmarried men slept on mattresses under the athletic show stage, and Diane De Elgar/George Searles slept on the stage in the blow-off section of the sideshow tent. After the last show of the day, she would pull a mattress out from behind the stage and set up living quarters on the stage. In the morning she would stow everything away again.

Frear's did not have good dates and revenue was poor. By September 1948, Ward and Harry decided to leave Frear's and rejoin Dailey Bros. where they stayed for the rest of the season and all of the following year.

Selling the Show:
The Art of the Bally

CHAPTER 7

It was on the midway of Frear's United Shows where Ward learned there were big differences between performing a bally for a carnival sideshow than a circus sideshow. "They are as different as a dark night and a bright sunny day," he notes.

Ward quickly found that while turning a tip on a carnival show is much tougher, the revenue potential is much greater than on a circus because on a carnival midway, you can stay open for more hours. On a circus, guests would congregate at the bally in front of the sideshow tent to await the opening of the big top. There was virtually nothing to do until the doors for the big show opened, so most of those gathered at the bally (called a tip) would buy a ticket and go inside the sideshow tent. Convincing people to buy a ticket and go in is the process of "turning the tip." The sideshow would shut down when the circus began, sometimes to reopen briefly after the circus performance, meaning it may operate for only one to two hours during the day, compared to 10 or 12 hours of continuous operation normally found on a carnival midway.

Hall and Leonard Show empty bally stage, 1954.

The process is much more difficult at a carnival because there is so much more for people to do. A tip can be built, but the people will only stop if they are curious or fascinated by what is taking place on the bally stage, not because they have nothing else to do and are waiting. On a carnival midway, there are plenty of ways to spend money, such as riding the rides, eating the food, and playing the games. The carnival sideshow had major competition while the circus sideshow had few distractions.

"Ladies and gentlemen, the show is going to start in exactly three minutes. In that time if you are quick enough, fast enough to reach the ticket box, I'm going to ask our ticket sellers to put away the regular $2 tickets of admission and for those three minutes and three minutes only, if you get a ticket or are in line to purchase a ticket, we're going to invite you to go in for half price. Please don't walk away, go down the midway and get an ice cream cone or ride a ride and come back in 15 minutes and expect to get in for this price. The special sale is right now for three minutes and three minutes only. Come in stay as long as you like and see as much as you wish. Hurry along. It's half price time now."

During the first turn on the bally on the first night of their run with the Frear's carnival, Ward had gathered a tip of 80 potential customers. When the bally was over, 72 walked away and only eight came in. He was devastated. "Now what do I do?" he asked Harry. "Go out there and do it again, and then again, and then again," Harry said.

Ward works the crowd from the bally.

Selling the Show: The Art of the Bally

The bally, an essential part of selling tickets, takes place on a stage or platform in front of the entrance, usually next to the ticket box. The exaggerated spiel espoused from that stage is created to sell the acts inside the tent. It is called the bally and can either be done live by the talker (not called a barker) or played from an endless tape loop which plays the same bally over and over. Ward likes to say, "We used to be called barkers, but most fairs don't allow dogs on the midway."

Legendary sideshow entertainer Harley Newman says a good bally is not only a joy to listen to but is somewhat addictive. There's a big stage in front of a colorful tent, Newman visualizes. There's Ward standing on that stage. "He looks so normal, so grandfatherly; he seems almost out of place. But he's in a bright colored coat, talking on a microphone. There's a crowd gathering. Nobody can walk by without stopping to listen. The closer you get, the better you hear him. The better you hear him, the more you have to hear him. You MUST listen! He describes the wonders inside the tent - mummies, sword swallowers, pain-proof women, midgets and human immensities! And you have to listen. You have to buy a ticket. You have to see for yourself!"

> "The lady on the stage inside right now is no freak of nature. She was not born to be strange. She is a man-made monstrosity. To keep other men away from her when she was young and beautiful, her husband would mark her body. Today, this lady is an old widow but she still has all the marks her husband put on her. Come inside now, and she will explain those markings to you."

Washington Post writer, David Mills, called Ward a "master of gruesome seduction."

Ward's oratorical talent has been considered the best of the best for the past 40 years, but he acknowledges he has "never articulated an original" line. "I've worked with the best, including Doc LeRoy, Milt Robbins, and Mush Wonder, and I've stolen a little from each one."

In his autobiography, *The Talker – The Life and Times of the World's Greatest Carnival Sideshow Man,* West Coast showman Bobby Reynolds writes that "we all learned our craft from other talkers," and that all successful talkers borrow the words and the style of all the talkers who preceded them. "It's the voice and intonation, along with (the use) of metaphors and similes that creates each talker's individual style."

"I'm an entertainer," Ward told *Network News* reporter Lavinia Edmunds in 1980 while the show was set up at the Smithsonian in Washington, D.C. "We're creating fairy tales. Like Jack Sprat, the skinny man, and Little Tom Thumb. We create colorful, humorous word pictures."

Todd Robbins, sideshow performer, musician, actor, and world record holder for eating the most light bulbs (5,000 and counting) said Ward's success as a talker comes from his wit, his sense of humor and his ability to understand people. "When he is up there explaining what people will see inside the tent, he uses a combination of expertise and imagination to paint word pictures that excite the imagination."

Robbins, who has been on the bally stage countless times during his own career, teases that it really is easy, once you get the drift. "All it takes is to stand on the bally stage, build a crowd and get them to do what you want them to do. It's like being a politician or an evangelist, only in a different context," notes Robbins. Reynolds adds that "it takes guts and guile plus lots of energy to make people listen and buy from you."

Ward talks while Poobah (Pete Terhurne) eats fire on the bally.

In 2009, journalist Lynn Waddell visited the World of Wonders sideshow at the Florida State Fair while preparing a chapter in her book, *Fringe Florida,* titled "Showtown's Last Showman." Of course the subject of the chapter is Ward Hall – King of the Sideshow.

As she approached the sideshow, she noticed immediately that the showman was in his loud, chaotic, colorful and strange element. She describes her first impression of Ward on that bally stage. "In any other dress or environment, Ward would cut a grandfatherly figure. He's short with a broad face, receding gray hair, big-framed shades propped on a broad nose, and hearing aids the size of quarters in ears that are a cartoonist's dream. Here on the sideshow platform, he's giving such a spirited bally, as showfolks call the pitch, that you would never guess he's eighty."

"Nothing has changed in the philosophy of the bally since the very first one," Ward said. "You exaggerate and they congregate and then you use your skills to sell them a ticket."

> "My friends, in here today, you are going to see the thin man – the human skeleton. He is so skinny you can actually count the ribs in his body, right through his skin. He will collapse his stomach to such an extent that you can see the front side of his backbone, right through the skin. On stage, right now on the inside."

Circus historian Lane Talburt has watched Ward bally to large crowds. "He can stand out there and read a tip. Before tickets go on sale, he seems to know exactly who will and who will not buy a ticket and who will and who will not enjoy the show. He knows his crowds."

Todd Ray, owner and talker for the Venice Beach (Calif.) Freakshow said he has always considered Ward Hall to be one of the greatest talkers of all time. "Something about his voice and his choice of descriptive words always hypnotizes the crowd. He calls it painting mind pictures. I call it magic!"

> "Now ladies and gentlemen, while you are gathering down this way, we're going to have some entertainers come out, here they come now, and we are going to have a little fun here on the platform."

Gathering a crowd in front of a bally is a work of art and a good talker can make or break a show by what he says and how he says it. To help out the talker, there is usually at least one act on stage during the bally. A lady with a snake is a good draw during the day. The midget eating fire is a good draw after dark; and the build-up to a sword swallower taking it "down the hatch without a scratch" always works, night or day.

Ward is proud of his oratorical skills. "I learned from the best and I enjoy being up there. I know what to do and how to do it to get the best results possible," Ward said. When asked to rank his skills, with one being terrible and 10 being the best, without hesitation he answered. "In total humility, I would have to put me in there as an 11. I think I am one hell of a good talker."

World of Wonders front showing tall banner line.

Visualizing the Show:
Value of the Banner Line

CHAPTER 8

The line-up of colorful canvas or vinyl banners in front of a sideshow is known as the banner line. In addition to the bally it is the principal way a sideshow advertises its attractions. The longer the banner line, the bigger impact it has on those walking along the midway. The weirder and more exaggerated the claims painted on those banners are, the more effective they are in attracting attention. Banners live within a world where everything illustrated is the biggest, greatest, and tallest. Today, they portray the same oddities as they did 50, 60 or more years ago.

Sideshows don't advertise in traditional ways and have always depended upon the draw of the circus, carnival or fair for business. Instead of traditional promotional methods, the sideshow has banked on "major illustrations, an orator and sometimes, music, to attract crowds," wrote John Polacsek in *Freaks, Geeks & Strange Girls*. "The sideshow has relied upon major illustrations, an orator and in sometimes, music, to attract (needed) crowds."

In the same book, Dale Slusser notes that the combination of a good bally and a bright and colorful banner line that features "amazing wonders with blended elements of the grotesque, bizarre and erotic" is essential to awaken the "desire and curiosity in the passerby."

Johnny Meah is a multi-talented sideshow veteran. In addition to owning his own sideshow at one time, working for others, and performing in shows as a sword swallower, blockhead and talker, he is a renowned banner painter, responsible for more than 2,500 different banners since he began painting them in 1957. "You capture the essence and you exaggerate. Anyone shorter, taller or wider than us is perfect for a good banner," he said, noting that traditionally, the banners on the outside are always much better than the act inside.

Meah painted many banners for the units Dick Johnson operated for Ward. Johnson is quick to compliment his work, saying "Johnny has the great ability to paint a banner that can sell tickets. His style is very intriguing and whimsical and evokes a sense of curiosity that in turn pulls people into the show."

During the early eras it was not unusual for a show to have new banners painted each year, even if the acts inside remained the same. It

1940s banner line with the cast posing on the bally.

gave the perception of a new show, and it was affordable. Today, with painted banners being considered an art form in the "Americana" and "Folk Art" genres, the prices prohibit yearly change-outs.

Meah said banners were originally painted with oil paints on canvas and were usually 8-foot by 10-foot in size. In the 1950s when he started painting, those banners sold for under $300 each. By the 1970s, they were going for $500 to $600, and today, few painters will create them for less than $1,000. Of course, smaller ones by lesser known artists are less expensive. As the last-standing vintage banner painter today, Meah's work starts at $3,000. "I do mostly commissioned pieces today for people who want customized sideshow banners in their home or office," Meah said. "I've priced myself out of the sideshow market."

Circus sideshows often contained animal acts, menagerie exhibits, minstrel shows and novelty acts, while on a carnival it was essential to offer more edgy shows, such as freaks and human oddities. On the Dailey Bros. circus in 1949, an act featuring Susie the lion was part of the sideshow. "She was a very good cat and was trained to attack the bottom of a chair. When you held up a chair she would attack the legs. When you set the chair down, she would become very docile," Ward recalls. Susie's cage wagon was parked just inside the door of the tent and a curtain could be pulled back to show the wagon and the lion inside.

One day, Ann Wesley, Susie's trainer, put her hand in the wrong place at the wrong time, and Susie scratched her badly and Wesley had to go home to Atlanta for medical treatment. Ward had watched the act

Visualizing the Show: Value of the Bannerline

many times so when Wesley left the lot, Ward dressed up, picked up a chair and became the sideshow lion tamer. After performing it for a couple weeks, along with his other acts, he asked for a $20 a week raise, which would raise his weekly take to $55. Circus owner Ben Davenport sent word that he would not give "that dizzy punk kid no $20 a week more to work that cat act." The lion tamer in the big top took over for $10 additional per week and Ward continued to bally the act.

> "And the first act in the show today is going to be that daredevil who fights the untamable lion. A lion who has already killed three of its trainers, and today you're going to see the man enter the cage without gun, without whip and you will see the man fight the lion and the lion fight the man. Who will be the winner today, only time will tell. It's show time right now so everyone is invited to get your ticket and hurry along. Look, there he is in the safety cage, he is getting ready to step into the lion's den now."

While on Dailey Bros. during the summer of 1949, the entire circus crew was apprehended by police on suspicion of murder. A dead body had been found rolled up in the canvas of the big top and the police were called.

"Most of us had gone to bed for the night when policeman came onto the train and told us we were all under arrest," recalled Ward. "We

Banner line of the Hall and Leonard's *Sensations of 1959* show.

got dressed and joined the rest of the circus crew, about 450 in all, and we were taken to the courthouse for questioning." All the women and children were taken to the library and the men taken to the laundry. After four hours they were put into a single line and as they walked out, they were asked in which department they worked.

Everyone who said they worked in the prop department ended up behind bars for about two days. It wasn't until the following fall that a man confessed to the murder." However, Ward added, "This guy was not guilty. He was working the poster truck and was 1,000 miles away. I think he just needed a place to stay for the winter and jail was as good as any – and free." Ward never heard of that man's fate.

Hitting the Boards:
Ward Gets Theatrical Experience

CHAPTER 9

During fall 1949, after Dailey Bros. closed for the season, Ward met Dick Dixon in New Orleans, who became his theatrical agent and long-time friend. Dixon immediately booked Ward and Harry onto the *Frisco Follies* revue at the Rio Theater in New Orleans, for the rest of 1949 and spring 1950.

During this production, Ward's first-ever theatrical experience, he was on stage for 40 minutes of the 45 minute revue. He performed his vent and juggling acts in addition to contributing to the comedy and production numbers. It was hard work, performing five shows a day (six on Saturdays), "but I never tired of it and loved every minute of it."

It was common in those days for theatrical show people to join up with circuses and carnivals during the summer while their (non-air-conditioned) theaters were closed during the hot months. Likewise, it was common for circus and carnival variety acts to play the theater circuit during the winter months when their shows were shuttered in winter quarters.

Following its huge success in New Orleans, the *Frisco Follies* moved to the Broadway Theater in Tampa's Ybor City. One afternoon while working backstage, Ward turned the corner and was surprised to come face to face with the

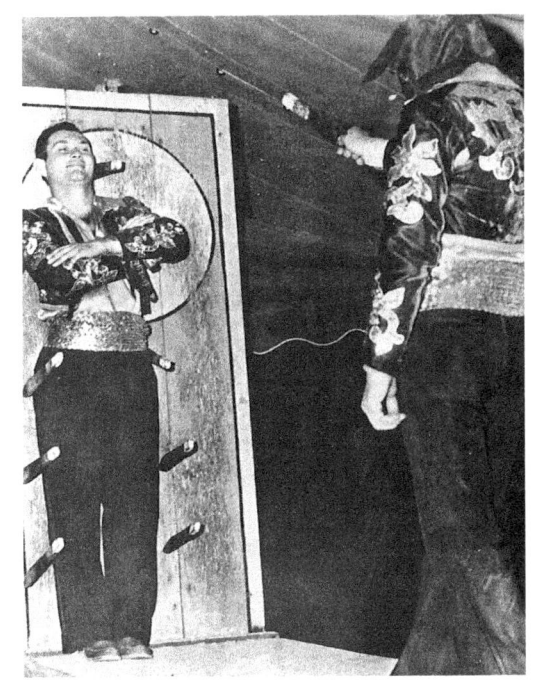

Harry threw knives at Ward for 17 years and only hit him 7 times.

WARD HALL & LEONARDO

famous Gypsy Rose Lee, by then a world-renowned star of the burlesque stage. Sunny Knight, star of the *Frisco Follies*, had worked with her in New York City in a Minsky's burlesque house. Gypsy was now the high priced star of the Royal American Shows and was in the Tampa area vacationing prior to joining the carnival for the Florida State Fair, and she stopped in to visit with her long-time friend Knight on several occasions. "I loved exchanging show business stories with Gypsy. "She was a delight," Ward said.

Gypsy told Ward a story that he loves to retell about how she became the highest paid burlesque dancer ever with Royal American Shows, the largest carnival in the country at that time. Sally Rand had starred on the Royal American midway the year before but Carl Sedlmayr, the show's owner, decided for the 1949 season he wanted the star power Gypsy Rose Lee could bring to them. Gypsy knew that Rand had been making $5,000 a week so she told Sedlmayr she was "a bigger star than Sally

Rand and expected more money." She asked for $5,010 a week, and got it. She obviously held out so she could claim that she made more than Sally Rand, who was at the time a world-famous burlesque dancer known for her ostrich feather fan dance.

During the run of the *Frisco Follies* in Tampa the stagehands went on strike and, to make their point to management, sabotaged the show by throwing stink bombs into the theater during a performance. The run closed early. The *Frisco Follies* next date, the Joy Theater in West Memphis, was still several weeks away, so Ward and Harry joined the Benny Fox Star Spangled Circus, and played several indoor shows on military bases during the layover.

The Joy Theater run in West Memphis went well. Following that experience, Ward and Harry figured they had found a new path for their talents and would stick with the theatrical side of their art from then on forgoing the circus sideshow business. However, nightclub and theater dates started getting harder and harder to get, with bookings few and far between. Short on money by this time, the two pooled their resources, bought a *Billboard* and went searching in hopes of finding a future under canvas once again. It didn't take long. They found an ad, obviously written with them in mind. It read: "Want sideshow manager with acts for Bud Anderson's Seal Bros. Circus." At the bottom of the ad was printed: "Ward Hall and Harry Leonard please answer."

Hall and Leonard's car and trailer in Cedar City, Utah, 1951.

Hitting the Boards: Ward Gets Theatrical Experience

Telegrams were exchanged, a deal was cut and the boys were off to North Dakota to spend the 1950 season with Bud Anderson and the Seal Bros. Circus. As they driving north there were, shall we say, transportation complications. They hit a pothole in the highway, cracking the axle and flipping over the trailer holding all their props. "I was doing about 50 when the trailer hit the hole and the trailer flipped, but there was not a lot of damage." What occurred next sounds like a setup for a joke, but Ward insists it's a true story. "A carnival advance agent, a beer truck driver and a priest all stopped to help. With all of us pushing, we were able to right the trailer and move it off to the side of the road."

When the priest arrived in the next town, he dispatched help to the crash scene. A helpful mechanic drove out, assessed the damages, went back to his shop, and came back with the needed parts and "we were on our way in a couple hours." They made it to the Seal Brothers lot on time and the 1950 season began.

Ward and Harry had a percentage deal with the circus. With such deals it is customary for all receipts to be turned in to the circus office at the end of the night, then once a week the circus would pay what is owed to those working on a percentage. Circus owner Bud Anderson, who was known for his honesty, was having a hard time making payroll each week and wanting to be fair, Anderson advised Ward to take out his percentage before turning in the day's receipts, assuring that he and Harry would get paid. It was good advice that Ward took seriously and continues to take seriously. "I have followed that advice all my life and several times it has prevented us from coming up on the short end."

Two beautiful Asian elephants, Babe and Palm, were on the Seal Bros. Circus under the control of Wimpy, their trainer. Babe and Palm were so well mannered that they followed Wimpy around on the lot without any encouragement from the trainer. But there was a problem in that the elephants were often too large to fit through the areas in which Wimpy was walking. That didn't faze the pachyderms one iota.

Ward recalls that on one spot that summer the house trailers were positioned about five feet from a wall toward the back of the lot. As Ward was shaving and preparing for the afternoons show, his trailer started trembling and rocking. As he looked out the window he saw gray elephant skin rubbing the side of the trailer as Babe and Palm followed Wimpy through the maze of trailers. "Wimpy, you idiot, I'm going to break that bull hook over your head," Ward yelled out the door. "Ward, you ain't going to do one damn thing," answered Wimpy as he continued his little parade. "I laughed till I cried," said Ward. "I saw great humor in that moment."

Bud Anderson died a few weeks into their run when his brakes failed on his truck and he went over a cliff during a jump to Miles City, Mont.

He was thrown from his truck and his trailer carrying his trained horses landed on top of him. Within a few days, in-fighting between Anderson's wife and his son, combined with a poor revenue stream, created a morale problem amongst the troupe, and it was clear to Ward that the circus was doomed. On July 3, 1950, the close notice came. Ward immediately sent off a telegram to his friend Bob Stevens, owner of the Steven's Bros. Circus, telling him of he and Harry's availability.

Creative Showmanship:
Ward Makes a Baby

CHAPTER 10

They joined up with Steven's Bros. Circus two days later, with Ward being hired as sideshow manager. He had turned 20 in June of 1950 and his family of friends was larger than it had ever been. He had been accepted. He knew that he fit in with the others he worked with. He was happy.

Business was bad from the beginning. As they worked their route through Wyoming, storms knocked down the big top eight times in seven days. Once, they had to reset the canvas twice within a 12-hour period. But as the show moved south, business picked up and Stevens told Ward he was thinking about adding another act to the big top.

Ward made Stevens a proposal. For no additional cost to the circus, Ward would provide a juggling act in the big top (himself) in exchange for being permitted to exhibit a two-headed baby in the sideshow.

Ward wanted to offer the baby show as a blow-off, an extra attraction that customers would pay additionally to see. Not only did Ward offer his juggling act, but he promised Stevens 25% of the "contributions" collected from the baby. Stevens agreed immediately.

This is how the burgeoning showman described his first baby exhibit. "I bought two rubber dolls from a toy store. I stuck some adhesive tape over the cry whistle in the back and vulcanized the second doll's head onto the first. I gave the thing a coat of paint and placed it in tea-tinted water in a Tom's Peanuts jar, and I was in business." For $3.84 he created an exhibit that paid for itself within hours. (Editor's note: Remember this WAS 1950.)

**HALL & LEONARD
SIDE SHOW Wants**
Talkers, Ticket Sellers, Acts and Annex
Attraction for Gooding's State Fair route.
Contact Ward Hall, Nashville, Tenn.,
now.

He created a back story for that poor rubber baby for his bally:

> "Behind this curtain you will behold probably the strangest freak on exhibition. A baby boy from Mysor, India, Kashmir Singh, who has two ears, four eyes, four ears, two noses, two mouths, and one body. The widowed mother of Kashmir lives in Mysor where she is the sole support of her other nine children. We do not charge an admission to view this child. All we ask is a donation, all of which will go to the widowed mother. So please open your pocket books, open your hearts. Whatever you give is greatly appreciated. I collect the donations when you go behind the curtain."

Today, Ward laughs at the pitch. "I'm not sure if they believed it, but surprisingly there were no complaints." Bob Stevens found the pitch humorous and couldn't believe people fell for it. When other showmen would visit the circus, Stevens made it a point to take them to the sideshow to hear Ward's baby pitch and to see "the best $3 investment in circus history."

The trade-out prospered and not only did Ward make big money off the baby show, but it put him in the center ring of big top for the first time in his life on a regular basis. "That was an exciting moment for me," Ward said. "It never got old either. I found myself looking forward to those few minutes of juggling every day."

He also learned how to walk the wire that season. He befriended Cha Cha and Alfredo Sanchez, part of the Mexican family who had the wire act on the circus. Between shows he would join them during practice and they taught him how to walk the wire. He occasionally joined them on performance days. Ward and Harry did well with Stevens Bros., and ended up having a profitable year.

During off-season, they ran into Norman Anderson, who had taken over his father's Seal Bros. Circus and was in the process of revitalizing it and renaming it the Wallace and Clark Circus. He asked Ward and Harry to join him for the 1951 season to operate the show-owned sideshow. They thought about it and with nothing else lined up, joined up with Anderson in Venice, Calif., following several months of playing nightclubs in New Orleans and Baton Rouge.

That was the first time Ward had been in California and he basked in all its glory for a month before the circus opened for the season on April 1, 1951 in Elsinore. Surprisingly, with an "improved version" of the two headed baby exhibit, he soon became the top gross maker on the Wallace and Clark Circus. One day the ringmaster didn't show up and Ward was asked to fill in for him. Nothing is free on the midway, so Anderson "paid"

Creative Showmanship: Ward Makes a Baby

Ward for his ringmaster role and juggling act by allowing him to keep 100% of the baby show blow-off. Harry was watching Ward juggle during the performance one day when Norman Anderson walked up to him and pointed to Ward, noting, "That is the most expensive act I've got in this show." Harry asked how that could be because he knew Ward was not getting paid a penny from Anderson. "No, I'm not paying him, but he is now getting 100% of all the two-headed baby money."

"Perhaps I had too good of a financial arrangement with Anderson, and perhaps I was saving too much money at that time," Ward said. "But the urge to own something of my own was gnawing at me." He started looking at For Sale ads in *Billboard*.

Having been both successful and frugal for several consecutive years, and with a small stash of money, Ward and Harry purchased their first sideshow on July 3, 1951, from the Greater Rainbow Shows carnival. At 21, Ward now owned his first sideshow. He was the youngest show owner in the country.

They paid $1,000 for a complete show, with a nearly-new tent and banners and, for another $500 they bought the truck. "I wanted to own something," he said, noting that the extra money he had was "burning a hole in my pocket." He felt that owning a successful sideshow would be his first step to owning a circus, which was still his dream. Now, all they needed was a carnival on which to book. Once again, they turned to the *Billboard*.

In retrospect, Ward said buying the sideshow was "probably the most foolish thing I did in my entire life. I knew little about running a carnival sideshow and even less about where to take it. We walked away from making a lot of money and we walked away from many of our friends, our support group."

The new Hall and Leonard Show, consisting of only Harry and Ward, opened five days later in Ogden, Kan., on the Don Brashear's American Midway Shows, a carnival that proclaimed in *Billboard* it had "a winning route

of 24 fairs and celebrations." The bally would start with both of them. Then as Ward sold the tickets, Harry would go inside and perform the Punch and Judy show. Harry would then go out front and replace Ward as ticket seller and Ward would come on stage and do magic and his vent with his wooden friend Perky Perkins. He would then walk a sword ladder and eat fire. As a finale, Harry would close the front, come in and throw knives at Ward.

That inaugural spot for the Hall and Leonard Show was a bust. Heavy rains flooded the show's premiere and the resulting mud kept it trapped in one very messy spot for two weeks before they could move on to the less than stellar "winning route" that had been promised. The next date was also a bust but things slowly began to get better and, along the way, the two were able to make physical improvements to their equipment.

It didn't take long for them to realize they didn't belong on the American Midway Shows. There were girl shows, which didn't bother them, but the games concessionaires took great pride in cheating and stealing from the locals. That did bother the two and they agreed it was time to move on. The incident that made up their minds to jump the show still stands out in Ward's memory. "We were sitting around in the cookhouse one day talking about business and I brought up the fact that Harry and I weren't making any money. A couple of the crooked games operators laughed and said (making fun of the farmers and country folk's innocence) that 'if you can't make it in Coffeyville (Kan.), you can't make it anywhere.'"

There are now laws forbidding it, but it was once commonplace that nearly every circus and carnival had crooked games called grift joints or flat joints, operated by grifters. There was no possible way anyone could win these games unless the operator wanted them to. On the carnival, there were flat joints, or flat stores; games that looked simple but in reality were rigged against winning. On the circus, the Three-card Monte (run by what was called the broad mob, because the three cards used in the games were usually queens) and the shell game (run by the nut mob, which signified the walnut shells originally used in the game) were the two favorite gambling games run by grifters. Ward had read about grift joints but admits that when he joined up with Dailey Bros. in 1946 and saw grifters in action, he was surprised how foolish and clueless the locals often were at the hands of these professionals. Both the Nut Mob and the Broad Mob operated on the midway and inside the sideshow on Dailey Bros.

Earlier in their run with the American Midway Shows, an incident occurred that made them first think of staying away from any show that had grift. A group of lumberjacks had arrived in town to spend their paychecks and apparently to let off a little steam. One accused the man running the Three-card Monte of cheating him. The dealer politely told him he would have to go outside the tent and talk with his boss, Joe, who was the fixer for the two mobs (nut and broad) on the show. Joe, who had probably imbibed as much as the lumberjack by that point in the evening, told the guy that if he wanted his money back, he would have to go in there and take it back himself.

A big fight ensued and, along with the "security" attached to each mob, the fight spilled into the midway where more of the locals joined in. "It was quite tense," Ward recalled. "And it is a wonder that things like that did not happen more often. We wanted to stay away from scenes like that."

Ward on Steven's Bros. Circus, 1950.

Having made the decision to jump from the American Midway Shows, Ward and Harry headed south to Louisiana in late August, booked on with Groves Greater Shows and finished up the season with good business. Owned by Ed Groves, the carnival had no girl shows and cheating and stealing from the locals was not permitted. "We finished our first year as show owners with six weeks of good fairs on a nice clean carnival. We were very tired, but we did well financially."

Ward on Steven's Bros. Circus, 1950.

When Groves Greater Shows closed down for the 1951 season, the Hall and Leonard Show remained on the road, booking dates as independents on less than stellar lots, knowing it was cheaper to stay open and bring in some money than it was to close down, come off the road and take up a seasonal residence somewhere. They were able to do it because they had no payroll. Ward and Harry still performed all the acts and did all of the grunt work themselves.

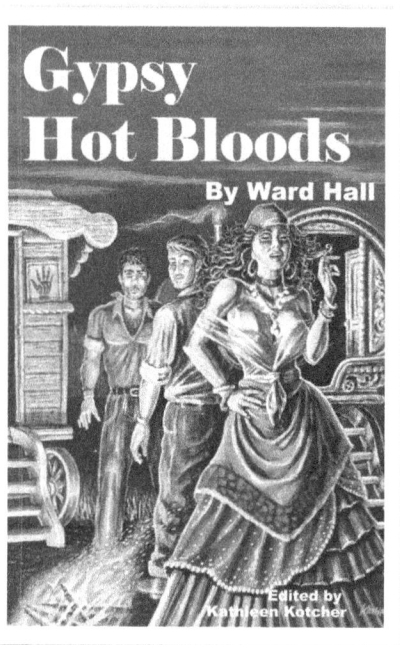

Instead of booking nightclubs during that winter as they had done in the past, Ward and Harry signed on with Barney Tassel who booked rides and shows throughout Florida for winter fairs and festivals. They headed over to Louisiana and joined the Buff Hottle Shows for the 1952 season.

Inspiration for the novel Ward would write nine years later, *Gypsy Hot Bloods,* came on the same day he arrived in Covington, La., to join Buff Hottle. A wedding was taking place joining two prominent Gypsy families. A large big top had been erected and the wedding took place during a three-day period. A member of Gypsy royalty died during that time and his wake lasted two more days. Prior to this time Ward had no association with the traveling Gypsy troupes but he was fascinated by the rituals they followed.

Gypsy Hot Bloods is not based on any real life events but only on his knowledge of Gypsy culture. It is a gay romance novel and quite explicit at times. "It is a very spicy and sexy story, probably too much for the public when I wrote it in 1961. I have letters from six of the finest publishers in the country," he explains. "They are all rejection letters." Ward's "dirty little book" (as he calls it) was edited by Kathleen Kotcher, then editor of the *Shocked and Amazed!* series of journals and was published by Dolphin-Moon Press in 2005. "It was the first book I wrote and the last one I had published," jokes Ward.

As the Buff Hottle Show was playing near a U.S. Naval base near Memphis, Ward thought it would be a good idea to add a girl show to his lineup, seeing that there would be a great many young men walking the midway.

"Our beautiful ladies will make the old feel young, and the young want to feel."

Only after he created the show and hired "Luella" to run it did he find that Buff Hottle would not book it. Luella's husband was on a show in Kentucky running several gambling joints and she said he could get the girl show booked there. One phone call and it was done. The boys left the Buff Hottle Shows, with their new girl show, and Luella, in tow.

Harry and Ward joined the Gladstone Exposition Shows in Eminence, Ky., in time for the July 4, 1952 celebration. It was a warm and clear day for a summer holiday. A nice crowd appeared in late morning but had thinned out drastically by mid-afternoon. To Ward's astonishment, the carnival started tearing down and loading up. Puzzled by the sudden chain of events, he asked why.

"You won't want to be open tonight when all the drunken hillbillies come back to destroy the place," he was warned. "They will come back when they realize the flat stores robbed them of their money." Ward had watched his new girl show bring in some good money prior to the unpredicted teardown and was disappointed that he had to call it a day.

> *"If you want to see a beautiful young lady in here today
> wearing a beautiful costume, you will be disappointed;
> because the beautiful young lady you will see today,
> live on stage, live on the inside right now, wears nothing."*

Ward witnessed that Luella, the lady running his girl show, couldn't read or write but was good at counting and giving change. "Except, that is, when she was counting out my share of the take. I guess it ran in her family." For the rest of the summer, business ranged from "bad to worse," he recalls.

When fair season in Louisiana started, they re-joined Groves Greater Shows where they did reasonable business but were off from the year before. When Groves closed for the year, they decided to extend their season again and joined Southern Valley Shows for several dates. By mid-November, with little choice but to stay open and get any cash they could, they limped to Georgia and joined Lone Star Shows, owned by "Myrtle the Girdle" McFadden. That show was doing even worse, and they shortly left and joined up again with Barney Tassel for a short run in Florida before they laid off for the holidays at Sailor Katzy's Road Side Zoo, just North of Gibsonton, Fla.

They booked the 1953 season with Al Wagner's Cavalcade of Amusements, a 35-car railroad carnival. The owner's wife, Hattie Wagner, whom Ward describes lovingly as a "plumpish, middle-aged Jewish woman with a vocabulary that would put a drunken sailor to shame," operated

Hall and Leonard's truck, 1952.

the cookhouse and was a friend to all the sideshow people on the carnival. The day after Ward and Harry's show arrived, she mentioned to Ward that his sideshow was a welcomed addition to the midway, but "being a big railroad show" she though the sideshow should be larger. It needed more acts. At that time, the Hall and Leonard Show still consisted of only Hall and Leonard, but on Hattie Wagner's advice, they both decided that yes, this would be a good time to grow. They were charging 25-cents admission and the baby show blow-off cost an extra dime.

Hattie Wagner's suggestion that Ward and Harry expand was heeded. "We started getting bigger immediately and I enlarged the banner line front to 150 feet, ordered a larger tent and put an ad in *Billboard* looking for additional acts," Ward said. Diane De Elgar (George Searles), the show's original half-and-half from 1948, re-joined them as a mentalist and fortune teller.

One of the acts hired from the *Billboard* ad was Burt and Vera Morey who had a performing dog act and a comedy juggling routine. Velma, Ward was told, dressed in a "cute little" bellhop costume. It turned out to be a mediocre act. "They arrived with six dogs. One who was trained and five nuisances," Ward recalls, adding that the bellhop costume "must have been discarded by its original owner many years previously."

They also picked up tattoo artist Ralph Johnston, a great talent who not only had a tattoo concession on the sideshow but became the carnival's painter as well as the sideshow's tattooed man. Ward notes that

Hall and Leonard's house trailer, 1952.

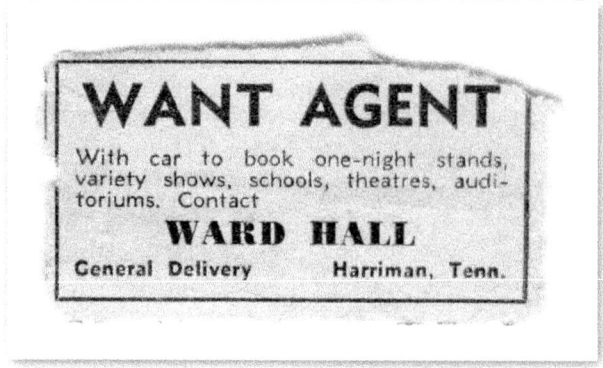

Johnston's artistic proficiency was very popular and in each town word quickly spread and locals lined up for hours to get fresh tattoos. "His business flourished and the tattoos cost from $2 up to $100, depending on what the person wanted. Ralph gave me 20% of his take. It was good to finally have an act that paid ME," Ward notes.

Tattooing was so lucrative for Johnston that he quit his job as the show painter and concentrated on his money-making concession. Needing a new painter, Ward brought on a "hillbilly painter," Ted Owens, who, unfortunately, painted his words as bad as he mispronounced them. "I asked him to paint a sign that read: "Continuous Performances." He painted a sign that read: "Cuntinnyous Performances." "I told him he had spelled it wrong and he argued." Owens told Ward, "That's not wrong, that's exactly how I say it, a cuntinnyous performance." The hillbilly's sign stayed that way until Ward could get another painter.

The real reason Owens was on the show was his wife, Frances Lee Owens, the show's bearded lady. Ward described her as "somewhat homely with the same twang in her talk that her husband had, but she had a real, full beard." It was obvious that the Owens' beat-up car needed work and was not dependable, so for the first jump, Ward drove Frances ahead to their next fair to make sure she was there on time. Her husband stayed behind for several days getting the car repaired. Ward was paying Frances $75 a week, a good salary.

Her "wealth" immediately attracted a young merry-go-round operator at the new spot, with whom she quickly began a full-scale affair in the short time it took her husband and the jalopy to make it to the fair. Then, ironically, wanting to be "pretty" for her young paramour, she shaved off her beard which left him totally uninterested in her and, in turn, Ward had no place for her on the show, at least until she grew her beard back.

When Ted the husband arrived, he quickly appraised the situation and the last time Ward or Harry saw either one of them, Ted was chasing Frances down the midway waving a pistol and shouting at her.

In late August 1953 in Gary, Ind., the city's vice squad decided to inspect the train and the midway of the Cavalcade of Amusements. They found nothing "objectionable" in Ward and Harry's show, allowing them to set up and operate, but the rest of the carnival took a hit. There were two girl-shows on the midway, operated by Fred Miller and his son Mike. It was Mike who first saw the raid coming. He jumped off the bally, grabbed the money bag from the ticket seller and disappeared in the crowd. He showed up at Ward's bally, gave him the bag of money for safe keeping, then went to find the show's fixer so they could go downtown and bail out his people who were at that time being arrested.

Meanwhile, the authorities predictably closed down the gambling games and, surprisingly, the funhouse and dark ride, citing that the "darkness was an immoral environment." By the time the raid was over, the minstrel show and the big musical revue had been shuttered, and the health department had shut down most of the food vendors.

The cookhouse was the last to be closed and when Hattie saw them coming, she greeted them in loud and continuous profanity until they left. Totally upset, she ordered her husband Al to close down the show, load it up and head to their next stop in Evansville, Ind. This time, the fixer didn't do so well "fixing" the spot.

A fixer, or patch, on a carnival or circus is exactly what it sounds like. He is there to bail anyone and everyone out of trouble, to make sure everything is solved in a way that is beneficial to the show, to arrange with the local authorities to allow unlawful games and attractions and to pay-off any inspectors or officials who have a problem with anything on the show.

Ward and his partner enjoyed good business during 1953 and after September's Tennessee State Fair in Nashville they joined Gem City Shows in Cape Girardeau, Mo., for several dates. Then, unhappy with that show's poor locations, they jumped to Gooding's Amusement Co. and finished up the season with Gooding's in Athens, Georgia. They stored their equipment in Macon and headed to Miami for a well-deserved "vacation."

Ward's promotional photo, 1957.

They never got to Miami. Instead, they stopped off in Sarasota to visit a few friends and, while there they discovered that the Loyal-Repensky

At The SOUTHLAND Club

Barrancas Ave.

OPENING
TONIGHT
BRAND NEW
FLOOR SHOW

★ Presenting the Beautiful

LISA RENEE

In her famous dance

"Fantasy of the Fans"
ALSO
CONGO and LATIN AMERICAN DANCES
PLUS

WARD HALL & LEONARDO

WARD does a very amusing ventriloquist spot. LEONARDO thrills the audience with his fantastic manipulation of knives. In one number WARD acts as target as LEONARDO blindfolded cuts his silhouette out of paper. WARD also does a commendable M. C. job.

LISA RENEE

DINE and DANCE
To The Music Of
EDDY'S ORCHESTRA
50c Per Person Cover Charge Show Nights
Phone 9172 for Reservations
Club Now Under New Management
Make Up A Party — Come Out Tonight

---

family, who had been a featured bareback riding act with Ringling for many years, was planning on creating a European-style, one-ring circus (a rarity in America at the time) and taking it on the road in 1954.

"The family needed two things, a quality sideshow and additional cash. We were able to provide both," said Ward. He and Harry's investment of $2,000 helped get the circus on the road and garnered the two a small piece of future revenues. They were also to get 60% of all sideshow revenues. The excitement of finally owning a circus, albeit only part of it, energized Ward into action and he didn't mind skipping a couple months of relaxation on Miami Beach.

On Feb. 25, 1954, Hall and Leonard opened as the featured sideshow on the Loyal-Repensky European Circus in North Miami. Business was brisk here as it was at the subsequent Florida locations they played, but as the circus started heading north, attendance began to wane and the financial situation got worse by the day. In Leeds, Ga., in early April, the circus didn't have the funds to buy gas for its trucks to drive to their next spot, family members on the show had not been paid, and it wasn't much better for Ward and Harry. Following its abrupt closure on April 2 the show limped back to Sarasota where the talented Repensky family was invited back to the Ringling show.

"The circus was beautiful, very deluxe and the acts were all of a high quality, but what killed them was the advance - the booking, promoting and advertising. They didn't understand that part of the business. They were entertainers." Ward and Harry owned the sideshow but neither had any say in the management of the circus operation. They never got their $2,000 investment back and their revenues from the sideshow didn't amount to much.

"By the time they closed the circus down, we were running very low on cash and needed to do something very quickly." Ward and Harry were left with no place to go. Diane (George Searles) suggested Ward call Al Wagner to see if they could re-join the Cavalcade of Amusements which was to open its season in a couple days hence at Pensacola, Fla. Ward was hesitant because he expected Wagner would be upset that he and Harry abruptly jumped the show the year before, leaving a large hole in the midway. Desperate for a location, Ward reluctantly sent Wagner a telegram. He expected a harsh, or no, response. Instead, a couple days later Ward received an answer that simply read. "Come on Home, Al."

"When we arrived at the fairgrounds in Pensacola we found that the carnival had been attached by the IRS and was still at winter quarters in Mobile, Ala.," Ward notes. Five days later, after the Wagners turned over their two new Cadillac cars and a box of jewelry as payment, the show was released. It hurried to Pensacola and opened to poor business.

Three days after opening in Pensacola in April 1954, the show painter shot and killed Al Wagner during an argument over unpaid wages, then 10 days later the show folded. The local sheriff's office posted guards around the grounds to make sure none of the equipment, including that owned by the independents, was removed from the lot until it was assured that all local bills had been paid in full. "We observed that the guards changed each morning at 4 and at that time they would all leave for a short time for coffee," Ward said. "We got all the sideshow vehicles loaded and ready. All our personnel waited anxiously in the dark and at coffee time, we fled Pensacola." They made a clean get-away. Ward didn't feel guilty because all his local bills had been paid.

When the Cavalcade of Amusements was finally released by officials, it was loaded onto the train and sent back to its Alabama winter quarters. In time it was auctioned and most of the better equipment and railroad cars were purchased by the Royal American Shows.

The weekend after fleeing Pensacola, in late April 1954, Hall and Leonard opened with Gladstone Exposition in Mississippi. Business was terrible and they needed money so badly that Ward reduced admission price from a quarter to a nickel. The next stop was Jackson, Tenn., where they set a good-weather record for bad business that still stands: $12.50 gross for an entire week. Gladstone closed down later that season, never to open again.

"Gladstone was the third show we had been with that folded that year," Ward said, noting that his booking prowess still needed fine-tuning at that point. Nearly broke, they found another gig with the World of Today Shows, owned by Izzy Wells and Curley Reynolds, two men that Harry had worked with before. There was only one hitch to that booking; Harry and Ward didn't have enough money to pay for the jump. Wells and Reynolds sent them a couple hundred dollars to help get them to Bartlesville, Okla., where they joined up with the show. Although it eked its way through the summer, this was also to be World of Today Shows' last year on the road. Number four.

Gem City Shows, on which they closed the season, was the only show that Ward and Harry booked with during 1954 that didn't fold. Ward admits to thinking seriously that maybe he was a jinx. Was he bad luck? "No, it was just a bad year. At least that's what I convinced myself to believe," he recalls.

Despite what sounded like a tumultuous summer, Ward and Harry made money and they were able to buy their first semi-tractor and trailer. Their rich man/poor man journey, quite typical among nomadic entrepreneurs, continued. Earlier that spring while playing the Wilkin County Fair, a small expo in Breckenridge, Minn., Ward met a dwarf named Pete, a little man who became a big part of Ward's life.

Ward Meets Pete:
How a Dwarf Won the Heart of a King

CHAPTER 11

Poobah, Little Pete, King of the Pygmies, the Human Volcano, the Fire Eating Pygmy, or the Last of the Munchkins, he answered to them all.

No matter what he was being called at the time, Norbert "Pete" Terhurne was the smallest but most noticeable feature on the bally platform of Ward Hall sideshows for 55 years. Photos of Pete in newspapers and magazines from coast to coast over the past half century probably outnumbered photos of Ward two to one!

Pete's life in show business began while Ward and Harry were playing Pete's home town of Breckenridge. Geri Burke, one of the sideshow bally girls, asked Ward if he had seen the little dwarf selling newspapers downtown and, when he said yes, she asked if it was okay for her to try and recruit him for the show. Ward agreed.

On the lot, about an hour later, Geri showed up with Pete. Ward laughs when he recalls that he put Pete in clown makeup so the locals wouldn't recognize him as he took their tickets. "That was a really foolish thing to think. Each person who handed him their ticket would say 'Hi, Pete, I see you are working the fair.' He was quite sad when we left town and left him behind."

Ward, Pete and Harry in Sarasota, 1965.

Two weeks after leaving Pete in Breckenridge, the show pulled onto the lot at the North Dakota State Fair in Fargo and there was Pete waiting for them. Ward contacted Pete's mother who said it was okay that he was with them and that Ward should just "put him on a bus and send him home" when the fair was over. Instead, Pete insisted that he stay with the show. Other than the few odd jobs he picked up in his small town, Pete's only "real" job in his entire life was with a Ward Hall-produced sideshow.

He was born Jan. 19, 1930, joined the show in 1954, retired in 2009 at age 79, and died on July 30, 2012 in Brandon, Fla. at age 82.

No story of Ward, Harry or Chris Christ (Ward's partner following Harry's death in 1964) would be complete without multiple mentions of Little Pete. He was always there and he became a part of the nuclear family.

Reporters love to tell stories of the unusual and what is more unusual and eye-catching than a 3-foot, 7-inch dwarf eating fire? He also climbed a sword ladder, played with snakes that outweighed him by 100 pounds, was a target for knife throwers, and in his favorite role, he was an impressive white-faced clown known simply as the "Lovable Little Clown."

In 1991, Washington Post reporter David Mills wrote an in-depth piece after a visit to the World of Wonders show when it was playing the Clarke County Fair in Berryville, Va., in early August. The first two words of that article were "Little Pete." The reporter explained that he first saw Pete sitting on a small patio chair on the bally with a python on his lap. "People interrupt their strides to approach the platform. They stand and

Poobah (Pete Terhurne) would eat fire up to 50 times a day on the bally.

stare. Or they point. Some of them smile and wave at Little Pete. His sweet grin rests upon a large, jutting jaw. Across his knotty fingers, the python is slowing squirming, flicking its tongue."

Harry took on the job of teaching Pete to eat fire, juggle, lift weights with a hook in his tongue, take care of the snakes, and to be the target in Harry's knife throwing act. "We were very careful not to teach him anything in which he could hurt himself, such as sword swallowing and the blockhead act. We kept a close eye on him." During those early years, Pete's "angel face and curly blonde hair" attracted a lot of women. "And he loved every one of them," Chris said. "He also knew how to spend his money impressing the ladies." Pete loved doing his own laundry at the Laundromat and it took Chris awhile before he realized why. "He would sit there while his clothes were being washed and ogle the women around him and he would make friends with them all."

There are literally thousands of stories about Pete's love for women, his love for beer, and his love for the sideshow business. An entire book could be written about him. Pete first lived with Ward and Harry during the off season and then with Ward and Chris until he went into an assisted living home following his retirement.

Ward protected Pete against most evils, and Pete saw Ward as a father figure even though they were nearly the same age. Pete couldn't read or write but was quick to learn to do the chores he needed to do on the midway. He was busy during the season, practically living on the bally stage eating fire, being the brunt of Ward's bally humor, or sitting peacefully with a snake on his lap. During the typical day on the bally, he would eat fire up to 50 times. He was the star of the Pygmy Village as well as the Midget and the Monsters shows that Ward fielded over the years. During a seven-year spring date at Madison Square Garden with the Ringling shows, from 1960-1967, Pete was featured as the Lovable Little Clown. In make-up, his role was to simply stand on the bally, shake hands, talk with the crowds and sell photos of himself.

"I would guess in those seven years we played Madison Square Garden, Pete sold 35,000 photos of himself," Ward said, adding that those years in New York City were probably the happiest in Pete's life. "He had his own hotel room. He had the city to play in, and there was never a lack of pretty girls in his life to romance. He kept a good size box filled with small photo albums of hundreds of his girlfriends."

> *"The little man has a tiny voice and you'll need to be closer so you can hear him speak."*

Pete didn't talk much when he was younger and it was difficult for most people to understand his speech as he got older. He had a sweet smile,

Ward Hall - King of the Sideshow!

Pete loved his ladies!

but he had a quick temper. Ward recalls many times the little guy would get very angry with him. "It was his Minnesota Swedish background."

Ward added that Little Pete "was the most wonderful little guy in the world who had a million friends. I have never heard anyone say anything bad about Pete, and it appeared to us over the years that there was not one person out there who disliked him."

Pete was in dozens of television shows and movies, including *Carny* with Jodi Foster in 1979 and *Passion Play* with Mickey Rourke and Megan Fox in 2011. He was part of many publicity tours with Harry and Ward for the kiddie films created by K. Gordon Murray's Trans-International Film Company, in which he dressed as Puss 'n Boots. His natural bent for comedy landed him several roles in theater productions, including the two musicals created by Ward, *Saigon Doll* and *Million Dollar Doll*. Pete's character was murdered in both of Ward's productions.

"I never paid him much, but he made a lot of money selling photos and collecting tips," Ward said. "We set up a joint bank account with him to help him manage his money." He had a happy life and was healthy right up to his last couple of years. Chris and Ward took great care of Pete, and the closeness of the three is legendary within the sideshow community.

Poobah
King of the Pygmies

1930-2012
He will be missed!

House Guests:
A Poem to Ward and Pete

CHAPTER 12

Poet Martha Talburt wrote this piece shortly after Pete and Ward paid her and her husband Lane, a visit in June 2008. She wrote it because, "I'm fond of Ward – find him a delicious character." Reprinted here with her permission.

We had two visitors last week,
A carny man and his sidekick, Pete,
a dwarf who swallows fire and swords.

I fed them steak and greens, they swore
They'd never had a better meal
And leaning forward then regaled
With tales of sideshow freaks:
lizard men, hermaphrodites,
one-ton ladies and other types.

I acted polite
but felt annoyed
to learn of lives I'd sooner avoid
When three-foot Pete looked up at me
And spoke about community
And how for fifty years or more
He'd had family.

Before they left I heard the men,
Both late septuagenarian,
Agree they'd do it all again.
I understood
As best I could.

Program of Events
Presented by the

FROMAN BROS.

FEATURING
IN PERSON

SHOWBOAT
OPENING NUMBER

MISS DE ELGAR - Mistress of Ceremonies

★ LITTLE LORD LEON ★
★ 4 FEET OF FUN ★

WARDELLOS
Unrivalled
Juggling Feats

★ PRINCE RAJAH ★
ORIENTAL
★ NOVELTY ★

Harry Leonard's
Original
Old London
PUNCH-&-JUDY

★ LADY DIANE ★
Worlds Foremost
★ LADY MAGICIAN ★

WARD HALL
and
"PERKY PERKINS"
The Poor Man's
Charly McCarthy

★ MARIA MORAY ★
Contortionist
★ SUPREME ★

THE LEONARDOS
Australian
Impalement Artists

★ HUNK and DORY ★
LAUGHS
★ A PLENTY ★

GRAND FINALE
Havana Mardi Gras

A Society Circus:
The Froman Brothers are Born

CHAPTER 13

Hall and Leonard stashed their sideshow in Oxford, Ala., at the end of the 1954 season and created a new two-man show they called the Froman Bros. Society Circus. They played small indoor shows, usually school assemblies and town halls, performing three or four shows a day, often with each show being in a different town. Who were the Froman Bros.? "I have no idea," Ward said. "I guess we just liked the name."

Ward loved the performing and the schedule they had created, but by February 1955, the cold Midwest was getting to them and the two headed south again. The Froman Bros. Society Circus was a success and they made money. Ward and Harry vowed that the world had not seen the last of the Froman Bros.

Seeking warmth, they headed to Alabama to work on their stored equipment before they were to join the W.G. Wade Shows later that spring. The big job on hand was to paint the new semi they had purchased that summer. As they were painting, friends Byron and Thelma Gosh stopped by and asked Ward and Harry if they would join their All American Indoor Circus, set to open two weeks hence. Not known to ever pass up a paying gig, the two signed on to perform several of their acts, finished their painting and joined Gosh.

The first half of the show featured the knife throwing of Harry, with Ward as the target, and Harry's Punch and Judy Show. In the second act, Ward performed his vent and juggling act. Byron Gosh had put the knife throwing toward the start of the show, in the third slot, because of the popularity of the art in general and because he knew Harry's knife act was quite dramatic. Ward would stand up against the target and a large paper screen would be placed between him and Harry, blocking his view of the target and of Ward.

Ten knives were thrown, all going blindly through the paper; five down one side, five down the other. On opening night Ward wasn't paying attention, miscounted and stepped into the path of an oncoming knife that hit him square in the forehead. As a real trouper, he finished the act, stepped through the paper to take a bow, with blood streaming down his face. He was taken to the hospital and received a few stitches. Needless to say, he didn't finish the show, which ended up three acts short that night.

Ladeez and Gentlemen!
The Greatest, Most Stupendous
SHOW on EARTH

*On STAGE
In PERSON*

Fun for the whole family

Froman Brothers
present

TOBY TYLER;
or
Ten Weeks With A Circus

A COMEDY-DRAMA IN THREE ACTS

WITH ALL STAR BROADWAY CAST

Dramatized by
RICHARD YOUNG

From the story by
JAMES OTIS

FEATURING

WARD HALL

Harry Leonard

LITTLE LORD LEON

DIANE DE ELGAR

SEE
America's Greatest
CIRCUS
HEADLINERS

A Society Circus: The Froman Brothers are Born

The next morning, when Ward caught up with the group headed to their next stop, he noticed that Gosh had changed the order of performances, putting knife throwing last on the bill, just in case.

When the outdoor season began in May 1955, they returned to Oxford, dusted off their sideshow equipment and banners, rounded up a few additional acts and headed to Michigan to join the W.G. Wade Shows where the season proved to be a good one, with the exception of just one day. The July 4 date that summer was one of the worst Ward ever experienced. "We were in Negaunee, Mich., and were waiting all week for the expected large Fourth of July crowd," Ward said. "The day came, but the people didn't. We grossed $8, and the rest of the midway brought in $20. We never could figure out what happened or where the people went." Following the Michigan State Fair in Detroit in early September, Ward and Harry headed south where they played the big fall fairs with Gooding's Amusements, closing out the 1955 season.

Prior to the opening of their outdoor show in spring 1956, Ward and Harry performed as a juggling and knife throwing act in Opa-Locka, Fla., in a show called *The Arabian Nights Pageant,* which also featured the well-known entertainer, Cab Calloway. Pete stayed with Ward and Harry that winter, working in the act while they played the Miami area. One act featured Pete as the target for Harry's knife throwing. Harry would pin Pete against the board and when the throwing was over, Pete would walk away, with his pants stuck to the board by the knives. Ward said to this day that act was loved by the crowd as much as any he saw through the years.

A large gathering of socialites was being held at the West Palm Beach Yacht and Country Club and the organizers were looking for a dwarf to dress up like a clown and serve as a photo opportunity as the guests entered. The agent told the organizers that the only dwarf available was Pete, but they would have to hire the entire act, which they did. According to Ward, the real star of the evening was Pete. "One of my biggest regrets in life is that I didn't ask the photographer for a set of prints. That night, Pete, as a clown, had his photo taken with many of the biggest names in society, including Joseph and Rose Kennedy with their sons John, Robert and Ted!"

Harry didn't want the responsibility of a large operation in 1956, so Hall and Leonard's big sideshow remained parked and they opted instead to create and operate several small single-o shows, which featured only one attraction each. They played hard-to-get when Rod Link asked them to join his World of Pleasure Shows for the season, citing fuel costs and bad tires on the equipment as a reason they might not be able to tour. In fact, before deciding to downsize, they talked about not taking any of their shows out for the season.

At first, Link promised them enough gas to get to the first spot. When Ward said he didn't think he could make enough with just one small show to pay for the larger jumps on Link's route and he wasn't sure if the tires on his vehicles could take another full season of travel, Link gave in graciously and offered free gas all season for all of Ward's vehicles and threw in all new tires for good measure. With new tires and a bottomless gas tank, they rejoined World of Pleasure Shows where Rod and Ward cemented a trusting friendship during that season that lasted until Link died, at 70, on Oct. 31, 1993.

In place of their 10-in-one large show, Ward created a new snake show known as The Midget and the Monsters, with Pete seemingly imprisoned in an 8-foot by 16-foot cage surrounded by live snakes. The monster show was a grind show and pretty much operated with only Pete and a ticket seller. Not being needed at his own show, Ward helped out Link by being the outside talker on the Louie Weiss managed girl show, a task he ended up liking.

> "They'll twitch it and twatch it all while you watch it. You're going to see her do the dance of the rock and roll. She's going to rock it up one side and roll it down the other."

"I confess, this 26-year old guy had the most fun of any job in my life, during the weeks I talked the girl show. The bally for a girl show is quite different than for the sideshow," Ward notes. "It was more fun teasing the crowd with the girls than it was trying to sell the crowd on what oddities they were about to see on the inside." A big part of a girl show bally was bringing a man up on stage and having one of the good looking show girls tease him and embarrass him.

Sally and Sandy, a tattooed couple dropped by and mentioned to Ward that they were looking for work and "out came the two-headed baby and we framed a three-banner baby show," Ward said. Sally sold tickets and Sandy operated his tattoo parlor inside the baby show.

> "One body, two heads. Two heads are better than one.
> Only 10 cents!"

During mid-season 1956, they played several fairs that did not permit girl shows, so Louie Weiss left Link and the girl show to go work other spots. When the girl show started up again, Link hired Ward as manager and, as they headed south, Link asked Ward to frame another show because some of the large Southern fairs called for two girl shows. In response to Link's request for a new show, Ward built and operated

"Sultan's Harem" a smaller girl show which, when combined with the baby show and the snake show, made money. All the girl shows had a blow-off that promised various and exciting things for those who paid a little extra to step through the doorway into the small back room. Sometimes the girls flashed, but most of the time they just danced a bit more provocatively than they did in the regular show.

"Most of the time the law kept the girls from flashing," Ward said. In those cases, they would wear what was known as a "'twittle-twicker," a small piece of a fur coat cut into a small triangle and attached to a flesh covered strap. During the blow-off and under the lighting, the girls would "flash" that piece of fur coat and the men in the audience thought they were seeing the genuine thing. While never being "officially" raided, Ward recalls that on several occasions, he guided the police into the back room to show them how a twittle-twicker worked.

Another valuable friendship developed for Ward that summer of 1956 on the World of Pleasure Shows. Henry Valentine, who operated the show-owned sideshow, and Ward became quick friends. In later years, Valentine would not only work for Ward on several occasions but also bailed him out of trouble several times.

Ward and Harry, along with Pete, teamed up again with Gosh and his All American Indoor Circus during the fall of 1956 and played indoor clubs, including the popular Carmichaels Supper Club in Birmingham, Ala.

Following dates in and around Birmingham, the show headed to Georgia. After Gainesville, the show jumped over the mountains to

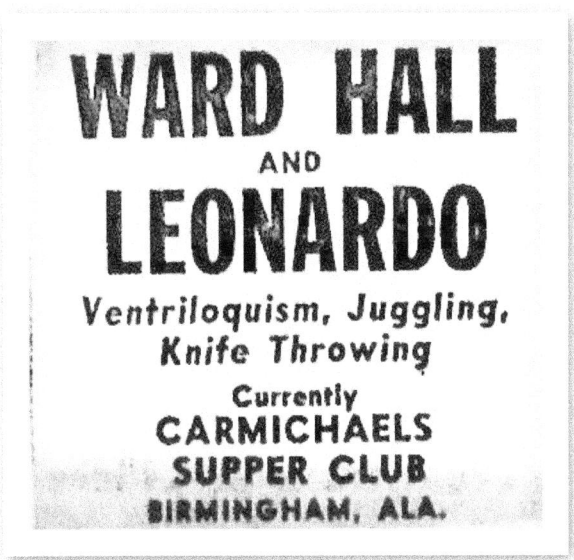

Burnsville, N.C., without most of the acts, who, for some reason, left the show without notice. Other than Harry, Ward and Pete, only Hans and Rosita Clair with their juggling and balancing act showed up. The advance sale was good and no one wanted to cancel, so Byron Gosh went to the sponsors and told them that the truck carrying the animals broke down going over the mountains, rather than admitting that his acts didn't show up.

Luckily, he had a projector and a one-reel circus film called *Hurry, Hurry, Hurry,* starring W.C. Fields. Just before show time he announced the change in the program and that if anyone wanted their money back, he would personally refund it. No one left, and the film, along with the remaining acts, seemed to appease everyone. "When we were packing up to leave, one of the sponsors came over and asked if there ever was an animal truck. I stuck with Byron's excuse that there really was. He believed me," Ward said.

During the winter of 1956-57, Ward and Harry played theaters and hotels in and around Miami Beach with their juggling and knife-throwing acts. While not on stage, Ward kept busy writing, creating and producing the *Broadway Sensations Revue,* a production in which he invested every available cent, on an agent's promise that it would be booked into a 700 seat theater in New Orleans during Mardi Gras in February.

He was deceived big time. When they arrived in New Orleans they discovered the theater was actually in the warehouse district far from Mardi Gras activities, that 300 of the 700 seats were in a condemned balcony and that the "good sized stage" had a permanent movie screen which the revue had to play in front of. The show bombed and the boys gave what little money they had left to their performers to get home. "We smuggled our props and costumes out of the theater at 5 a.m., unable to pay our local bills," Ward admits. The rest of the spring was not much better. "We left New Orleans and went to work for Ben Davenport's Merchants Free Circus, but by late spring we figured we needed to take out our own big show again."

With $13 between them, the partners prepared for opening and headed out to their first stop in Union City, Tenn., with Tennessee Valley Amusements. In addition to the low cash reserve, they had no permit to drive their truck in Tennessee. "We sneaked by the official highway checkpoint and got within six blocks of the lot when we were stopped by a portable truck check point. We were fined $10 of our remaining $13 for not having the proper permit," Ward recalled.

A late spring snow dusted the carnival, causing very slow business on opening day. Ward sold the girl show for $40 to get food money. Business began to improve and by the end of the second week they had

A Society Circus: The Froman Brothers are Born

saved $50 and were headed to Kentucky. Their feel-good mood about the success in Tennessee ended quickly when their truck was stopped as they entered Kentucky and they were fined $37.50 for not having a fuel permit for the state. They squeaked through the fall of 1957 billed as Hall and Leonardo – The Impalement Artists, with a string of one-nighters at night clubs and schools.

In December 1957, the two joined the Tom Packs Circus for a series of dates in Cuba. The circus was sponsored by President Fulgenico Batista and Cuba's first lady, Marta Fernandez de Batista and was principally brought in to entertain specific arms of the government. One day, the troupe would perform for post office workers, another day for the government office workers, etc. All performances were held at the Palace of Sports in Havana.

> Ward Hall and Harry Leonard have completed their dates with Byron Gosh's All-American Circus and they now are readying a side show they will take to Havana as part of **Tom Packs'** Circus.

It was an interesting, albeit somewhat scary, three-week run. "We had the equivalent of a Cuban secret service man in each ticket box and an armed guard inside the big top at each end. In back of the sideshow was a 12-foot high wooden structure manned by soldiers with machine guns," Ward noted. They were there during unsettling times and great caution was required around the clock, no matter where one went or what one did on the island. Ward and Harry broke even on that experience. They didn't make much money and they didn't lose much. Ward had to rebuild and refurbish parts of the show after being hit by a hurricane late in the run, but they came home unharmed.

In May 1958, Ward produced a small musical revue stage show for a sponsor in Hazard, Ky., which went over well and sold out all performances. The only real problem in Hazard was the night the entire crew assembled on the stage following a performance. They inadvertently left the souvenir stand unattended and it was subsequently stripped clean by the audience.

The musical revue was entitled *Sensations of 1958*. Ward was over zealous, as usual, and had too many posters printed but later in the spring, changed the sideshow's title to correspond with the revue's posters and used up the surplus during the next couple of years. He had a new 10-foot high, 30-foot long banner made which increased the sideshow's banner line to 200 feet. At the time, Bill Chaulkas had the largest physical plant of any sideshow with 200 feet of banner, so he was compelled to increase his to 220 feet when Ward increased his own to 200 feet.

Ward never increased his banner line to keep up, but he later got the 220-foot banner line when he bought the Chaulkas show in 1970 when Bill Chaulkas retired. "There has never been a larger banner line in the history of the sideshow than that 220 foot line," Ward notes.

The only change needed the following year was updating the title banner of the sideshow to read *"Sensations of 1959."* In January they were invited to join the Al G. Kelly & Miller Bros. Circus, a large truck-show headquartered in Hugo, Okla. Ward and Harry had already booked the full season with the William T. Collins Show carnival which had a route of large fairs that could be very lucrative. However, Ward thought he would throw an outrageous financial deal out to circus owner Obert Miller, a deal he was sure would be rejected. "I asked for a deal that would be too good for me to refuse, but I felt I should respond (to Miller's request) since he had reached out to us. To my surprise, it was accepted."

It was off to Hugo, Okla. for Ward, Harry and of course, Pete. By the time they joined up with the circus, Miller had sold out to his son Dore, but all financial deals remained the same. Using the tent which the circus once used for its menagerie, Ward and Harry put together a strong performance of working acts, plus a six-member sideshow band. In early summer 1959, Ward, Harry, Pete, Diane and Tex Arnold left the sideshow at the circus under good management and the six of them went over to the William T. Collins Show to fulfill their obligation, spending the rest of a successful season with them.

Ward described show owner Bill Collins as a "very gruff" man who was known to dislike sideshows in general. "When we had our first opportunity to work for him, I asked others how to best get along with him." Never argue with Collins was the advice he kept hearing. "He will come in and tell you how to run your show," one Collins veteran replied. "Just stand there and listen, agree, shake your head and say that's a good idea. He will be happy, and as soon as he walks away from you, he will forget about the conversation and you'll never hear about that issue again." Ward followed that advice and notes that "my relationship with Bill worked out exactly like that and we became great friends." The season saw the typical successes and disappointments to which both Ward and Harry had become accustomed. Finally, they appeared to be on a course that had the potential to lead them to success and maybe even prosperity.

Following the fair seasons in both 1958 and 1959 Harry and Ward kept busy with their *Froman Bros. Broadway Varieties* revue which they booked quite successfully into clubs, schools and theaters. Performances consisted of Ward, Harry, Pete, and sometimes Diane, who became less of a hermaphrodite during the winter and more of a magician. Pete was often billed as "Little Lord Leon, a celebrated comedy star." Harry, who was most often publicized as Leonardo, threw knives and performed "an original Old London Punch and Judy Show." Ward juggled and performed his vent act with his right hand dummy, Perky Perkins.

In an effort to make the troupe look like it had more performers than it actually did, they went by a variety of different names for the different acts they performed, similar to what is done under the big top. It was always Ward Hall and Perky Perkins for the vent act but, when he juggled, Ward became Wardelo the European juggling sensation, or Walendo the Society Juggler. Harry and Ward's knife throwing act was billed as The Leonardos - Australian Knife Throwers; and Harry's puppet show was Leonards Old London Punch and Judy Puppets.

They ended their Miami-area club dates on Christmas Eve 1959, attended a local live production of *My Fair Lady* on Christmas night, and the next day headed to Mexico in a new Cadillac for a short vacation. They then drove up the West Coast to Portland, Ore., where Ward visited with his mother for the first time in 10 years. While there, they got booked to play a 17-day run with the E.K. Fernandez Circus in Honolulu in February.

It was going to be a tight schedule because eight days after they were set to close in Hawaii they were opening in New York City's Madison Square Garden for their first run with the Ringling Bros. and Barnum & Bailey Circus. Nate Eagle had the contract for the Ringling sideshow and hired Ward to provide the acts (a gig that would last from 1960 to 1967 for a six to 10-week showing each spring).

Ward nearly became a dead legend before he had the chance to become a live one. The circus was set up in Kapiolani Park in Waikiki and the beach was just a few feet away. Not knowing how to swim, but having never seen anyone surf before, he was intrigued with the surfing scene. He figured he would rent a board, paddle it out and ride it back on his knees, without worrying about his lack of swimming skills. Predictably, he fell off the board and was going down for the second time when a lifeguard "pulled me safely to shore profaning my stupidity at each stroke."

He stays clear of the open waters today, but when he's at his Gibsonton, Fla., home, you can often find him in the cool waters of his own pool on hot afternoons. Has he learned to swim? "No, I still can't swim, but I have a rope attached to both ends and I hold on to that rope the entire time I am in the water."

The Hawaiian dates were very successful. Fernandez tried to get them extended but the local authorities would not allow it as Lent was to start the next day. They flew back to the mainland, went to New Orleans to pick up the equipment, and drove to New York for their first appearance with Ringling.

April 1960:
First Time on Broadway

CHAPTER 14

It was a good run that first year in New York City, not only for the sideshow but for Ward as well. He had time to see shows and learn more about Broadway musical productions and legitimate theatre. He had a chance to think creatively. He had a chance to savor his life, his friends and the fact that he finally fit in with so many people who looked up to him and respected him. This was all new for this Nebraska misfit and it felt good.

During that initial Ringling run in 1960, the sideshow was presented one act at a time, each on a separate stage. Tommy Hart was the inside lecturer and he would lead the audience from stage to stage talking about the act they were about to see. Ward and Harry were on the first stage with their knife throwing act, and later, Ward showed up on another stage with a vent act. Other acts included Tiny Hicks the fat man; Jean Carol the tattooed lady; Lydia the contortionist; Mario Manzini the escapologist; Estelline Pike the lady sword swallower; Bobby Reynolds with puppets; and Eddie Carmel, the Jewish Giant. Eddie would end up performing on the Ringling dates at Madison Square Garden with Ward through 1967. Pete was in white face as a clown and he too would be a part of the New York show for all seven years.

Eddie Carmel was billed by Ringling as the Tallest Man on Earth at the height of nearly nine feet tall. He was more realistically in the 7-foot, 3-inch range. "While not as tall as many of the giants, Eddie was gangly with huge hands, two elements that made him a great attraction," Ward recalled. In 1970, a popular photo of Eddie by the legendary Diane Arbus, entitled "A Jewish Giant at home with his parents in the Bronx, N.Y. 1970," brought him wide fame and immortality. Suffering from gigantism resulting from pituitary adenoma, he died in 1972 at 36 years of age.

The Madison Square Garden lineup did not change much from year to year and it was usually a smooth and profitable run. It was also a relatively easy gig, with short hours. The sideshow only ran prior to the big top performances. When the whistle blew, connoting that the big show was ready to start, the sideshow had to shut down immediately no matter which act was being featured and the audience would be directed to their circus seats. Ward and Harry would then be finished for the evening. "It worked out well. We were done every night by 7:30 and curtain time for the

Ward Hall - King of the Sideshow!

Broadway productions was 8 which allowed us to see most of the shows," he said. During off hours while in Manhattan that year Ward attended a course in theater management and joined the Motion Picture Publicists Guild, a union relationship that would serve him well in the years to come.

Later in 1960, while the sideshow was booked with the Collins carnival in Jamestown, N.D., Dick Brisben joined for the first time as the "Penguin Boy," a role he would lucratively fill for Ward until he retired in 1986, bought a home and lived a somewhat normal and affluent life in California.

Dick Brisben was 20 years old the day Ward met him. He was 3-foot, 4-inches tall and had no legs. His ankles were connected to his hips. On his right side he had an arm, but no hand, and he had one finger sticking out at the end of the arm. On the left, he had no arm, just a stub. He was on welfare and attended a school for the physically disabled. Ward spotted Brisben in a wheelchair on the midway, invited him over, and offered him a job. Brisben said yes, but that he would have to check with his brother with whom he lived. The next day Brisben's caseworker came out to the fair to talk with Ward, asking him immediately why he had offered Brisben a job.

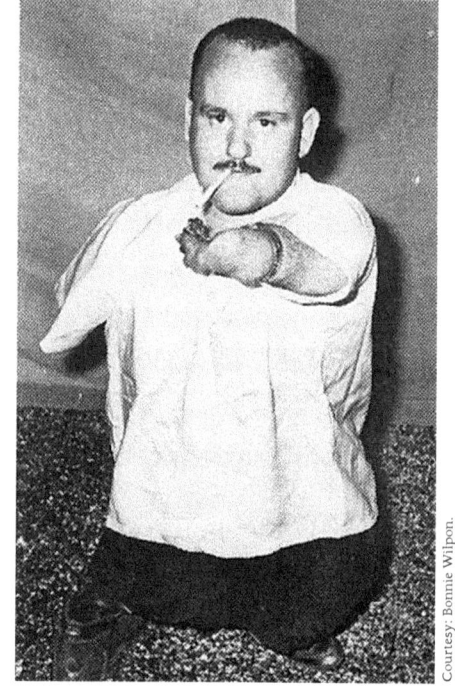

Penguin Boy Dick Brisben.

"Because he can make me money and he will make some money, too," Ward said. The case worker liked Ward's honesty and said she would approve it but asked Ward not to sign Brisben to a binding contract for at least a month so he would have the option to return home anytime he wanted. Ward replied: "I will never sign him to a contract. I would shake his hand, if he had one."

Dick Brisben as the Penguin Boy starred on Ward's midway for 26 years. Marc Hartzman in his book *American Sideshow* described Brisben's act. "He waddled across the stage – like a penguin across polar ice caps of Antarctica – and lit a cigarette with his limited appendages." Brisben was

April 1960: First Time on Broadway

easy to get along with and enjoyed what he was doing, Ward notes. For his act, he would talk about himself and would show how he could use the typewriter. Ward never postured any of his acts as, "Here I am, come look at me because I am a freak." Rather, he wanted to showcase an act that said, "Here I am, come look at me. I am a freak and look what I have done and how I have overcome these handicaps."

While travelling with the Collins show that summer, Joe Queen was booked to operate his tattoo parlor inside the sideshow. In Okmulgee, Okla., a young man just discharged from the Army wanted Queen to add a few things to the large existing tattoos on each arm he had gotten inked while in the service. When the young man got home, his mother saw an opportunity for what she thought would be an easy payday and called law enforcement complaining that her son, who was under 21 years old and under the legal limit to be tattooed in the state without parental consent, received fresh ink at the carnival.

The next day, Joe Queen was arrested and hauled off to jail. Within an hour, another policeman showed up on the Collins lot and presented Ward with a summons to show up in court. Ward and Harry were being sued by the mother for $100,000 for criminal negligence for "allowing a minor to be tattooed" in Ward's place of business. After some investigation, the police released Queen, telling the mother that if she wanted to arrest or sue someone, she should start with the U.S. Army, since he got his initial tattoos while in service to his country. The judge dismissed the case against Ward and Harry and their insurance paid for the $52 in court costs.

Following the regular season, Ward and Harry were booked at the popular Hubert's Museum in New York's Times Square during the holiday period of 1960. They live in rock and roll history today as a result of that short date at Hubert's.

Each act that performed in the famous museum would get a space on the wall near the stairway to hang an 8x10 promotional photo of themselves. Harry and Ward did as dozens of acts before them and stapled their photo on the wall. As fate would have it, the cover photo of the Rolling Stones' *Exile on Main Street* album, released in May, 1972, was of that wall of photos and prominently showed the photo of Ward and Harry.

One of Ward's performers saw it shortly after the album was released and brought the jacket to show Ward. "I was both amazed and baffled to have our picture on the cover. We didn't get paid anything for it and I really didn't know much about the band at that time. I don't even like rock and roll."

When they finished at Hubert's on New Year's Eve 1960, they headed south, preparing to be the featured act at the prestigious Copa City Night Club in Miami Beach but, once again, plans were foiled. "That was to be

Advertisement for Harry and Ward, but the show never happened.

our entrance to the big time. When we arrived in Florida, having driven almost continually in a blizzard from New York, we learned that the club had been padlocked by the IRS for back taxes," Ward said. With the "big time" again temporarily on hold, they drove across the state to Tampa and played the Florida State Fair in February booked with Dick Best on the Royal American Shows midway.

Financial problems once again visited and, following the state fair run, they managed to make a meager income at a couple smaller fairs. They were forced to sell their truck tractor for $100 to raise money for the trip to New York City to play their second date at Madison Square

April 1960: First Time on Broadway

Garden. They knew they would be okay financially once they played that date with Ringling, which turned out to be another great year for them in New York City.

Stability, a word not used up to this point in the story of Ward Hall, started to become reality in late spring 1961. Ward and Harry, along with Pete and Dick the penguin boy, were booked for a season-long run on Sam Alexander's sideshow at Belmont Amusement Park in Montreal, Quebec. Driving to Canada, while listening to big band music on the radio, Ward and Harry were excited about their upcoming gig. Alexander provided everyone with a nice apartment about a mile from the park. Hall, Leonard, Terhurne and Brisben performed throughout the summer at that one spot, enjoying their most relaxed summer yet in the business.

Things ran smoothly all season in Montreal. The entire show was performed in French, so Ward's duties, outside of being a target for Harry's knife throwing, were quite limited. With little responsibility, he had time to tap into his literary leanings and wrote his first novel, *Gypsy Hot Bloods*. It would not be published until 2005 because of its racy, gay-romance theme. He also started writing his first musical, *Million Dollar Doll*, which he finished the following winter. He finished the music first and had a local piano player and drummer record the score. *Million Dollar Doll* would later be reworked and would resurface in 1989 as *Saigon Doll*.

Ward thought it would be a good opportunity to learn the French language, and a couple of the locals working on the show offered to tutor him. Andre, the front talker, taught him one phrase: *"Voulez-vous coucher avec moi?"* and told him to go out and practice it in front of others who spoke the language. Ward had requested to learn, "Hello, how are you?" He went up to Lisa, an 18-year-old bally girl, proudly enunciated the phrase and nearly got clobbered. "I should slap you," she said coyly. "I should say no, but I will say yes." She smiled and added, "You have no idea of what you just said do you?" Everyone laughed and he soon learned that he was the brunt of a well-played joke. He had asked the lady to go to bed with him. He abandoned the urge to learn a second language.

The long Montreal run, which finished in August, was followed immediately by a successful gig in Toronto at the Canadian National Exhibition (CNE). Instead of the comforts and leisure time they experienced in Montreal, everyone stayed on the grounds directly behind the sideshow tent at the CNE. The housing proved very convenient, as the troupe worked from morning until midnight every day of the run, allowing no time for commuting or, for that matter, leaving the show grounds.

In addition to overseeing his own show at the CNE, Ward was busy lecturing Lou DuFour's (real) two headed pickled baby show, working the blade box, and performing his vent and magic act.

From Toronto the show moved to the Western Fair in London, Ont., where the "weather was hot and business was good." That was the final fair of the season. They stored their show equipment at the Conklin Shows' winter quarters in Brantford, Ont. and returned to the States having regained their financial stability.

They had a week off before they needed to board a plane from Los Angeles to Hawaii to join E.K. Fernandez for several island fairs. In a newly painted car and Ward's first-ever tailored suit, Ward, along with Pete and Harry headed to the West Coast, but first stopped in Trenton, Neb., Ward's hometown, to visit his aunt Alda. She had arranged a small dinner party for Ward's father Glen, the local family members and a few circus fans. It was a triumphant return.

With the appearance of success, Ward mesmerized his aunt and her gathered friends with stories from the road. He also played them the soundtrack recording of *Million Dollar Doll*. With hugs, smiles, waves and a sense of achievement, the boys headed off to Los Angeles where they parked their car and boarded a flight to Hawaii. Those few hours in Trenton was the last time Ward saw his father.

The three landed in Hawaii and immediately joined the Fernandez family, who had discontinued the circus and were now operating a large carnival. They were to work Sam Alexander's sideshow in Hilo and on several different islands. Business was only moderately good most of the time and they were beset with rain as they travelled through the state. Halfway through the run, Alexander was admitted to a hospital in Los Angeles and Ward took over management of the sideshow.

While the carnival and sideshow equipment traveled by barge from one Hawaiian island to the next, the sideshow performers flew to each of the islands, which allowed them several days of free time while they waited for the barges to arrive. "There were many tourist treats to make life enjoyable!" Ward recalls.

Sam Alexander was known as the "Man with Two Faces." He had half his face blown off in an explosion years before. One side was a mangled and hideous face and one side was more normal. For several decades he wore a half-mask in public. Tired of hiding his disfiguration under a mask, he decided he could capitalize on it and joined the sideshow operated by Pete Kortes, where he obtained his sideshow moniker. He had 72 surgeries in an effort to rebuild his face, which was accomplished to the point where he did not wear his mask in public anymore. He died in 1997.

Overall, the Hawaiian adventure of 1961 was a successful one. They made money and, when the tour ended in late November, they headed back to Portland, Ore., where they stayed with Ward's mother while they played local club dates throughout the holidays. During the Hawaiian engagement, Ward had sent information about his acts to a Portland

April 1960: First Time on Broadway

booking agent and once back in the U.S., he found the agent was anxiously waiting with many dates booked.

One of those Portland dates stands out in Ward's memory, a Christmas show at the Veteran's Hospital auditorium. "I had not noticed the sprinkler system in the area above the stage and during the fire juggling segment of the act I set off the sprinklers," Ward recalls with a laugh. "The water destroyed the stage and orchestra and soaked about 25 guys in wheelchairs in the front couple of rows." While noting that the event was "most embarrassing," he added that they finished the show after the water was turned off and the fire trucks, summoned by an automatic alarm, left. To no one's surprise, the show ended to no applause.

Shortly after that debacle, they were playing a date in Burns, Ore., and by the time the curtain came down, a heavy snow had started in the area. They had a matinee date in another town the next day so they headed out immediately but didn't get far and ended up stranded in a motel far from their gig. That December 1961 matinee was one of only two scheduled dates during his 70-year career as an entertainer that Ward did not make.

After the Christmas holidays, Harry and Ward headed to Hobbs, N.M., where they had a week-long engagement at the Fontainebleau Supper Club. "We were excited. With a name like that I expected plush curtains, and crystal chandeliers," Ward said. One can only imagine his dismay when he pulled up in front of the club. It was a large, steel, nondescript Quonset building.

They discovered that the inside was as uninteresting as the exterior and the only people they saw when they entered were a few cowboys gathered around a bar in the corner. The manager was a tall man in snakeskin boots. Before he could greet Ward properly he had to spit out a big wad of tobacco. "I told him we were there for the 4 p.m. orchestra rehearsal and I pulled out the music for our show." The manager looked at Ward, looked at the music, and told him calmly, "No need for that mister. I'm also the band leader and none of us can read music." Biting his tongue, Ward simply nodded. "That's okay, just play something peppy." Believe it or not, it was a great week for everyone and Ward and Harry had a great time. Ward looks back now and thinks that week was better than when he played the "real" Fontainebleau in Miami Beach.

Now at 32 years old, Ward had become an established variety show performer, a successful businessman, playwright, musician, composer, co-owner of a well-known sideshow and a man who appeared ever-more comfortable driving new Cadillac cars and wearing tailor-made suits.

During early 1962 as he was preparing for New York City and the date with Ringling, Ward received word that his father had died. Due to his schedule, Ward was not able to attend the funeral. At least that's what he said publicly. In reality, he had no desire to go. Today he looks back and acknowledges that he should have taken better care of his father during his later years.

"He never remarried after divorcing mother and he was a lonely man living by himself in Trenton (Neb.)," Ward said, adding that twice he got his father to come on the show to work but both times Ward had had to ask him to leave because he didn't get along with the others. He and Harry did not have the time, money or the desire to make the trip to the funeral.

Nor did he attend his mother's funeral many years later. "She was living in Oregon in a nursing home and I went out when her cancer worsened and stayed with her for a short time, but had to leave to go back to Florida for an appointment I had with my heart doctor." Two days after he left her, she died. Before leaving though, he told her that he would not attend her funeral because he refused to see her "in a box." Although he helped support her financially, he feels today that he should have done more for her as well, stayed with her when it was obvious that she was at death's door, and thinks he should had made an effort to go to her funeral. However, when the lady who had taught him so much about the arts, his aunt Alda, died, he made sure he was there. "She taught me so much about music and about life that enabled me to do what I have done. She was a great woman and a great teacher."

Starting in 1962, Ward and Harry began heading to Philadelphia with their acts immediately after closing with the Ringling show in New York City, to play 10-day stands with the Clyde Beatty Circus. The first year there, the Nerveless Nocks sway pole act was part of the opening bally for the sideshow and that created huge crowds, according to Ward. "Both Ringling and Beatty were early spring dates and really got us off to a good start. By the time we finished up with those back-to-back circus dates, our bankroll was in pretty good shape."

On the way to Florida to pick up their own equipment following this first Clyde Beatty Circus run in 1962, they stopped in Macon, Ga., where they got a "good deal" on a used GMC truck tractor. They bought it on the east side of town and it promptly broke down on the west side. They were to open with the William T. Collins Shows in Austin, Minn., and once they picked up their equipment, they headed north. For the first half of the journey, Ward estimates the truck broke down every 100 miles; every 50 miles for the second half. "By the time we reached Minnesota our bankroll had nearly been depleted," he said. Once they got set up, the changes they needed to make as a result of the local electrical inspectors cost them what they had left. As Ward and Harry should have expected, the electrical inspectors at the next stop in Rochester, Minn., condemned everything the Austin inspectors insisted upon.

April 1960: First Time on Broadway

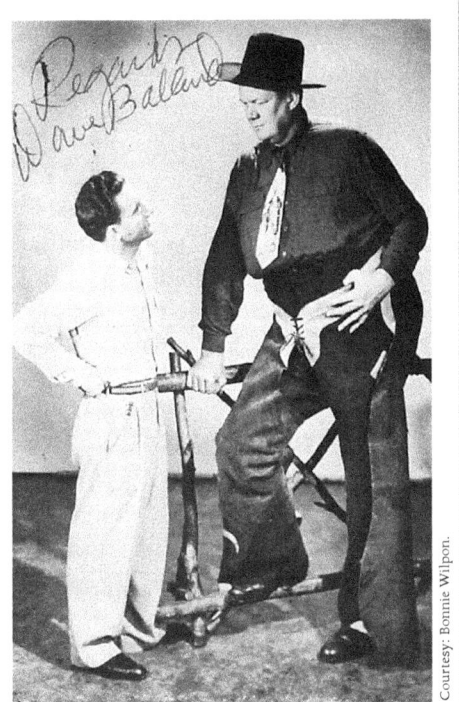

Dave Ballard, the Texas Giant.

During summer of 1962, they took out a smaller show than they had in recent years. The banner line was cut from 200 feet to 135 feet and no live bally was used on the northern fairs. Ticket seller Tex Arnold was out front accompanied by Ward's pre-recorded bally.

Inside, Harry threw knives at Jane, Tex's wife, performed his Punch and Judy and worked the blade box illusion with Jane. Pete ate fire. Ward did his vent act, sold a package of magic tricks, juggled and presented Jerry Dowel for the blow-off attraction as the Alligator Skin Boy. The normal skinned Dowel created an alligator effect by painting his skin with green glue which would crack and peel, giving him the look that easily fooled the customers. Dave Ballard, The Texas Giant, was the featured act. Admission was 25-cents, with an additional charge of 10-cents to see the blade box girl and 15-cents to see the green-scaled Dowel.

The Texas Giant lived in New York City and did a great deal of off-season film work. Although Ward said he was a bit difficult to work with, he was a good draw and stayed with Ward through 1968. "He was close to the vest with his money, and he made a lot," Ward recalls. "I paid him $300 a week and he had the privilege of selling giant rings. He would not live in our accommodations on the grounds so we had to get him a hotel room, plus furnish him transportation to and from the show each day."

Financially, 1962 was the best season Harry and Ward had up to that point and, when they went back to Houston for the winter, they opened up their first-ever checking account. Surprisingly, he and Harry had gotten along fine without a checking or savings account. "We were in a cash business and we paid our bills in cash and we got paid in cash," Ward said. "By putting a couple thousand dollars in an official bank account made us feel a bit more secure."

His creative endeavors continued that fall when he began the arduous task of casting, booking and launching a national tour of his *Million Dollar Doll – a New Musical Mystery*. A.J. "Doc" Barry was hired as the ever-important booking agent; Spain Thorne was brought on as director; and Mannie Edwards was cast as the leading lady.

It was now nearing December and the entire cast was gathered in New York. They had one day of rehearsals under their belts when Ward learned that his booking agent, whom he refers to as a "good hillbilly show agent," was unable to land even one booking for the show. Figuring it was too late to get another agent and get the show on the road for the winter months, he sent his cast home, upset that this first attempt to get his musical produced and a tour booked had failed.

In early December 1962, Ward received a call from Leonard Simons, his old friend from the Rogers Bros. Circus. He was now promotion manager for K. (Ken) Gordon Murray Productions. Ken Murray was fondly known as the "King of the Kiddie Matinee" and had several kiddie films on tour. Each of the low-budget films travelled with costumed characters that doubled as advance men who visited schools and malls and appeared on local televison to promote the upcoming shows.

Simons wanted Ward, Pete and Harry to help promote a Santa Claus movie when it played in New Jersey. Ward took his first-ever helicopter ride when he escorted Santa to a mall for a special appearance to promote the movie. Then in January and February, they helped promote *Little Red Riding Hood*. Harry was the Big Bad Wolf and Ward the straight man. "It was a job much to our liking, taking us through the winter until it was time to start hitting the spring fairs with our shows again," recalls Ward.

Following the promotional film tours in early 1963, Ward and Harry headed to Miami Beach for a couple club dates and along the way, stopped in Sarasota to see fellow sideshow operator Dick Best. He asked Ward and Harry to work the Florida State Fair for him again in February, which they did following their Miami obligations. Ward ended up on the bally for Best during the fair when his talker went on a drunken binge after getting his income tax return.

Following Tampa, they started out with successful circus stands in New York and Philadelphia. Harry's health had begun to decline in early 1963 and it was decided to create a smaller show that they would take out following the spring circus dates. Pygmy Village was created to be small enough to load into the car and house trailer. Inside the tent, Harry lectured about Pete, the pygmy, while Ward made bally and sold tickets. "It was a clever little frame up and was capable of making us a nice living with a minimum of problems," Ward said.

April 1960: First Time on Broadway

Both the 1963 and the 1964 seasons are remembered by Ward as "very agreeable," with only he, Pete and Harry to support. Since they carried everything in their house trailer, pulled by their Cadillac, they didn't have to stop at weigh stations or conform to Department of Transportation rules. "We were quite independent," he said.

In Pygmy Village, Pete, performing as "Poobah the Pygmy," dressed in leopard skins and performed six different sideshow acts with no other "pygmies" in sight. He juggled, ate fire, danced barefoot on broken glass, did the iron tongue act, handled the snake and Harry threw knives at him. Some people felt they were being cheated, expecting to see a plethora of pygmies dancing and prancing. Out front on the bally stage, dressed in a flashy red sequined suit and a top hat, Ward would be joined by Pete, who had a canvas bag over his head, handling a snake. Soon Ward's voice was booming out over the growing crowd that stopped to see what he was selling.

"I want you to meet Poobah who, as you see, is a pygmy.
He is the featured attraction of the Pygmy Village.
In this show you will see all the acts pictured in these
paintings. You will see the pygmy juggler who juggles
everything but the kitchen sink. Here the pygmy dances
barefoot up and down a ladder of sharp knives and jumps
into a box full of broken glass without pain or injury.
The snake Poobah is holding here is a six foot, 10-pound
boa constrictor. This is the smallest snake in the village.

"The pygmy fire-eater will eat and breath fire and flame.
He could bend red hot iron bars over his tongue or bite
the ends from red hot horse shoes. He could drink
burning gasoline like you or I would drink ice tea.

"The show is ready to begin. Six acts, all alive.
You see them all for just 25-cents.

"I sell the tickets here. Come in now."

At that point, Ward would move to the ticket box and begin selling tickets while a taped bally continued to extoll the virtues of the show, while recorded jungle drums pounded in the background. Later in 1963, the first year the Pygmy Village was on the road, Bill Collins of the William T. Collins Shows heard that Ward had a midget show and booked him into the Nebraska State Fair, Lincoln. Ward showed up, put up the tent and the five-banner front. When Collins came along and asked Ward where the midgets were, Ward pointed to Pete. Collins had expected, as did many others who paid to enter the attraction, a bevy of dwarfs.

Collins had the famous three-legged Frank Lentini's big sideshow booked at the fair as well and when he discovered that Pete ate fire in his act, he told Ward he had to get it cleared with Lentini because Lentini might see it as a conflict with his contract. Ward had met the three-legged man before, but he had never worked with him. Frank Lentini was born in Sicily with his unborn brother's leg growing from the base of his own spine. He had two sets of genitals, 16 toes and a fourth foot growing off the third leg. The three legs varied in length by as much as two inches, but Lentini could do just about anything he wanted. He drove a car; he got married and sired four normal children and he ran his own empire, making a great deal of money operating and starring in several of his own sideshows. He died in 1966 at the age of 78.

Ward approached Lentini, explained the pygmy show to him and asked if there was a conflict. Lentini responded (add thick Italian accent). "That's all right. You go back over there and you do the best you can with what you've got." Ward went back and Pete did it right. They out-grossed Lentini because being from Nebraska, "I knew how to work the Lincoln crowds." Ward said he witnessed big crowds attending Lentini's shows, not necessarily because it was a great sideshow, but because they had heard of the three-legged man and they had come "to see a great performer and a true gentleman."

In November, once Pygmy Village was closed for the season, but before heading back to Florida for the winter, Ward and Harry booked several of their acts, including knife throwing and juggling, at the Rivoli Burlesque in Houston. In addition to being Harry's target, Ward sang a couple numbers back stage while a stripper was dancing out front. A live orchestra provided the music.

On Nov. 22, 1963, U.S. President John F. Kennedy and his political entourage started the day in Fort Worth, and while riding in the official motorcade in Dallas, the President was assassinated by Lee Harvey Oswald. Ward was in Houston, in the wings at the Rivoli Burlesque waiting to go on with his ventriloquist act when one of the showgirls told him the president was dead. "What president?" queried Ward as he headed into the spotlight, without hearing an answer.

Reality hit seven minutes later when he finished his act and came backstage. "I was shocked and disturbed as the entire nation was," he said. President Kennedy had been campaigning in Houston the day before and Ward had read about his visit that morning. As they gathered around a radio backstage and heard more details, management cancelled the evening performances and the theater remained closed until after the presidential funeral. Ward, Pete and Harry headed home.

April 1960: First Time on Broadway

Upon returning to Florida, they pulled into La Tosca's Trailer Park in Sarasota to lay off the road for a while and visit with friends. They were confronted by the park manager who notified them that "no midgets" were allowed in his trailer park. "I was astonished and quietly took the trailer to another park to end the immediate problem of midget discrimination," Ward recalled. "All I asked (the manager) before we left was how tall must one be to qualify to stay in your park."

Harry, Ward, and Pete went back to work that winter promoting kiddie films for Ken Murray. While on the road, Harry was interviewed by Ronnie Fox of the *Herald-News* in Patterson, N.J., on Jan. 30, 1964, and the headline read "Wolf Meets Fox." Harry was in his Wolf suit and reporter Fox had fun with the interview. "Leonard has been playing dramatic parts as well as animal roles since his debut as the front portion of a two-man horse 40 years ago," reporter Fox wrote.

In spring 1964, Harry and Ward once again operated the Nate Eagle sideshow for the Ringling Bros. and Barnum & Bailey Circus at Madison Square Garden. Betty MacGregor, known as "Stella the Bearded Lady," worked the show for $50 per week with the rights to keep what she made from selling photo cards of herself. When the photo sales weren't going well for her, she jumped the show, skipping out on her hotel bill. Ward and Eagle covered the bill and vowed not to allow MacGregor back on the Ringling show.

The following year, Bernie Rogers, a drag queen who worked as "Brenda Beatty the Bearded Lady," was featured on the show instead of MacGregor. He/she sold a great many photos and was quite happy. However, five days before closing, law enforcement came into the office with a warrant for Rogers with the declaration that it was illegal to perform in drag in New York City. While Ward talked with the officials, Nate Eagle discretely found Rogers and sent him back to the hotel.

Not being able to locate Rogers for themselves, the police

Brenda Beatty the Bearded Lady.

returned to the office, showed Ward and Eagle the complaint that Betty MacGregor had filed against Bernie Rogers and the conversation went something like this:

Detective: "Is the bearded lady a female impersonator?"

Eagle: "If she tells me she's a lady and she looks like a lady, that's good enough for me. (He pointed to Dottie Williams who was working in the office.) She looks like a woman. She told me she is a woman and she dresses like a woman. She has worked for me for 20 years and I have never once asked her to lift her dress and show me whether or not she is really a woman. Now sir, you look like a man, but don't be dropping your pants because I don't want to see if you are a man."

Detective: *(laughing)* "Doesn't the circus close in five days?"

Eagle: "Yes, it does."

Detective: "Is the bearded lady leaving with the circus when it leaves town?"

Eagle: "Yes, she is."

Detective: "Good. I will write a letter to Ms. MacGregor telling her we are looking into it, and by the time she receives the letter, you'll be gone and we will consider this a closed case."

While Betty MacGregor was a genuine bearded lady, she was not a great attraction. Her wardrobe was nice but drab, according to Ward, she wore no makeup and she was not flashy. Her photo cards reflected that drab image. On the other hand, Brenda Beatty wore a beautiful wardrobe, wore ribbons in her beard to accentuate the curls, and was always in exquisite makeup. Her pictures sold very well and she had a good income. Beatty (Bernie Rogers) was a great asset to the show, brought in nice crowds, and was attracted to several of the boys who worked for the circus. Soon after joining Ward, she boasted that she had a boyfriend. Ward inquired if he was a performer. "He sure was last night," said Rogers over his/her shoulder as he/she walked away.

Closing out 1964 with the Pygmy Village booked with Nolan Amusements playing mostly the smaller fairs throughout Ohio and the Midwest, Ward learned something new. "By presenting a smaller show in smaller spots, we did better than we had done for several years playing bigger shows at larger spots."

That fall another attempt was made to launch *Million Dollar Doll,* but despite a promise by a new promoter of "at least 60 dates" for the show, only five, scattered across the country, were booked, making a tour very costly and inefficient, so once again the musical was shelved.

April 1960: First Time on Broadway

When Ward Hall spoke – not only the midway crowds paid attention, but the media would listen, follow, and chronicle him. There probably has not been an entertainment entrepreneur, other than P.T. Barnum and Robert Ripley, who has received more publicity for his body of work than Ward has. Sideshows and human oddities are colorful and not a common sight, so by nature they attract the media. Add the gregarious Ward to the mix, and any reporter had a potential front-page story.

When Ward talks, people listen.

He started becoming a media darling in the early 1960s. The Pygmy Village was a part of the 1964 television documentary, *Carny,* produced by NBC News and narrated by the well-known burlesque fan dancer, Sally Rand. It was on this show that Sally Rand crowned Ward "The Silver Throated King of the Carnival Talkers." It was the first major accolade for his bally banter.

In the early 1980s when his show played at the Smithsonian Museum in Washington D.C., the review of the show in the *New York Times* noted that, "When Ward Hall talks, people listen, even when they don't want to." *Network News,* covering the same event, wrote that, "Ward looks as normal as a U.S. flag, balding and burly in his brown shiny shoes, but you can tell by the diamond ring on his plump pinky that he's somebody special. He started at 15 and has talked his way around the carnivals of North America."

Amusement Business called Ward "the living counterpart of P.T. Barnum on earth." *Variety* noted that, "P.T. Barnum was the Ward Hall of his day." *Life* magazine asserted that, "Ward Hall is the Ziegfeld of the cornfield." Consistent (and frequent) press of this sort helped make Ward a legend and a media darling, which he remains today. Dean Jensen, author of several circus-related books, was the art critic for the *Milwaukee Sentinel* when he made the assessment on Oct. 1, 1980 that, "(Ward) is a guy with a lot of honey on his tongue who only has to open his mouth to have people swarming like bees around his ballyhoo stage."

Sideshow historian James Taylor looks at Ward and his legacy differently than most. "It's quite the compliment that Ward is called the modern day P.T. Barnum. The 19th century had its Barnum and the 20th and 21st centuries did not. We didn't need another Barnum. We had Ward Hall. We got what we needed," Taylor said.

A mobster friend of Johnny Meah knew of Ward as well. When Meah brought up Ward's name one day in a discussion, the mobster smiled and said yes, he knew Ward, describing him as a "panderer of human flesh."

If he had not become the King of the Sideshow, Ward suggests he would have been either a trial lawyer or a television evangelical minister. He has created his own persona as not only a successful sideshow operator but as a legend who loves the public and his fans.

While he has been as successful as any other sideshow operator in the history of the genre, Ward's multi-dimensional love for the arts, show business and especially Broadway musicals, makes him stand out amongst all the others. It's not hard to believe that if he weren't on the midway, the natural evolution of Ward Hall would have led him to Broadway. Meah predicts, "I think when Ward dies and is re-incarnated, he will come back as either a Hollywood star or a Broadway producer."

11/24/1964:
Ward Suffers Tragic Loss in New York

CHAPTER 15

Harry Leonard, Ward's partner of 19 years, died of a heart attack on Nov. 24, 1964. "It was, and still is, the saddest, most tragic time of my life," he recalls. "In those 19 years we were never apart." The two were staying in New York City's Belvidere Hotel while on their way to Boston to help promote Ken Murray's *Little Red Riding Hood* film. Harry became ill, was sent to the hospital and nine days later he died. Ward spent that entire time at Harry's bed side.

Ward took Harry's body back to Toledo, Ohio, for viewing at a local funeral home and burial. Harry's sister took care of all the arrangements and Ward spent a great deal of time calling friends to inform them of the tragedy. Friends gathered at the chapel to say their goodbyes. It was a Catholic service and the Mass was in Latin and from what Ward can remember, it was quite impressive, but he didn't understand it. It was a cold, dark and rainy winter's day.

Harry's death ended an exciting and often turbulent 19 years of show business and a close personal relationship for Ward. Often penniless, the two were always able to continue and pursue their first love – show business and performing. They performed together and had owned several shows and sideshows through the years. Harry was happy just being a performer. That's all he really wanted. He didn't necessarily want to be an owner, according to Ward. "For 19 years, he went along with my dreams and supported me, just as Chris has done for the past 48 years." Harry's knowledge and Ward's youthful enthusiasm combined to make them strong enough to have persevered against all the hardships they faced. It was a fortuitous relationship that put Ward on a direct path to become the best loved and longest running sideshow operator in the country. Harry was a strong male influence in Ward's life, something he had never had as a child.

In January, 1965, a period that he calls the beginning of a "whole new era in my life," Ward was in Toledo promoting one of Ken Murray's films and made a side trip to visit Harry's grave at the Calvary Cemetery. The visit caught the attention of Seymour Rothman, a columnist for the *Toledo Blade,* who interviewed Ward about his relationship with his late partner.

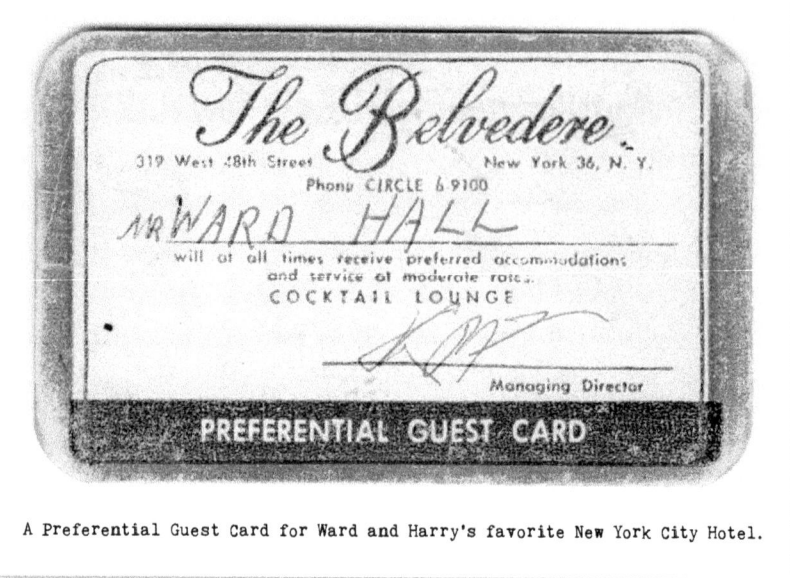

A Preferential Guest Card for Ward and Harry's favorite New York City Hotel.

"Harry was the best knife thrower in the business. I was his target," Ward told Rothman in the Jan. 11, 1965 edition of the paper. "He cut me just seven times in those 19 years and five of those times it was my fault."

Noting that he "really needed to be occupied" after Harry's death, he went back to work almost immediately. He and Pete headed to Des Moines the week before Christmas to promote *Puss'n Boots*. They continued the promotional tour during the winter and ended up promoting the film on nearly 50 television shows.

Following the Des Moines promotional tour, Pete flew home to Minnesota to visit his parents for the holidays and Ward decided to go to Oregon to visit his mother. While there, Ward received a bill for Harry's New York hospital stay that totaled $10,000. Harry did not have insurance and Ward told his mother he had no idea how he was going to pay for it.

Both Harry and Ward had been covered by a group policy with the American Guild of Variety Artists, of which both were members, but just months prior to Harry's death, Ward had received a letter saying that the guild was discontinuing their medical coverage, but for $18 a year, it would continue on an individual basis with a private insurance carrier. Ward sent in his money, but Harry didn't. Ward's mother was the credit consultant for a major hospital in Oregon at the time and urged Ward to contact the insurance company and tell them the entire story. He did and they wrote back that for $18, they would re-instate Harry's insurance for the remainder of the year, and would cover all medical costs. Ward quickly mailed a check.

11/24/1964: Ward Suffers Tragic Loss in New York

Ken Murray had loaned his attorney to Ward to work out the financial side of Ward and Harry's will, which they had drawn up 10 years earlier. It was a joint will and Ohio was the only state at the time that would accept a joint will shared between two persons not legally related. After tracking down the witnesses who had signed the will, probate was smooth and swiftly completed, although doubt still loomed whether the will was actually valid. During testimony, Harry's sister Clara said it best when she commented to the attorney that the will should be legal. "This is the way it should be. They shared the same bed every night for over 18 years."

Harry had not been in contact with his two brothers for many years, but six months after his death, Ward received a letter from one contesting that he now owned half of everything Ward had. Ward sent the brothers a copy of the will and the probate papers, but noted that he and Harry did have a joint bank account in New York City with $16 in it and, being a generous man, he would send them a check for $8. He never heard from them again.

Hall and Leonard's 10-in-one, the big show, had not toured since Harry's health had started to decline and Ward felt that it was time to bring it back out again in 1965. As he was assembling a crew for the show, he began corresponding with a young magician, C.M. Christ. It was arranged that he would join Ward at the Ringling dates in New York City to test the waters to see if he liked the business. The young man came to New York City during his Easter vacation that year from high school in Buffalo. It was a short stint but he discovered he genuinely enjoyed circus life and liked getting to know others in the business.

C.M. "Chris" Christ (pronounced Crist as in crisp, not Christ as in Jesus) told Ward he would like to work for the show. He came back that summer for three months and then went back to Buffalo for his senior year. He joined Ward again briefly for Easter break during his senior year, and then joined him full time in spring 1966 following graduation.

While still in school and thinking that he wanted a life in the circus, Chris had saved a list from the *Amusement Business* magazine that listed all show owners, their specialties, and geographic areas in which they played. Chris had written letters to 22 of them asking for a job. Ward wrote back. Chris chose him over the other respondents because the six-page letter "was filled with more bullshit than all the others combined."

On the day Chris was to arrive in New York City, Ward left Madison Square Garden between shows to meet Chris at the hotel. "I had never seen a more nervous person in my life," said Ward. "But there in the lobby was this tall, gangly kid with beautiful hair and a fair complexion who was ready to get to work."

Big Screen Action:
Ward as a Celluloid Hero

CHAPTER 16

Ward would eventually appear in seven full length movies, countless videos and documentaries, and nearly 100 television shows. His celluloid stardom stretches over five decades and an entire volume could be written just about his time in front of a camera. While not exactly concise, this chapter will highlight some of the projects in which he has been involved, in chronological order.

It is fun to point out that while Ward is a darling of virtually all media, he has never been much of a movie-goer or television fan himself. In a 2013 interview, he noted that the last film he had seen in a theater was Water for Elephants in 2011, and that was only because his crew insisted that he go with them. The last film for which he bought his own ticket was in 1989. The film? He can't remember, he just remembers going. His favorite television show for the past couple of decades has been the reruns of the *Lawrence Welk Show*.

Ward's first venture into film was in 1962 while he was operating the sideshow for Ringling at Madison Square Garden. He appeared in *The End of Bimmy Jay*, produced by Larry Crane and Naddar Productions. He jokes that in his first role in a professional film he played a sideshow talker. He surmises that it was obviously a type-casting decision on Crane's part. Also in New York City that same year, Ward appeared on a serial radio show, Footprints in the Sands of Time, in four episodes playing various characters including Edgar Allan Poe and P.T. Barnum.

During 1964, Ward's popularity as a talker and extrovert got him cast in another film, *Teamwork,* another quickie production created by Larry Crane. Shot in Manhattan late at night, Crane's films were able to benefit from the fact that many Broadway actors who wanted to earn extra money could work under assumed names, after their regular show performances were over for the evening. "I never made much money doing those and didn't get credits, but they were good training for me," Ward said.

Carny was an NBC-TV produced one-hour special that aired on April 12, 1964. The network had visited six carnivals during the previous summer, filmed more than five-miles of 16-mm film and spent nearly $100,000, a typical budget for a television documentary at the time.

"Step right up and go behind the glitter of the midway. NBC News explores the world of the carny – an American phenomenon - in one of the season's most delightful programs. With Sally Rand as hostess."

Ward's Pygmy Village featuring Pete as Poobah in all the starring roles was one of the featured scenes in the documentary. "Once inside we find only one pygmy, but then Mr. Hall didn't promise six pygmies, he only promised us six acts," Sally Rand declared. Ward appeared in the show as himself, the talker fronting the show.

Pete, Ward and Harry performed as costumed characters and advance and promotional men for several of the kiddie films produced by Ken Murray for many years. In July 1964, they had their first chance to actually be in one of his film shorts. They went to Santa's Village theme park in Dundee, Ill., a Chicago suburb, in July and worked for two weeks on the film, *Santa's Magic Kingdom*. Later it was renamed Santaland and released in 1966. Both Harry and Pete, in costume, had leading roles and Ward served as a production assistant.

Years later, it was all cameras and lights again for Ward (along with Chris this time) in 1972 when Ken Murray called and asked them to work on the movie *Daredevil*, starring George Montgomery and Terry Moore. It was shot in the Tampa and Gibsonton areas and their home was used in several scenes as was Ward's limousine. Ward played a hotel clerk and Chris served as a link between the film company and the community in finding people and things needed in a hurry and on the cheap. He also was Montgomery's stunt double in one scene. Chris and Ward got 45 of their friends employed as extras on the film and they all participated in the premier gala at the Tampa Theater.

In the months to follow Ward and Chris were involved in the filming of commercials for Standard Oil and for Lion Dog Film's feature *Moonshiner's Holiday* that also included scenes shot in and around Gibsonton.

In August 1973, while playing in Indianapolis, Ward appeared in a television special called *On Location: Alan King at the Indiana State Fair*. Dick Johnson's unit was playing the fair and had to close down during the shooting of the segment when Ward was being interviewed by King. The show had been doing well that day and Johnson got a bit perturbed that the interview was taking so long. Money was being lost for every second that Ward told stories. "Dick was getting impatient because he had customers, with cash in hand, lined up to come in," Ward said. Alan King kept talking, asking very basic and non-informed questions and it was obvious to Ward that King didn't quite understand, or like, the business. "I can't imagine why anyone would pay 50-cents to see this stuff," the comedian told Ward, referring to the sideshow acts. Taken aback, Ward retorted, "I can't imagine someone paying $5 to go to a nightclub to see your act." King bragged, "They pay $15." To which Ward responded: "That's actually worse!"

The network edited out that exchange, but it did serve the purpose at the time. The interview ended shortly thereafter and Johnson reopened the show. The edited segment effectively showed that freak shows "provide honorable livelihoods for handicapped men and women who otherwise might be unemployable." The show aired the week of September 24 as part of the Wide World of Entertainment programming on ABC and the ratings were high enough for network bigwigs to consider a follow-up show.

Shortly after returning home in early December 1973 from the International Fair & Expositions Assoc. (IAFE) confab in Las Vegas, Ward and Chris helped coordinate a television special with David Frost to be called *On Location with the Human Oddities,* a show that was an outgrowth of the successful segment Ward had taped earlier with Alan King. "We were led to believe that the show was to be about the entire community, not just the unusual people," Ward recalls. "Many of my friends donated their service and talents to the project because I was told the producers were going to donate a sizable amount to the IISA's Showfolks Retirement Village." He only had a verbal agreement on the project and had no promise on how much that donation would be. Finally, after writing ABC several times requesting the promised donation, they received a check for $500. Ward, as well as the others, was outraged but at this point, it was too late to do anything except to cash the check and be smarter the next time a similar opportunity presented itself.

Ward on the set of *Sideshow,* 1976.

During the 1976 season, Ward and Chris were joined several times by Jeff King and Martin Brest and their crew from

Sunrise Films, who made what Ward calls, a "beautiful documentary about our show" titled *Sideshow*. Unfortunately the studio decided not to release it, and both King and Brest went on to be major film directors in Hollywood. "They did a very good job on the film, but we never did get a good answer why it wasn't released," Ward notes.

Hollywood found the boys again in February 1979 when Chris and Ward contracted with Lorimar Productions to provide show equipment and sideshow people for the filming of *Carny*. On location near Savannah, Ga., from April 1 to July 3, the producers built six different show fronts and a front gate. The film, released in May 1980, featured two hustlers who came to town with a carnival. It starred Jodie Foster and Gary Busey, among others. One of the taglines of the show was, "When you're young and going nowhere - the Carny looks like a good way out."

On July 4, 1979, sword swallower John Trower, the fire eating Pete and Ward flew to New York City where they were joined by Dolly Reagan the Ossified Girl and author-historian Joe McKennon to tape an hour-long interview the next day with Tom Snyder on the *Tomorrow Show*. On July 5, Ward lunched at the St. Moritz with Irvin Feld, head of the Ringling organization, and in the evening they taped the show. NBC liked the ratings when the show ran and showed it again as a rerun that fall.

In March 1980, upon coming home from a trip to South America, Chris and Ward signed up 30 of their friends and provided equipment and locations for the Astral Bellevue Pathe movie *Being Different*. "We put up the big sideshow at our winter quarters and they filmed Johann Petursson the Viking Giant, Little Pete, Percilla the Monkey Girl, and Emmett the Alligator Skin Man. Then Chris took them to Niagara Falls, Ont., where they filmed Sandy Allen, the tallest lady in the world. In California they filmed Dick Brisben the Penguin Boy at his home," Ward noted.

They spent three weeks filming. He recalls one specific scene in which he starred. "It was a 20-minute take and I was dressed in a three piece suit, standing in the sun on an iron stage!" The film, released in 1981 and narrated by Christopher Plummer is a "beautiful story of people whose life revolves around sideshows because of their being different."

> "Step up close ladies and gentlemen for what you are about to see is a rare sight indeed, one of the last traveling sideshows in America today. It might amuse you. It might amaze you. Yes, it might even disturb you. But come, come witness it with your own eyes. For tomorrow it may vanish for good."

A film crew with the British Broadcast Corporation (BBC) Television unit followed the Chris and Ward-owned World of Wonders 10-in-one sideshow for six weeks during the summer of 1994 as the show worked its way back to Florida for the winter. The hour-long documentary was entitled *The Last American Freakshow,* and it doesn't take long when talking with Ward to realize that this was one of his favorite film projects. The cameramen covered all aspects of the show, from fat man Howard Huge (Bruce Snowden) taking a nude shower with a garden hose behind the tent, to the somewhat poignant end-of-the-season dinner at the Georgia National Fair in Perry during early October.

"We brought in an amazing line-up of talent from all over the country for the final show that year," Ward said. "When we got to Perry, we lined the inside of our tent with black plastic to make it light-proof so the photographers could play around and get unique shots of each of the acts." The night before the fair opened, the catered banquet was set up on a lawn next to the lake so as the sun set over the water all the acts sitting around the tables were silhouetted by the light. That was the final shot of the film. "It was really beautiful, and we had a lot of fun all gathered around enjoying a splendid meal," Ward said. Using his own camcorder, Ward taped much of the same scenes the BBC did, including the final dinner, and had it edited. "I called my version *The Final Sideshow* and put it on sale the following year," he said.

The documentary was to premiere on the BBC in London on Dec. 17, 1994 and the producers called to see if Ward could go to London for that opening event and meet with the press. Chris answered the phone and Ward heard him ask, "How much you paying?" Then he heard Chris start negotiating. The BBC had not planned on paying Ward anything aside from all his expenses, and that was not what Chris expected. "Needless to say, they came to an agreement and I was told to expect three intense days of meeting with the media when I got there," Ward said.

The show received one of the highest ratings any BBC show ever received during the 7 p.m. hour. That high rating came about, according to Ward, "not necessarily because the show was so good, but there was to be a National Lottery drawing at eight that night that had one of the biggest jackpots ever."

In 1996, Ward and Chris were involved in an even bigger production than the BBC documentary. Filming took place throughout the spring and summer at various locations that year for *Sideshow – Alive on the Inside.* The two-hour television documentary was narrated by Jason Alexander (George on *Seinfeld*) and aired for the first time on The Learning Channel (TLC) in February 1997. That first showing brought in the highest ratings that network had up to that point, said sideshow historian James Taylor who was a writer as well as a "talking head" for the production.

Ward played himself and he and Taylor garnered the most face time in the all-star production. Virtually every major and a few minor sideshow stars that ever walked a bally were in the show, either as a live interview

World of Wonders set up in the New Mexico desert for *Passion Play*, 2009.

or on archival footage. Taylor calls the program, which has turned out to be a cult hit, the best sideshow documentary ever filmed.

The last big production in which Ward and Chris were involved was the full-length thriller, *Passion Play*. It was quite an enjoyable experience according to Ward. World of Wonders closed its season at the Arkansas State Fair on Oct. 20, 2009 then moved it to the desert on the Zia Pueblo reservation, less than an hour outside Albuquerque, N.M., for the filming. "We had expected to go in, set up the equipment, get it filmed, and head on to Gibsonton by November 2," he said, noting that they didn't get out of there until late December.

"There was a great deal of hurry-up-and-wait and we had to stand by and be ready at any time," he said. "We had our tent, our banners and our bally stage set up, and there wasn't anything for us to do except wait, and get paid. It was a nice vacation after a hard season."

The film starred Mickey Rourke, Megan Fox and Bill Murray and centered on a special female act in the sideshow – the annex attraction who had angel wings. Ward was cast as a curmudgeon, and World of Wonders regulars Sunshine English, Tommy Breen, Little Pete, Red Stuart, Natalie

Big Screen Action: Ward as a Celluloid Hero

Verelli and Mike Vitka performed their acts for the cameras. Ward admits that most of them were bored after the newness of their situation rubbed off but they all received pay for every day their parts in the shooting were delayed.

Stephen Holden, film critic for the *New York Times* called the movie "a fatuous noir-flavored reverie with allegorical pretensions." The May 6, 2011 review added that the film "is barely palatable." Ward laughed when he read the review. "I could have told you that, but we got paid and had a lot of fun, so that's okay."

The popular History Channel show, *American Pickers,* visited with Chris and Ward during spring 2013. The episode, "Step Right Up," was taped in their Gibsonton back yard and at the Museum of the American Carnival on the IISA show grounds a couple miles away. The program's Mike Wolfe and Frank Fritz picked through winter quarter sheds and found a few treasures that they purchased on the show, plus several they purchased for themselves after the cameras stopped rolling. Even the cameraman got into the act and purchased an old trumpet that Ward had forgot he had.

"We get a call one day asking if we would be interested in being on the show. They had called the IISA and they suggested they call us," Ward said. "We said we would and they explained that we wouldn't get paid, but they would buy enough to make it worthwhile for us, which they did." An advance man was sent out about a week before the scheduled shoot to see what we had and on the day of the filming, the crew showed up around 11 a.m. Before Mike and Frank showed up, some things were pulled from the back of the shed to make it easier to find, and a large painted banner was brought in from a neighbor who wanted it sold.

A large motorhome pulled up in front of the house as did several support trucks. "They make it look like the guys just dropped by, found us at home and it was only them and their photographer who walked around picking out stuff," said Ward. "It was interesting to watch and yes, it certainly was worth our time. It was also good publicity for us and they were true gentlemen."

One item Mike "discovered" was a Devil Child, a grotesque creature made by the famous gaff creator, Homer Tate. He especially liked the creature and took it to the museum after they left Chris and Ward's home and talked with curator Doc Rivera about the item and about Tate's Curiosity Shop's history. Mike then donated it to the museum, which now has it on display.

"They were very fair to us and gave us very good prices for things," Ward said. "We told them what we wanted for some items and they said no, it was worth a lot more than we asked for, and they gave us a higher price." The episode premiered on June 3, 2013 and has been shown many times in repeat since. "I wish they would quit showing it so much," laughed Ward. "I want them to come back and do another show, because we have so much more I would like to get rid of."

Rain didn't dampen spirits in Gibsonton the first week of December 2013, when the AMC Channel brought their crew to town to tape an episode of its popular *Freakshow* series. Chronicling the daily life of Todd Ray's Venice Beach (Calif.) Freakshow, the television show premiered in February 2013 and this event, which featured Ray's show combined with Chris and Ward's World of Wonders show, was taped for the second season of the series. "They called us and it was not an easy thing to negotiate," claims Chris, who has always done the negotiating for Ward and himself. "It took two months, but we did it and it was an amazing show."

The World of Wonders tent and bally stage were set up behind the Museum of the American Carnival on the grounds of the IISA and individual performers were interviewed and taped. The next day, in a heavy rain, World of Wonders, with Ward as bally, started the free performance for the 420 guests who could get into the tent. Another 50 to 60 people were turned away due to capacity issues. Following the World of Wonders performance, Ray was the bally for the performance of his Freakshow troupe. All of it was being recorded. Each sideshow presented its regulars: Tommy Breen, Red Stuart and Sunshine English represented World of Wonders while shock artist Morgue and George Bell, billed as the tallest man in America at 7-foot, 8-inches, were among those who represented the Venice Beach Freakshow.

Ray said getting a chance to join forces with Ward and the World of Wonders group "was one of the greatest moments of my life. It was literally a dream come true. To have it happen in Gibsonton was the icing on the cake!" The combined effort gave Ray a special moment that he said he will never forget. "There was a moment, under the tent, when I saw in Ward's eyes that he was reliving the glory days of the sideshow. It seemed like he was remembering when he had the biggest and most exciting shows on the midway. I realized then that the sideshow was not dead and would never die. In fact, it is very alive and will always live in all of us."

"It was a great opportunity for many of our friends and the other locals to come out and see a free show," added Chris.

Act Needed:
Knife Thrower, Please Apply

CHAPTER 17

Following Harry's death in late 1964, Ward needed a knife thrower to help fill out the line-up for the 1965 Ringling date. He brought on Butch Clifford, a thrower, and his wife who served as the target girl. He also brought back Eddie Carmel, the Jewish Giant, who once again was allowed to pitch giant rings, a popular item at the time. The Cliffords were allowed to make the pitch for a plastic telescope they offered "free" to all children. The Cliffords kept a share and Nate Eagle, the sideshow manager, got a piece. "I'm not sure Mr. North would have approved if he had heard the pitch, but the telescopes were a big hit," said Chris.

> "This year, John Ringling North brings you the largest, most spectacular edition of The Greatest Show on Earth ever. And he wants to make sure you don't miss anything from your seats so he is providing, for free, these high magnification telescopes that make that high flying young lady appear to be in your lap. These are free, but we are asking 25-cents each to cover packing, handling and shipping."

Toward the end of Easter week when the crowds and the pitch money slowed down, the Cliffords went missing on the Friday of the show's final weekend. "They didn't show up for the Friday show, so I went to the hotel to check on them and found they had checked out," Ward said. "That was a serious problem because that left our first stage empty and we needed something out there."

About that time, "a nice Irish lad" asked Ward for a job. Ward hired him immediately. Pulling out a few props and an unused costume, the young lad became a strongman after Ward showed him a couple phony strength stunts. He did fine Friday night but during the Saturday morning show, Ward had to let him go because he had found out that the kid had jumped his menagerie job with the circus and went with Ward, which was against Ringling policy. The kid was embarrassed, Ward was apologetic, and the stage remained empty for the rest of the weekend.

Shortly after closing at Madison Square Garden in 1965, Chris headed back to high school in Buffalo and Ward trouped to Philadelphia for the

Chris, the knife thrower, and Ward, the target, July, 1965.

Beatty circus run there. Then, Ward headed out to Queens and took over management at the New York World's Fair of the Arabian Show at the Moroccan Pavilion, in charge of 27 Moroccan Arab performers. He only stayed for two weeks. "The management wanted to open late and close early, so I didn't think I would make any money." He left and decided to go back to Houston, pick up his own show and start the season.

What does Ward Hall do if he needs to get from New York to Houston? While most would probably fly, Ward went out and purchased another limousine. He would eventually own six during his career. People thought Ward liked limos just to show off but he had a very practical reason to have one. "I hired many fat men, fat ladies and giants through the years and we could not transport them in traditional vehicles," Ward explained. The day before he left for Texas, instead of waiting for the elevator at his hotel, Ward decided to run up the stairs. He fell and hurt his ankle. "It hurt quite badly, especially the next morning, but I had to get on the road, so I tried to ignore it and headed to Houston." He decided to not go directly to Houston, but to stop along the way and visit with friends who were working at various fairs.

Act Needed: Knife Thrower, Please Apply

In Columbia, Pa., just south of Harrisburg, he stopped to see old friend Milt Robbins who insisted that Ward see a doctor for his now swollen ankle. He did, and found that it was broken. Once a cast was placed on it he thanked Robbins and headed out. "It was my left ankle, so it didn't interrupt my driving."

When he got to Houston, where the equipment had been stored at the Old South trailer park over winter, he and Pete, along with friend Billy Judd, busied themselves preparing for the 1965 season. Within a couple weeks Ward opened Pygmy Village near Chicago, along with the two-headed baby and a fat-man grind show. Managed by Billy Judd, it featured Tiny Hicks who had been Ward's fat man for many years at Madison Square Garden. The show played several Midwest dates and was booked with Nolan Amusements for a couple early fairs in Ohio.

As Chris was heading to Chicago to meet up with Ward for the summer following his junior year in high school, a severe storm caused a blow-down that ripped the sideshow tent in numerous places. In all the excitement, Ward had not received the telegram from Chris asking him to pick him up at the bus station, so Chris, along with his two large suitcases, trudged to the racetrack where the show was playing. After the long, hard walk, the tired and somewhat agitated Chris found the sideshow.

It was an inauspicious sight for the haggard Chris. The tent was on the ground, the poles scattered. Chris saw Pete the dwarf and Tiny the fat man sitting on the ground sewing torn canvas. Then he saw Ward, hobbling around due to his broken ankle. Chris admitted to Ward later that if he would have had enough money he would have turned around and gone home after seeing the mess he had walked into.

Chris is straightforward about how little he knew when he joined Ward. He is a self-taught sword swallower and fire eater. "I learned the circus arts out of necessity. I paid attention and took advantage of on-the-job training," Chris said. When he joined Ward, there was no extra room for him in any of the trailers so he ended up sleeping in the tent inside the blade box for the duration of his first summer with the show.

One skill Chris quickly learned from Ward was driving. When he arrived he was just 17 and had not learned to drive. Realizing this would be an essential part of his duties with the sideshow, Chris picked up the basic skills from his mentor, using Ward's Cadillac limo on the back lot of a small fairground in Rocky Grove, Pa. As the show was tearing down late one night, Chris was carrying the giant mannequin dummy they had on display to the truck when he tripped over a tent stake and badly bruised his leg. Working through the pain, they made a successful jump to Gahanna, Ohio, an eastern suburb of Columbus.

Chris asked for a referral to a doctor to treat his leg and was sent to a Gahanna doctor named Sam Shepherd. Chris found out later that this was THE Sam Shepherd who had been sent to prison for allegedly killing his wife while they lived in Bay Village, Ohio. Dr. Shepherd had served 10 years in prison before he was acquitted by the Ohio Supreme Court and deemed an innocent man. He moved to Gahanna and resumed his medical practice. Chris saw him just a couple months after he was released from prison. Shepherd's case was the basis for the television series and the movie *The Fugitive*.

Following several more fair dates in Ohio the show closed its Northern route on Labor Day in Canton booked on with Megerle Shows, which was to be Chris's last stand that summer. On the last Sunday night the crew threw a big going away party for Chris and following closing on Monday night he headed back to Buffalo for his senior year of high school. He promised everyone he would see them the next spring during Easter Vacation.

As the show was preparing to head to Texas for a series of fall dates in 1965, the 10-in-one was readied and fully staffed, and the pygmy show was merged into the larger sideshow. Two grinds, the fat man show and the two-headed baby show, accompanied the big show.

Tiny the Fat Man was then 46 years old, weighed in excess of 600 pounds, and was afraid of being in the Southern part of the U.S., including Texas. Early in his 20-plus year career on the midway Tiny had been stranded by a carnival on which he worked in the South that had kicked him off the show and didn't pay him. Why? The carnival owner, not wanting to pay him, told Tiny, "Southerners don't like fat people and that's why they aren't buying tickets to your show." Alone and penniless, Tiny had to find his way back home to Warren, Ill., and vowed never to go into the South again.

He had a heart-to-heart talk with Ward who promised he would be watched over, there wouldn't be any trouble and he wouldn't be abandoned, and Tiny consented to go to Texas. The show was booked on the Bill Hames carnival midway in Abilene. Billy Judd drove and Tiny rode from Ohio to Texas in a car with no air-conditioning. It was a long, hot trip for Tiny and the weather in Abilene remained hot for the entire run of the fair.

Ward learned a lesson while in Abilene about running late and setting up fast. The baby show was the simplest to erect so it went up first and once it was in operation, with Judd at the ticket box, Ward and most of his crew went to work setting up the other shows. A few hours later, Ward checked with Judd at the baby show to see how business was. Judd noted that people were coming out, quite unhappy. Ward went inside to see what the problem might be. He came out laughing. "In our rush to open, we neglected to put the rubber babies in the jars. All people had seen were containers of cloudy water." Ward still laughs about that day.

So Tiny would be comfortable on the next jump, from Abilene to Amarillo, Ward purchased a ticket on an air-conditioned Greyhound bus for him. When Ward and his people pulled onto the fairgrounds the next morning he was greeted by Buster Brown, the Hames Show general manager, who had a hand written note in his hand from Tiny saying he was still afraid of the South and was heading home to Illinois. With no fat man, Ward quickly changed the fat show to a jungle mummy exhibit, utilizing the show's giant dummy figure and banners he had painted years prior.

The 1965 fair route ended for Ward and Pete in late October in Jasper, Texas and they parked the equipment back in Houston. Within a couple weeks, they made a deal with Buddy Williams, who owned a live freak animal show, to use the Pygmy Village as an annex attraction for his animal show at the Arizona State Fair. They agreed that Ward would keep all the money from the blow-off if he would oversee the animal show and lecture on the animals. Two other dwarfs joined Pete on the stage during that run, Glen and Billy Newman. Billy was both the talker and the attraction on the bally stage. Ward was inside lecturing on the animals and was able to build a nice tip for the Pygmy Village, starring Pete.

The first day they were set up, business was booming and Ward brought in a great deal of money. Once Buddy Williams saw the potential of the Pygmy Village he reneged on his deal with Ward and wanted half of the blow-off proceeds. Ward was upset that Williams didn't hold up to his original deal and threatened to pull out. In a cocky, "I-don't-think-you-will-do-it-voice," Williams asked Ward if he needed help loading up the equipment. "I looked at him, said no, we could handle it, and within an hour we were loaded and pulling off the fairgrounds, never looking back."

Prior to dispersing for the winter, the gang of Ward and the little guys, now with time on their hands after leaving the Arizona State Fair in Phoenix earlier than expected, decided to take a sight-seeing trip to the Grand Canyon, a place none of them had visited before. Then, because they were so close to Las Vegas, another place none had visited, they decided to visit that desert oasis. The dwarfs – Pete, Glen and Billy Newman, wanted to treat Ward to a night out on the town while in Las Vegas. They told him to wear a tuxedo. They washed and polished the show's limo. The dwarfs had matching red tuxedos with black shawl collars. Billy drove, with Glen in the front passenger seat and Pete and Ward in back.

They pulled into valet parking at the Tropicana Hotel and Casino. Billy got out, opened the door for Ward, and the four of them walked through the casino doors, attracting a great deal of attention. Management came over to see what was going on, and not wanting to have their gambling customers distracted much longer, Ward and the boys were officially escorted through the one-armed bandits to the theater where they were taken past the long line and were seated at an excellent table where they ate and saw Ward's favorite show, *Folies Bergere*.

The casino provided complimentary dinner for the well-dressed foursome. Ward loves to tell the story, noting that "Isn't it wonderful what three dwarfs dressed in red and a second hand limo can accomplish?" The next day Pete flew home to Minnesota. Glen and Billy headed back to Ohio. Ward went to Portland to spend the holidays with his mother and sister. It was a great end to an eventful year.

Over that winter, Ward and Judd built a torture exhibit they opened in late January 1966 on the Gene Ledel Shows midway at the Fort Worth Fat Stock Show. It isn't one of Ward's most pleasant memories of opening a new show."We used store mannequins," said Ward. "We refurbished them into victims and, instead of a traditional banner line, we used blow ups of the photos we took of the finished characters. It looked good and we had a good grind tape with sound effects."

As Ward and Judd would create each "victim," it would be taken back to Judd's motel room because they had no room to store them in the small space in which they were working. One day a maid opened the door of the closet and saw what she reported to the police as "the bloody bodies of women." Of course the officers who arrived laughed as soon as they opened the closet, realizing the so-called victims were dummies. Motel management failed to see the humor and it took some quick and smooth talking on Ward's part to not be thrown off the premises with their works of art. One day as Judd was working on the exhibit in their outside work area, a gust of wind blew up a piece of metal and cut one of his fingers off. Quick-thinking Ward wrapped the hand in a towel, picked up the severed finger and rushed Judd to the nearby hospital where it was sewed back on. Within a couple months, Judd once again had full use of his finger.

Opening day for the torture show in Fort Worth was 18-degrees, cold for the area, but business was decent. The second day, Ward showed up to prepare for opening, found that the man he had hired to watch the show overnight never showed up, and that kids "made shambles" of the exhibit. "We patched it up to get through the spot, which was the first, last and only one for that show." With a week before they were to open with the Bill Hames carnival in Houston, Ward and Judd reworked the exhibit into a jungle theme for the Pygmy Village and called for Pete and the Newman brothers to head to Houston. They also created a single-o for Watallah the Jungle Giant, using a large statue they purchased from Tate's Curiosity Shop of Arizona. The giant was exhibited laying down in a box with an open top for viewing. Several days after opening, a concessionaire from the other end of the midway came up to Ward carrying one of the giant's legs.

Not wanting anything else to be taken, the other leg was removed and both were stored away. Judd and Ward figured no one could heist the giant's torso as it weighed nearly 200 pounds. However (you guessed it!), Ward was taking a rest behind the show tent an hour later when he looked up and saw two locals carrying the giant crawl out from under the tent. He gave chase but the two thieves threw the torso over the fence and the two jumped into the get-away car that had pulled up, leaving the giant behind. The perpetrators were never found. Ward had several men go out and retrieve the body and put it back on display.

A smile comes to Ward's face when he recalls the fat man he hired that season to take the place of Tiny. The new fat man had a habit of sleeping while on exhibit. In response, Ward had a large sign made with a large pin attached. The sign read: *If the fat man is asleep, stick him with this pin. He will wake up and entertain you.* "It worked once and then the sign and the pin mysteriously disappeared."

Following the spring circus run in New York and Philadelphia, business was lackluster and by June 1966 money was once again tight making jumps from one date to the next more difficult. Chris had joined the show again in Manhattan during spring break and headed home after Easter. In June, fresh from high school graduation, Chris headed out to join up with Ward. "Instead of waiting for his graduation exercises,

High school graduation photo of Chris, 1966.

he joined us and brought along his savings – which were used to make the jump from Eastern Ohio to Anderson, Ind.," Ward notes. Chris was eager to get on the road. He recalls the year he joined Ward and Pete. "I was young and dumb," he said. During the first year with the show, the Selective Service came knocking but Chris failed his physical due to a bad back and ended up not going into the military. Ward had been too young for WWII and too old for Vietnam, so he didn't serve either.

Ward said he was impressed with Chris right from the beginning because he "wanted to do it all right now, big time, right from the start. I saw he had potential and that refreshing eagerness to learn." As a little kid, Chris always knew he wanted to be in the circus. He learned magic and that served as his door into the sideshow world. There was no sleeping in the blade box now that Chris was a full time member of the team. He moved into Ward's air-conditioned house trailer.

Chris, Ward and Pete spent most of 1966 with Rod Link on the World of Pleasure Shows. During the season, Link asked Ward if he would consider building a large sideshow for the following year and asked if $10,000 would be sufficient to create such an attraction. Ward said it would and Link told him to be at the showmen's convention in early December and they would work out a deal. Due to tax problems, however, Link had to default on his promise to fund the construction of the new show. Ward was devastated and a bit put off by Link's decision, but within days he found that all was not lost. They just had to look in a different direction. And Chris had to be the grown up.

Nearly 23 years after running away to join the circus, Ward Hall, with the help of Chris Christ, finally hit the big time in 1967, becoming owners of a high-quality sideshow. Here's what set the stage for the two to become the greatest force in American sideshow history.

During the fall of 1966 Duke Steinmetz had put his sideshow up for sale and Ward wanted it. Steinmetz had operated on both the World of Mirth Shows and Deggeller Shows. According to the photos they saw, Chris and Ward knew that it was in good shape and looked great. During the Showmen's League of America (SLA) annual convention at the Sherman House in Chicago, Ward and Chris went looking for money to finance the purchase after the promising deal with Link fell through.

Hal Eifort and his partner, Milt Kaufman, owners of Gooding's Million Dollar Midways, agreed to provide the $5,500 needed. The carnival showmen had financed the purchase of other sideshows for other people previously and had advertised that they would finance shows of merit."It was the turning point of my career," Ward said. "They (Kaufman and Eifort) not only didn't charge any interest on the loan, they booked the show on their route, which at that time was the best in the country." Chris

Act Needed: Knife Thrower, Please Apply

co-signed the mortgage papers and in doing so became Ward's business partner, a partnership that continues. Their first corporation was named World's Fair Freaks & Attractions Inc.

That initial contact with Kaufman and Eifort almost didn't happen. Ward was despondent that the original deal didn't work out with Link and he was ready to give up. Chris wasn't so easily dissuaded. While at the convention, Chris had sought out Eifort and set up a meeting, but, "I could not get him (Ward) to leave our room to go to our meeting with Eifort that I had set up," Chris said. "I had to literally pick him up and throw him in the elevator to get him there on time." With check in hand, the two purchased their new show – sight unseen. When they delivered the check to Duke Steinmetz in Port Huron, Ohio, the truck holding the equipment was buried under six feet of snow, so they weren't able to actually see it set up until after they picked it up later that spring. They took it out for the first time in spring 1967 and it remained their main show until 1972 and then their #2 unit until 1976.

In spring, the new sideshow owners headed off for their 1967 appearance with Ringling in Madison Square Garden. It would be the last for Ward and Chris, as the 43-year-old building was to be closed and demolished. When the new Garden opened, it was smaller and the circus had no room to present a sideshow.

Before heading to New York that spring, Ward and Chris put in a few weeks with Harry Beck's Indoor Circus performing juggling and knife throwing. Chris had worked with a couple knife throwers and had picked up the skill quite easily and felt comfortable performing the act. That is until one fateful day shortly thereafter as he and Ward appeared on a live national NBC-TV show, in which Chris was the thrower and Ward was the target. They were appearing at Madison Square Garden with the circus and the network asked them to come over for a guest spot on one of

Ward practicing juggling, 1969.

their shows. They took to the stage, the cameras were rolling and all but one of the knives Chris threw fell to the ground, totally unlike his typical performance. Chris and Ward took their bow as the somewhat embarrassed Chris doubted whether he should ever throw a knife again.

The problem had been that they weren't able to get their regular target board out of Madison Square Garden so they built a new one at a lumber yard and had it shipped to the television studio. Since it was new, the target board had not been properly conditioned by soaking it in water before its initial use. Shortly after the show, Ward received a phone call from his aunt Alda advising him to "never stand in front of that guy again." Embarrassment aside, it wasn't totally unsuccessful. "We got paid," said Ward.

The newly purchased and spiffed up Steinmetz sideshow, now the Hall and Christ 10-in-one sideshow, opened in mid-June in North Webster, Ind., booked on with the Key City Shows. Judd took out the "old" five-in-one show, now called the #2 unit, and toured it on the Prairie circuit in Western Canada with the Smith Wonder Shows. Judd's unit also included the baby show and the half-lady illusion that Chris and Ward had built the previous winter. The Prairie circuit was a hard schedule, with the show playing two towns a week, often with a long jump in between. Leonard Farley joined Ward's unit as press agent.

In late summer 1967, long-time friend and sideshow promoter Sam Alexander sent Schlitzie, the famous pin-head, and his nurse to Ward and Chris, all prior to the show joining Gooding's Million Dollar Midways in Allentown, Pa., in early August.

"You'll see Schlitzie the Monkey Girl, the strangest living human being in the entire world. Some people say Schlitzie is half-human and half-monkey. Schlitzie was discovered living with the monkeys in the Southern part of the Yucatan Peninsula of Mexico. She has a head the size of a coconut which comes to a point like an ice cream cone and when you feel the head, it is soft like a sponge. She has no more brains than a monkey. She's on stage now among the strange and unusual. The strangest of all is Schlitzie the Monkey Girl."

Schlitzie was already a big sideshow draw and Ward was ecstatic that he had a chance to feature her on his show. Schlitzie had star quality, having been a featured character in the 1932 film *Freaks*. Born as a male, Simon Metz in 1892, he suffered from microcephaly, a condition in which the head is much smaller and more pointed than normal and the person is usually feeble-minded and learning disabled. Schlitzie reportedly had the IQ of a three-year-old. While Schlitzie was, in fact, a male, he was always presented as a female because he had to be diapered, and it was easier to care for him when dressed in a muumuu.

As a very young child, he was adopted by sideshow operator George Surtees, and was exhibited across America. When Surtees passed away in the early 1960s, his family was unable to care for Schlitzie and dropped him off at a mental institution in California. Bill Unks, who worked as an orderly at the institution during the winter and then with Alexander during the summer, contacted Alexander and told him about Schlitzie. Alexander immediately started the process of becoming Schlitzie's legal guardian. The state of California concluded that the pinhead would survive much better in the sideshow surrounded by loved ones with whom he was familiar than if he remained institutionalized.

Schlitzie, also billed as the Monkey Girl, was presented with his head shaved except for a little tuft of hair at the very top. He had a very limited vocabulary. "But with his hand signals and grunts and sounds, he always was able to get what he wanted, along with entertaining us. He was very funny," Ward said, noting that the pin-headed attraction worked on the show throughout the rest of 1967 and the entire 1968 season before going back with Alexander in 1969. Schlitzie died at age 80 in 1972.

As the new Hall and Christ sideshow began its long, illustrious and prosperous life, the partners received a great deal of help that first year. Gooding's show painter, Jack Synrex, added "sparkle" to the show and Chris and his father, Norman, built colorful tracer lights. "We truly had one of the best looking shows in the business," Ward recalls. Business was good. In fact, that first season for the new Hall and Christ show was so successful that they paid off the mortgage by the first weekend of the Indiana State Fair in late August.

The stellar line-up on season one of the Hall and Christ show featured: Dick Johnson, vent and juggling; Mavis Johnson, whip cracking, electric act and the blade box; Shari Johnson, contortionist; a snake charmer; Kelly, the human ostrich; Chris was the sword swallower; Pete was the fire eater and performed the iron tongue; Frank Quinn, featured midget; and Dave Ballard, the giant. Ward was the talker. Señore Lydick and Carmen Del Rio were in the ticket booth, and Farley was the press agent.

Following the last date with Gooding's in 1967 in Tallahassee, Hal Eifort asked Ward and Chris to sign on for the total season the following year, which they did in a heartbeat. Obviously Kaufman was happy with the sideshow he helped finance. Gooding's was creating a second unit and they wanted Ward and Chris to create a new show that would travel with that new unit, but instead of committing their #2 unit to Gooding's they decided to build a new show from scratch. "Hal Eifort is the best carnival manager I was ever around," Ward recalls. "He had a calming effect and an

C.M. "Chris" Christ and Ward Hall, 1968.

ability to handle people and their problems, including his employees, in a very gentlemanly fashion." They remained friends up to Eifort's death.

Ward and Chris used animal freak show owner Al Moody's back lot in Gibsonton, Fla., as their winter quarters in 1967. Al and Barbara Moody were building a new home nearby and they offered to sell their current home – an eight-room house on a large lot – to the boys. "I explained that after building the new show we were short of money," Ward said. "He sold us the house for $7,000 with $10 down and $1,000 due each November on the balance." That property served as both their home and their winter quarters until they lost it in their 1985 bankruptcy. They then lived in their house trailer on leased property until purchasing their current home, which also serves as winter quarters, in 1999.

Pressed for time to get on the road, Ward and Chris signed a blank sales contract and blank mortgage papers and told Moody to fill in the numbers, make the transaction and to send them the paperwork. "Our trust was well placed and for the first time in my life, I was putting down roots," Ward said, noting that it was a feeling he never had before. "The idea that I was going to own a real home, the fact that the Moody's trusted me so much as to make that kind of deal and that I was going to fit in as part of a community, was amazing." However, settling in had to wait for the off season.

The show had only eight days to travel from Florida to Los Angeles where they joined the Al Dobritch Circus for a short run. Then, following a cross-country jump to Providence, R.I., the duo opened the 1968 season booked on with Gooding's in Allentown, Pa. The #2 unit made its premiere with Gooding's second unit in Tallmadge, Ohio, then jumped to Milwaukee for the first-ever Summerfest. The Johnson family performed in and operated Ward's #2 unit for nine years.

While the main sideshow was playing a fair in Berea, Ohio, a woman approached Ward and asked if he would provide a job for her son, Bob Collins, who was 7-foot, 8-inches tall. Ward immediately said yes and the boy giant joined the show. Ward now had an abundance of giants and he featured both the new kid and Dave Ballard, the Texas Giant.

> *"Dave Ballard stands eight feet, nine and one-half inches in height and when he spreads his arms – from fingertip to fingertip – it measures 109 inches, over nine feet! The fingers of his huge hand are so big that he can take off his ring and pass a silver dollar through it. And here today, you will see that he wears a shoe sized 36 quadruple E. If his feet were any larger, he couldn't wear shoes, he would have to wear the boxes they came in."*

Ward figured out a way to cash in on both of the big guys while keeping them on the same show. He dressed newcomer Bob Collins in a Roman outfit, complete with a high helmet, and sat him outside on the stage with a sign that read: "My name is Bob. I stand at 7-foot, 8-inches but if you think I am tall, see the Texas Giant inside." It worked and business flourished. Collins stayed on only for the remainder of the 1968 season. The show also gained a new fat man that season, Jimmy Dean, a former professional wrestler who by now weighed in at more than 700 pounds and was in no condition to continue his wrestling career.

In 1969, its second year out, the big show included: Mamie and Cliff King, a dwarf couple; Johnny, Marilyn and Kathy Munroe, knife throwing; Bud Rush, the human blockhead; Lady Patricia Zurm, sword swallower; Pete, fire eater and iron tongue; Rita Reed, illusions; Doreen Reed, albino girl; Albert Short, rubber man; Gladia Stump, frog woman; Milt Robbins, inside lecturer; and the spouses of Reed, Short and Stump in the ticket booth. Emmett Blackwelder, billed as the Turtle Man, also joined the show for the first time in 1969.

> "Inside today, you will see and hear Little Emmett. Born without any legs. Born without arms or hands. Just little stubs. Learn how he overcame this tremendous handicap. Watch him as he juggles three balls. How does he do it? Emmett moves across the floor in a way that resembles a turtle. That's why we call him The Turtle Man!"

Born in 1923, Blackwelder was forced at an early age to fend for himself and found both comfort and prosperity in the sideshow business. "He could juggle balls, just using those little stubs. It was amazing," said Ward, noting that Blackwelder was the one who kept the show's sound equipment working. "He could take apart and fix amplifiers, speakers and microphones with nothing but the tools he held in his mouth." The Turtle Man was also a smart businessman and received big tips because he worked so well with the people who paid to see and talk with him.

After each season closed, Blackwelder headed home to North Carolina and invested his money in rental properties which eventually funded his retirement. Once he got off the road in the late 1970s, he went home, married his childhood sweetheart and lived comfortably on his investments until his death in 1996.

"I really liked Emmett," said Chris. "He was a very interesting guy and he would usually ride with me on our jumps. We had some great conversations." Ward chimes in, "Emmett was probably the most remarkable man I ever met."

Act Needed: Knife Thrower, Please Apply

> *"Lady Patricia is the world's greatest living sword swallower. Watch today as she swallows swords, sabers, bayonets, ice picks and a screen door spring! Watch as the beautiful lady swallows a bright, glowing, neon tube. As our lights dim inside the tent, you will see the neon shining through her skin, from inside her body!*

A bit of class also joined the show in 1969 when Lady Patricia Zurm was hired as a sword swallower. "She had the best sword swallowing act out there and she ended nearly every performance swallowing a lit neon tube," Ward noted. "She was in every aspect a lady. She wore stylish gowns and always had on makeup."

According to Ward, Lady Patricia never talked in her act because "her squeaky Kentucky voice" did not sound good over the speaker system. Instead, she choreographed her performance to the song, Fascination, which would fade out as the lights went down as a cue for her to swallow a neon tube and end her act. With the lights dimmed, the glow of the neon would show through her neck. It was a very dramatic, albeit dangerous, act.

Prior to her seven years with Ward, Lady Patricia had worked for the best sideshows and circuses in operation, including several years with the Ringling organization in the 1940s. In 1951, she was featured as the sword swallower in Cecil B. DeMille's film, *The Greatest Show on Earth*. Ward and Chris became close friends with Lady Patricia. They, as well as her friends, called her Patsy. "She was great in the kitchen and would cook for us when she had time," Ward adds. She retired at the end of the season in 1976 and died in January 1986 at the age of 76. "Out of all the females who worked for me over the years, Patsy was my favorite," he added.

Dick Johnson's unit did well in 1969 with Reid Lefevre's King Reid Shows, and was the first sideshow in many years to be allowed into the Eastern States Exposition, in West Springfield, Mass. Hall and Christ operated five shows that year: two 10-in-one sideshows; two freak baby shows; and a fat man show featuring Jimmy Dean. Ward laughs when he recalls the antics of press agent Herb Pickard who worked with the Gooding's organization. "Herb would get fat man Dean stuck in a phone booth and then alert the press. That always garnered a lot of publicity," Ward confessed to Pete Pepke of *Carnival News* in 1998. Ward added that he learned the value of a good press agent many years earlier during his days on the Dailey Bros. Circus.

During off-season, Gooding's banner painter Jack Synrex was sent down to Hall and Christ's winter quarters in Florida to "add his magic

with paint and brushes" so the show would look its best when it hit the road in 1970. William Durks (often spelled Dirks), billed as the man with two noses and three eyes, joined Chris and Ward for only the 1970 season and was then as he is today referred to as one of the most successful human oddities who ever travelled the sideshow circuit. From 1959 through 1969, Durks was featured in Slim Kelly's single-o on the James E. States midway. During the off-season, Durks would work at Hubert's in New York City. He planned to retire in 1969, but showed up the following year with Ward. The bona fide oddity was born with a severe hair lip and a split nose. "He looked like he had been hit in the face with an axe," Ward said. Durks painted his third eye in each day.

"He was an easy-going man who from his hard-working days as a young man on the farm was very strong physically," Ward said. "As an attraction on our show, he was not expected to help erect and dismantle the show, but he enjoyed the physical labor, often working harder than anyone on the crew. I suspect he also enjoyed the extra pay he received for his labor." Durks died in May 1975.

Their new home in Gibsonton, Fla., was a perfect fit for Ward and Chris and they felt comfortable almost immediately in a community that embraced (and still does) showmen of all sorts. It was a friendly community, with most residents at that time connected to the entertainment business. Although delayed by nearly a year since buying the house, Ward and Chris were eager to put down roots as they continued to move into and decorate their first home. Chris's parents Norman and Betty visited that winter for several weeks. Norman helped frame a new baby show while Betty showered the guys with good home cooking. During that winter, Ward was elected to the Board of Directors of the International Independent Showmen's Association (IISA). Transportation-wise it was also a meaningful off-season. Tired of continual breakdowns, they purchased two new Chevy trucks, the first new vehicle of any sorts that Ward ever owned.

Chris was a member of the local volunteer fire department which consisted mostly of showmen. Al Tomaini, the giant, was the chief. That year, Chris recalls, the firemen had a busy winter fighting brush fires caused by the dry weather. Fighting fire wasn't the most dangerous part of the job, according to Chris. It was the abundance of rattlesnakes living in those open fields, all of which he luckily avoided. Huge boas performing on the bally, no problem; angry rattlers loose in a burning field, no way.

Later, Ward and Chris would both be instrumental in creating and producing the IISA's annual charity circus held each year in January. The 30th edition took place in January 2014 and it was the most successful of them all, at least creatively, said Chris, who took over all the PR and promotional duties more than a decade previously. Ward was the ringmaster and announcer for a couple dozen years, stepping aside from that duty in 2009. While enjoying domesticated life for the first time, Ward and Chris ventured out and played several winter fairs in Florida with Deggeller Magic Midways and David B. Endy Amusements.

Ward carries a big gavel shortly after being inducted as President of the International Independent Showmen's Assoc.

The Kudos:
Awards, Prizes and Honors
CHAPTER 18

Ward has received dozens of awards, kudos and accolades over the past 70 years, but three of them stand out at the top. He has been inducted into the Hall of Fame of both the Outdoor Amusement Business Assoc. (OABA) and the International Independent Showmen's Assoc. (IISA), both in 2008. Those were followed by the prestigious Circus Ring of Fame induction in 2011. He is the only person to have received all three accolades.

OABA, the trade association for the North American carnival industry, was founded in 1965 and Ward was introduced to the group in 1968. In 1971, he became the first show operator to be elected onto its Board of Directors, where he would remain for 17 years. On Feb. 9, 2008, Ward also became the first show operator to be elected into the OABA Hall of Fame.

"The OABA is a great organization and without it, there wouldn't be a carnival business as we know it today," he said. "They have been a watchdog for our industry and have challenged any legislation that they felt would hurt the industry, including minimum wages and trucking legislation. We all have benefited from their vigilance. At the time of his OABA Hall of Fame induction, "Ward was neither specifically a circus nor a carnival man and was able to succeed in bridging the two genres successfully," said Lane Talburt, a circus historian and a friend of both Ward and Chris. "He knows enough about both institutions to fill many books."

The OABA Hall of Fame honor totally caught Ward off guard, as he was not expecting it. However, the IISA committee wasn't as secretive in the preparation of their Hall of Fame award. "I wasn't surprised because I knew that I had been nominated and when they asked me for more information about my career, asked for photos and wanted to make sure I was at the banquet, I got a pretty good idea of what was going to happen," he said. "But knowing about it didn't dampen my excitement in receiving it."

Prior to the award, Ward was the only person who had served two terms as IISA President and, under his leadership the group had put into motion the creation of the Showfolks Retirement Center and had helped formulate plans for a carnival museum in Gibsonton.

Ward received a letter on June 23, 2010, from Floyd H. Kruger, president of the Circus Ring of Fame Foundation of Sarasota, Fla. "It affords me the greatest pleasure to notify you that you have been elected to the Circus Ring

Ward is inducted into the IISA Hall of Fame, February 2008.

of Fame." Ward of course was ecstatic at the news. Speaking of the Ring of Fame ceremony and the pomp and circumstances surrounding the Jan. 16, 2011 induction, Ward humbly said that it was the, "Most wonderful honor I can imagine." Overcome by emotion, the normally loquacious talker uttered what was probably his shortest speech ever.

Founded in 1988, the annual ceremony honors those who have made significant contributions to the circus. Those honored have a plaque installed in the park inside St. Armands Circle in Sarasota. The plaque honoring Ward reads: "Lured by the siren call of the circus, he joined Dailey Bros. at age 15, thereby embarking on a notable six-decade career in which he has enthralled, mystified, educated and seduced millions of circus and fair goers who were drawn to his bally platform as a sideshow talker, lecturer, and owner. He and his sideshows have appeared on scores of circuses, at hundreds of state, county, and town fairs and prompted the Smithsonian Institution to honor him for preserving 'A truly indigenous American art form.'"

The Kudos: Awards, Prizes and Honors

Red Stuart with Ward at the 2011 induction ceremonies
for the Circus Ring of Fame.

In 2002, he was the guest of honor and was named Ambassador of Wonder at the International Sideshow Gathering in Wilkes-Barre, Pa., and the following year was presented with the Lifetime Achievement Award by the same group. In 1997 The John and Mable Ringling Museum of Art in Sarasota inaugurated the Powers Behind the Scenes series honoring the outstanding people in the world of the circus. Six years later the museum's Circus Celebrity Committee selected Ward as its annual honoree. Due to health issues, Ward was unable to attend the Jan. 10, 2003 event, but Chris stepped in and accepted the honor for him.

Additional recognition he has received over the years includes the following: Honored Guest of the European Showmen's Congress, Hamburg, Germany, 1974; International Showman of the Year, New England Showmen's Assoc., Boston, 1976; Lifetime Achievement Award, IISA, Gibsonton, 1976; Achievement Award and Honored Guest at the Lone Star Showmen's Assoc., Dallas, 1983; Lifetime Achievement Award, Circus Fans of America, 2009.

In addition, Ward has been featured speaker at dozens of showmen's banquets and galas across the country, including the Circus Model Builder's Assoc., Circus Historical Society, Show Folks of Sarasota, and various local fan groups, called Tents, of the Circus Fans of America.

Only a few of the trophies Ward has acquired over the years.

Gibsonton:
The Utopian Society of Carnies

CHAPTER 19

Ward Hall calls the hamlet in which he lives "Grand and Glorious Gibsonton." Nestled on the banks of the Alafia River, 12 miles south of Tampa, Fla., the area has been attracting circus, carnival and show people to its environs since the early 1930s.

But it's more than the nice weather that attracts them, it's the zoning. Under the designation of "RSB," (residential show business), carnival and circus workers can literally bring home their work when they close down for the season. Corn dog peddlers can park their trailers in the front yard. Ferris wheel operators can set up their rides adjacent to their homes and work on them all winter long. Animals trainers can stake their elephants in the garden, and showmen of all sort can store their equipment "out back" for as long as they wish.

The backyard of Ward and Chris's home is chock full of current and retired props, trucks, trailers and signage. In the side yard of the house across the street, trailers with the wording and logo of the American Family Circus painted on their sides can barely be read due to fading and

Showtown USA!

rusting. It's the only area in the country that allows such accommodations to the show people, and it's the only village in the country where a giant over 8-feet tall and a dwarf under 3-feet tall served as fire chief and police chief, respectively, at the same time.

Diana Philips has lived in the unincorporated village of Gibsonton, or *Gibtown* as the locals call it, for nearly 40 years. She served as an associate producer of the 2000 award winning documentary, Gibtown. She says the fishing is one of the reasons the area became popular when it did. Another was its peacefulness, away from the bustling midway where "we all could come to be amongst our own."

Philips added, "We would be out all summer long and be very tired by the time we got back to Gibtown. We could relax here. We could let off steam here, and nobody would notice or care." The late Melvin Burkhart, blockhead and anatomical wonder, depicted his circle of friends as "a society apart from wherever we are (except Gibsonton). We are strangers going in, and strangers going out. We had to stick together." That's why, and how, this little village grew. *Los Angeles Times* reporter David Lamb profiled Gibsonton in a June 24, 1997 story. "Over the years, the little community has taken on the character of an extended family – tolerant and protective of its own, unbothered by the mistakes of nature in its midst that other towns might consider odd, be it a five-legged cow or a lady with a full beard." It was the perfect place for Ward and his family of oddities to settle.

Ward said when circuses started wintering in Sarasota, south of Gibsonton, in the 1920s, the circus people, lacking permanent homes elsewhere, migrated with their circus. But as Sarasota grew larger, many of the workers, from roustabouts to sword swallowers to dwarfs and giants, found the Gibtown environs a better fit for their lifestyle. "The area attracted thousands of performers who wanted to live in peace, while escaping the curiosity of outsiders," Ward said.

Philips said the still-busy train from the north down to Sarasota goes right through Gibtown, although they don't stop at the little station anymore. "The circus trains would stop here and many of the workers and performers would get off, and in the spring when the trains headed north again, they would be waiting at the station when they came through," Philips said. While they never took the train to Gibtown, Ward and Harry first drove through in January 1952 on their way to Miami. Chris and Ward bought their first house here in 1967.

The village was a bustling utopia for showmen from November to May, but became a ghost town when the showmen went back out on the road each spring. Like most showmen, Ward and Chris only got to enjoy their home for a part of the year. "We were on the road during the summer and up until the early 2000s we had spent only three or four summers in Florida. It's hot here. No one should ever have to live in Florida in the summer time," Ward noted.

The area especially attracted those without a lot of money or a permanent home. "When they got off the train, they would have enough money to pay for a sleeping cabin at Giant's Camp or another show business-friendly campground, and if they ran out of money, they could always fish. They knew they wouldn't starve if they stayed in Gibsonton," Philips added.

Al Tomaini, the 8-foot, 4½-inch tall giant, and his wife, Jeanie Tomaini, the 2-foot, 6-inch half-lady (she was born without legs) created the Giant's Camp in the mid-1940s and by the early 1950s, their cabins, a fishing camp and a restaurant known widely as having amazing home cooking, were iconic to the area. As the only 24-hour restaurant on Highway 41 between Tampa and Sarasota, the place flourished. Their friend, Francesco Lentini, the three-legged sideshow performer, suggested they name it the obvious, Giant's Camp.

Billed on the midway as the World's Strangest Married Couple, Al and Jeanie ran the business together until Al died in 1962. With the help of her daughter, Jeanie ran it until her death in 1999. The place closed for good in 2007 and was torn down, save for one of the sleeping cabins. Today, that one cabin and a tall monument, with a replica of Al's humongous boot, immortalize the Giant's Camp, marking its location at the spot where Highway 41 crosses the Alafia River. Philips, whose mother Carol spearheaded the effort to get the monument built, said the top of the monument on which the boot rests is the same height as was the giant.

Giant's Camp gets the credit for pulling the showmen into the area but it was back in 1924 when Eddie and Grace LaMay, cookhouse owners on the carnival circuit, came to the area, pitched a tent along the Alafia River and fell in love with the weather and the fishing. They spread the word about the paradise they found and soon opened a restaurant and bar known as Eddie's Hut. Together, the Giant's Camp and Eddie's Hut fed and sheltered the showmen when they came off the road for decades. Both are gone, but consistently spoken of reverently by the old timers.

Today, the Showtown Restaurant and Lounge is the year-round preferred eatery for the community's show people, both active and retired. You'll find a group of locals sitting around what is fondly known as the "liars table" every morning having breakfast and sipping coffee and telling tall tales, or cutting up jackpots, as show people call the telling of exaggerated claims about their life on the road. On any given day Ward and/or Chris can usually be found at that table.

Showtown Restaurant and Lounge serves as an unofficial art museum for the murals of legendary banner and show painter Bill Browning. Outside,

Showtown Lounge in its better days.

the entire façade is painted with scenes and characters who often frequent the bar. Unfortunately, the weather has taken its toll and the murals are quite faded. Inside, the murals have stood the test of time and are still colorful and unique pieces of this esteemed artist's body of work.

The bar at the International Independent Showmen's Assoc. (IISA), during the off-season, is also a popular watering hole and dancing spot. Most often referred to simply as the "Showmen's Club," its vast grounds host the annual Trade Show and Extravaganza, the carnival trade show. Each February thousands of showmen from around the country converge on Gibtown to buy new equipment, network with their fellow showmen, have a few beers, and breathe in a lot of tradition. A real gem and the real tribute to all showmen is the Museum of the American Carnival, located across the street from the showmen's club headquarters. Still in its infancy and still in need of operating dollars, the two floors of carnival and circus exhibits, rides, posters, banners and games offer an interesting look back at the industry.

While Gibtown, which is approximately 13 square miles in size, is a shadow of the excitement it used to be, the spirit lives on. "There are less and less shows and family-owned carnivals on the road today," said Ward. "That means less and less people are coming here each year. The townies now outnumber show people and there is fear that the RSB zoning will be removed and, if that happens, there will be a huge outcry. I don't know what we'd do with all our stuff if that happens."

Food concessionaire Larry Habeck, who with his wife Gala first purchased property in the area in 1973, said it's not just Gibsonton that would be hurt by a major zoning change; it would also affect the adjacent communities of Riverview and Ruskin, where many showmen still live. As more and more non-show people move into the new subdivisions being built, there is less and less tolerance for equipment-filled yards. As a result the current zoning is being stripped little by little, in both geographic area and in allowances, Habeck said.

According to Ward, in its heyday in the 1950s and 60s, Gibtown was home to more than 85 human oddities. Journalist Buck Wolf, writing for ABCNews.com in 2000, surmised that while few "professional" freaks and oddities still call the area home, it is still very much a show town. "Still, this town remains the largest concentration of carnies. Residents of Gibsonton and vicinity are ticket takers, ride and attraction mechanics, working clowns, acrobats, and animal trainers. These folk take a lot of pride in their profession."

Ward continually gets calls from reporters and circus and sideshow fans and historians from around the world wanting to visit Gibsonton. They want him to show them around "and they ask me how long it will take to see the human oddities, the circus performers and other interesting show people," he said. "I tell them that it's an easy tour. It will take 15 minutes. All we have to do is drive down the road and visit the cemetery. I'll point out the headstones to them." They are about 40 years too late if they want to see them alive, according to Ward, who added that even though a lot has changed, the outdoor show business industry will always be a colorful and dominant aspect of Gibsonton, Fla., 33534.

In February 1995 *The Cleveland Plain Dealer* sent reporter Brian Albrecht to Gibsonton to look around and capture the essence of the area. Sideshow performer and banner painter Johnny Meah told Albrecht that people are always asking him, with fascination, about the town. "I don't know what

Ward makes a point to Jeremy Weiss during a tour of the Museum of the American Carnival in Gibsonton.

people expect to be happening down here. There aren't 40 midgets walking down the street; no two headed cows standing in the field."

Things have changed over the years. Chris jokes that a "hurricane blew through Gibtown and did a million dollars' worth of improvements." For her book, *Fringe Florida,* author Lynn Waddell visited Gibtown, drank at its clubs, toured the museum and the club, talked with the residents and spent time with Ward and Chris conversing about the sideshow business and the community in which they live. She summed it up thusly: "Despite the griminess, old Gibtown has a bizarre kind of charm."

Landmark Cases:
Oddities Vs. State of Florida

CHAPTER 20

In 1970, the State of Florida had a law on the books that prohibited the exhibition of malformed, deformed or disfigured humans. Always a champion for the well-being of outdoor show people, Ward instigated a suit against the state to overthrow that law. A three-year court fight led by Ward (dba World Fair Freaks & Attractions) and other sideshow operators and performers resulted in overturning the 1921 Florida statute that banned exhibition of human oddities in the state.

That triumph was one of the most rewarding moments in Ward's career and it was a hard fought victory for every showman who does business in the state, he said. "Undoubtedly this was the biggest and best contribution I made to our business during my career." The Florida Supreme Court ruled the law unconstitutional because it deprived a deformed person of his or her right to earn a living. The court declared that a handicapped person or another in an "unfortunate position" because of physical handicaps or deformities "must be allowed a reasonable chance within his capacities to earn a livelihood." Under the old law, an exhibitor of such people was liable for a year in prison and a fine up to $1,000. Part B of the law, with the same approximate language, prohibited the exhibition of live freak animals.

During the late 1960s, several operators throughout the country, including the well-respected Kelly-Sutton Sideshow, were shut down at fairs for featuring human oddities. Each time that happened, the action received an inordinate amount of publicity, and each such event was fueled by the publicity from the prior event. Ward points out that none of those closures resulted in legal action, that each was more of a public relations stunt as a reaction by law officials to the complaint(s). During the court's actions involving Ward and the archaic law, it was found that only in Florida was there such a law. In fact, virtually every operator and exhibitor in the country was unaware that such a law existed until 1971 when a story about Frieda the Frog Girl ran in the *St. Petersburg Times* that cited the Florida edict.

Miami attorney, Royal Flagg Jonas, was hired to "fight the statute because we thought it was so unconstitutional. Most of us had never been challenged, but it could have happened at any time, so we wanted to get it off the books," Ward said. The four prominent operators of sideshows at the time, Chris and Ward, Kelly and Sutton, Dick Best and Pete Kortes, put in an initial $1,000 each to begin the effort. Once the lawsuit was filed, the Outdoor Amusement Business Assoc. (OABA) paid back the showmen and took over financing, as the outcome could affect all showmen statewide and potentially hurt all showmen in the U.S.

To get things rolling, attorney Jonas filed for a license for Chris and Ward's company, World Fair Freaks and Attractions, to present their show in Miami. The license was denied on the grounds of the law regarding freaks. It was the rejection on which Ward had planned. "That opened the door for us to sue the state of Florida," he said. Plaintiffs were Norbert Terhurne (Pete) the "dwarf," and Stanley Barent, "Sealo the Seal Boy."

The case was to be heard in Dade County where the state's attorney was Richard Gerstein, who by chance was also a prominent member of the Miami Showmen's Association. Gerstein didn't want to prosecute the showmen, but Jonas made it clear that not only did he (Gerstein) need to prosecute, but he needed to do whatever he could to win this case for the state. "Once we lost that case, which we wanted

Stanley Barent as Sealo the Seal Boy.

to, it would be off to the Appeals Court," Ward said. Gerstein built a "masterful brief to the court that upheld the law in favor of the state," Ward said. The state won and the case was taken to the Appeals Court as hoped for. It was defeated again and, at that point, the showmen had the state right where they wanted – in a showdown in the Florida Supreme Court in Tallahassee.

In the Supreme Court, five of the six justices ruled in the showmen's favor and the law was repealed. It took two years of wise diplomacy and deep pockets, but the law was taken off the books in 1972. Ward is quick to point out that "in a court of law one must never try to second guess the verdict," so he and the showmen were prepared to stage a protest of sorts, in case they lost in the court of last resort.

Landmark Cases: Oddities Vs. State of Florida

Jim Zajicek and Ward at the 2014 Florida State Fair.

The Miss Universe pageant was to be televised live from the Miami Beach City Auditorium within a week of the final verdict and the showmen saw that event as an opportunity for a little press if they had lost in Tallahassee. Ward said, "If we had lost, Jonas was ready to file an injunction to stop the pageant, citing the law and declaring these women could not be exhibited. They were malformed, having breasts larger than an average female."

Of course the pageant went on as planned, but it could have been an interesting showdown.

Florida's 1921 law had two parts. Part A concerned human oddities and Part B concerned live freak animals. Originally the showmen wanted to fight both parts at the same time, but Ward and the others could not round up any freak animal exhibitors who wanted to serve as plaintiffs, and not wanting to delay it any longer, decided to fight that battle later and concentrate on human oddities first.

Part B says that whoever "shall exhibit for pay or compensation any crippled or physically distorted, malformed or disfigured beast, bird or animal in any circus, show or similar place, or any other place to which an admission fee is charged," can be fined $500 and imprisoned for no more than six months. Other than for a few smaller deformed animals that they exhibited in the mid-1980s, Ward and Chris stayed away from live animals, preferring taxidermy, illusions, human oddities and working acts instead.

Several years after putting the Part B challenge to the side, Ward was asked at an OABA Board Meeting if something should be done about that portion of the law and he said yes. By then, one of Ward's former managers, Dick Johnson, had purchased a freak animal show and agreed to be the plaintiff if the OABA and Ward wanted to go forward and would provide funding.

Johnson booked his show at the Manatee County Fair in Palmetto, Fla., in January 1978 and the local law enforcement officials were tipped off about the law by the Manatee Humane Society. Officials came in late on a Friday and closed Johnson down, citing the freak animal law as the reason. A local attorney had already been briefed and retained. Instead of losing the case locally and allowing it to go all the way to the Supreme Court as Ward and OABA had wanted, this attorney fought the battle too well and won the case for the showmen. That meant it was now legal in Manatee County but illegal in the rest of the state.

The state appealed the outcome in the circuit court and lost again, but in May 1984, the state Supreme Court overthrew the actions of the two lower courts and found that it was indeed illegal to exhibit freak animals in the state and the high court's ruling still stands to this day. Ward said the big proponent in keeping this law on the books is the Florida Cattleman's Association. "They are the ones who had it put back on the books in Manatee County and have fought us all the way to the Supreme Court." One fear is that people will breed all sorts of deformed animals just so they can exhibit them and try to outdo each other. A fear that just might not be too outrageous, say the proponents, if you have read the 1983 book by Katherine Dunn, *Geek Love*.

Most fair managers or police officials aren't even aware of this law. At the 2004 Florida State Fair in Tampa, Jim Zajicek's Big Circus Sideshow, which features live freak animals as well as stuffed and pickled freaks of nature, was doing a brisk business until officials busted him, citing the 1921 law. An animal activist who had a radio show in the market tipped off authorities that such a law existed and she told them about Daisy Mae, a two-nosed cow Zajicek had on display. He was forced to take her out of the exhibit and send her back to the farm for the week. Zajicek told a reporter from the *St. Petersburg Times* that he didn't think he was hurting her by sharing her with others; on the contrary. "I told her that I considered Daisy Mae pretty lucky, considering that most people eat cows and don't keep them as pets." He exhibited again at the 2014 fair, with no problems. Daisy Mae came back as well, but as a taxidermied pet, having died of natural causes in 2009.

It's ironic that "Florida, a state where people can take their orangutan to Hooters, is the only one in America that explicitly prohibits the display of live deformed animals," notes Lynn Waddell in her book *Fringe Florida*. Under "Miscellaneous Crimes," the 2013 Florida State Statute 877.16 confirms the law is still in place, but to anyone's knowledge it has not been enforced since Zajicek's bust in 2004. "That's the problem," Ward said. "As long as it is randomly enforced, the law will be misused by local authorities or organizations who want to make a statement." At this point, if someone complains, lawmen must react. It's the law.

1971:
Off to St. Thomas

CHAPTER 21

In addition to seeing to their civic and home-owner duties, Ward and Chris were kept busy overseeing a major expansion to their #1 show for the 1971 season. They hit the road with an entirely new banner line which measured 165-foot long and towered 32-foot tall, from the midway to the flag tips.

During an early spring 1971 date with the Maki Shrine Circus at Tropical Park Racetrack in Miami, Ward's good friend Charlie Cox, a former promoter with the Clyde Beatty Circus, came by and made arrangements to take the show to St. Thomas, Virgin Islands, in April. Island sponsors wanted a baby elephant act but agreed on a chimp routine after Ward said he couldn't get an elephant but knew of a trained chimp for sale. He bought Simon the chimp from Peter J. Hennen. Dick Johnson worked with the chimp long enough to gain Simon's trust and was able to put together a good act before departing to St. Thomas.

Ward was apprehensive about the island gig for two reasons: the earning potential of an unknown market and the security of the expensive equipment he was going to take. The money issue was quickly resolved when the sponsors offered to pay him a flat fee which included round trip transportation for the performers and shipping of the equipment. That flat fee guaranteed he would make money and pay expenses, or so Ward thought.

To avoid the issue of excessive abuse on the show's best equipment, Ward and Chris quickly put together a "new" show comprised of bits and pieces from their various older shows and equipment they saw as dispensable, just in case it didn't make it back. Simon turned out to be a big hit and, as a whole, the audiences were polite and appreciative. It seems that most of the people had never seen a chimp and were delighted with Simon's antics. However, the kids who didn't have the money for a ticket or just had an inclination to vandalism peppered the canvas and the ticket boxes with stones throughout the run.

Bill-posting is an important aspect of any circus promotion, and as it turned out, Ward had the posters, but no one had ever posted on the island. On a search for a building or a surface to put a poster promoting the show, Ward came across a large semi-trailer parked next to a major highway. It was an ice house and, after some negotiation, Ward got the permission he needed to paper the trailer. On completing an exhausting five hours of posting the entire side of the ice trailer, he was quite pleased with himself. The next morning he went out to look at it only to find not a single poster on the trailer. It turned out that the man from whom he gained permission failed to mention that the trailer was switched out every two weeks for a new one full of fresh ice. The switch had taken place that morning. Following the three-week run, Ward was not able to get the promised financial help from the promoter to ship the show back to Florida so he ended up selling most of the equipment to Charlie Cox for $1. Ward kept the sound system and a few of the banners.

Pete Kortes was selling his 10-in-one in early 1972, a deal which also included a hippopotamus show. When Ward asked Hal Eifort of Gooding's Million Dollar Midways if he would finance the purchase, it didn't take the veteran showman long to answer. "Yes, the sideshow, but don't buy that damned hippo." Ward responded, "We sure won't. That hippo eats all winter." To which Eifort added, "Yes and it stinks all summer!" However, Kortes ended up deciding not to retire and he kept his show and his hippo for another season.

Hitting the road as true independents in 1972, the Hall and Christ shows did not book with Gooding's for the season, opting instead to hopscotch both units around the country playing the best spots they could find. Early-season rain put the damper on business at several spots for both units, but the big whammy came while the #1 unit was booked on with the Kenn-Penn Show in Dubois, Pa. It ended up under eight feet of flood waters, suffering extensive damage. Luckily they were able to drive the house trailers to higher ground at that spot, before the waters got too deep, saving them from destruction.

The Sky Wheel, a double Ferris wheel that was set up next to the sideshow tent and trailers, started to precariously lean toward the sideshow as the waters rose and as the crew stripped the show tent, placing as much as they could on top of existing vehicles. "They actually sent SCUBA divers out there to dive below the wheel and to re-block it to keep it from falling," Ward said. "If it had fallen, it would have wiped out our two semis and our tent and stages."

The show lost two weeks, as it never opened in Dubois, and then it took a week to get its trucks and gear into shape to be able to move out. Cleaning the mud out of the props and the wardrobe were additional tasks that occupied time and cost additional, unbudgeted money. Once they cleaned up and got everything running, they headed out to join Gooding's in Brockton, Mass. Clear skies and good business greeted them in Brockton, Mass., but they were visited by their rainy nemesis at their next spot in Fairport Harbor, N.Y. The rains turned the lot into a quagmire

1971: Off to St. Thomas

and they couldn't go anywhere until the National Guard showed up and pulled them out of the mud with an Army tank.

Lane Talburt, a writer, videographer and fan of the circus, once asked Ward how circus people could always look so good when the reality behind the glitter is often mud, rain, and cold weather. "Rain gear and mud boots are very important," Ward replied, noting that it was much harder to keep looking nice during the earlier years than it has been during the modern era. "It's simple. You have a show to do and you have to look your best. No matter how we looked during setup, by the time the public got here, we were ready."

In "those days," getting cleaned up meant going to the water wagon and getting a cold bucket of water with which to wash. "Sometimes, if you had an extra dime to pay the keeper of the water boiler in the cookhouse, he would provide you with hot water. That was nice," Ward said. "Now of course, we have running hot and cold water in our private living quarters."

Several weeks after getting out of the mud, while playing a spot near Cincinnati, Ohio, Ward became ill, went to the doctor, got a prescription filled, and went back to the lot. A couple days later he woke with an excruciating pain and went to the emergency room at the local hospital where he had an emergency kidney operation. He spent the next 28 days recuperating in the hospital. With Ward out of commission, the show closed on Sunday, packed up and headed north to Cleveland on an overnight jump, about a six-hour drive. Chris was behind the wheel of their new Cadillac, pulling their new house trailer. Doc Hankins, one of the show's talkers was riding with him.

About 80 miles into the northbound journey, a speeding semi-tractor crashed into the back of the house trailer. No one was hurt, but Ward's dog Rascal became scared, jumped out of the car into the traffic, was hit and killed. As well, nearly all of the personal belongings of both Ward and Chris were destroyed. "It was around 3 a.m. and very peaceful. Hardly anyone was on the highway, when out of nowhere I saw a truck gaining on us very quickly from behind. Before I knew it, he smashed into the trailer, which served as a shock absorber, and that probably saved our lives," Chris said. "The trailer literally exploded and as the car was spinning out of control, I kept hold of the wheel and tried to keep from rolling. The trailer did roll and ended up on top of our Cadillac." When the police came, the truck driver was arrested for being doped up. Chris settled with the trucking company out of court for a nice settlement but thinks he could have gotten a lot more if he would have gone to court with it. "With us traveling all the time, it just wasn't feasible to go to court with it," he said.

One of the few things that survived was Chris's Bible, which had landed right outside of the driver's side of the car. He picked it up as he was climbing out of the car. Authorities helped him rent a Winnebago and he and Doc Hankins were back on the road by daybreak. He called Ward the next morning and told him what happened. "It didn't scare me at first, because it had already happened and there wasn't anything I could do," said Ward. "Of course the dog's death bothered me but mostly I was thankful no one other than Rascal got hurt."

Ward's long-time friend, Henry Valentine, had two of his children working on the show at the time. Mike was a sword swallower and Sue was the illusion girl. They immediately called their father for help when they heard of the accident and that Ward was in the hospital. Henry was a good friend of Ward and a former sideshow man who left the road when he got married to settle down and raise a family. Knowing that his friends needed help, Valentine left his full time job in Iowa and helped the show in its jump from Cleveland to Columbus and the setup at the Ohio State Fair. And although he went back to his job in Iowa, Valentine would later become vice president of the company when he and his wife Shirley joined Ward and Chris full time in 1975.

Toward the end of the 10-day Ohio State Fair, Ward was released from the hospital and joined his team in Columbus while still recuperating. He was able to spend only a couple hours on the lot and the rest of his time was spent in bed in a hotel room reading and watching television. Upon closing in Columbus, Ward travelled with the show to its next stop, Knoxville, Tenn., but saw only the inside of his hotel room there as well.

Ward, 1970.

The kidney problems were only the start of various illnesses that put Ward out of commission for various lengths of time during the years. Did his itinerant lifestyle cause the maladies? "No," said Ward. "Circus people in general probably have better immune systems than most. They travel around and they drink from different water sources, they eat food prepared differently with various ingredients. With all that going on, our systems build up immunities to the different bacteria."

1971: Off to St. Thomas

The South Carolina State Fair, in Columbia, was the show's next stop. An incident there the previous year dictated Ward's next move. It was simple; he wasn't allowed to go back, so he made other plans for 1972 while the main unit played the date in Columbia. The fair president in South Carolina, Dr. Cantney, enjoyed Ward and his sideshow team and made his annual visit to see them the prior year. He walked in as he usually did, but before he got to see Chris or Ward, Duke Mayhood, the ticket seller collared him, told him to get out saying that he "doesn't care who he was, he needed a ticket to get in." The show was booked on with Gooding's Million Dollar Midways, so it was show owner Milt Kaufman who was called into Cantney's office to discuss what had just taken place. Kaufman knew the ticket seller was correct in throwing out someone without a ticket, but since that someone was the fair's president the situation became a bit sticky. It was a good spot for the show and Kaufman did not want to lose it.

Ward, 1970.

"They came up with a deal that if I turned over control to Chris and stayed away from the fairgrounds, and if Mayhood had his credentials rescinded, all would be good. I was held ultimately responsible for the action," Ward said. "It didn't bother me a bit and gave me more time to recuperate and visit our other shows," he notes.

Feeling well enough to travel on his own by early October 1972, Ward headed to Beaumont, Texas, to visit the Johnsons and the #2 unit while Chris took the big show to the South Carolina State Fair. On his way to Beaumont, Ward stopped off in Dallas to visit the State Fair of Texas, a major fair that he had never played. He took the opportunity to catch up with some old friends who were playing that date. On the last weekend of the fair, Ward was sitting in the cookhouse on the midway jackpotting with friends when Lowell Stapf, the fair's midway coordinator, dropped by and joined the conversation. As one can imagine, Ward is exceptionally good at cutting up jackpots.

As the two chatted, the owner of the sideshow who had the contract at the fair walked by and laughingly commented that "look at those two, nothing good could come of this." Stapf looked at Ward and asked him loud enough for all to hear, if he wanted to "look over the contract tonight or come back in the morning to sign it." Ward noticed that the sideshow owner's face got red as he hustled off without another word. The next morning Ward signed a contract to play the 1973 State Fair of Texas for the first time, a location his shows ended up playing for 17 straight years. "After that first year, we never had a contract and we operated only on a handshake for all those years," Ward says with pride.

After losing their house trailer in the wreck in Ohio, Ward and Chris decided, since it was late in the season, they would spend the rest of the year in hotels until time to return to Gibsonton. That idea didn't last long because they did not feel comfortable staying off the lot at night. So they turned one of their two semi-trailers into a combination office and living quarters where they lived the rest of the season. Chris acquired a chimpanzee named Toby that summer and he, too, moved into the living quarters with them.

Toby the chimp quickly became a member of Ward and Chris's family and, as any child born to new parents, Toby was a difficult critter to figure out. At first Chris was unsuccessful in teaching him backflips. He tried and he tried with no success, until their friend Rudy Lenz, a chimp trainer, came to visit. Lenz had Toby doing backflips in a couple hours. Chris and Toby had matching suits they wore when performing together on the bally stage and the two grew to have a strong bond.

Chris and Toby, 1972.

1971: Off to St. Thomas

Toby became quite protective of both Chris and Ward and that came to light one day when Ward fell off the bally stage and broke his wrist. As the ambulance came to take Ward to the hospital, Toby sensed something wasn't right. He started screaming and going crazy in his cage, which had only a partial view of what was going on. Before Ward got into the ambulance, he went over to Toby and the chimp settled down, reaching through the bars to gently touch Ward's hurt arm. "Once I acknowledged to him that I would be okay he settled down. He was very concerned and knew I was in pain."

Several years later, despite the bond and love they had for Toby, Chris sold him to another performer whose chimp had just died. He needed a chimp and the two knew Toby would have a good home and be lovingly cared for.

Pete Kortes announced his retirement in late 1972 after 50 years of continuous presence on the midway and put his sideshow up for sale (sans hippo and for real this time). Ward didn't hesitate and made arrangements to purchase the show.

Among those who stayed when Kortes sold were Dolly Reagan, the ossified girl, and her husband, Scotty McNeal, both of whom remained with Ward and Chris for many years. Reagan stayed off the road in 1978 due to her husband's declining health and in 1979, a few months after Scotty's death she came back out and went with sideshow operator Slim Kelly. She returned to Ward and Chris in 1980 where she stayed until retiring in 1983 due to her own declining health.

> *"At first she appears to be normal. She has a normal head and has perfect control of her speech, her hearing and her sight. Her right hand and arm are normal. But, ladies and gentlemen, you will see that she has no control over the rest of her body because that body has turned to stone. Right now, on stage on the inside is Dolly Reagan, the Ossified Lady."*

First hired into the business as a "stone lady," Dolly Reagan, who was three feet, nine inches tall, adapted to the business quickly. She could not stand or walk and was confined to a wheelchair her entire life. She could move her right arm and hand and her head, but the rest of her was frozen due to ankylosis of her joints.

Although she didn't work for Ward until he and Chris bought out Kortes, Ward had first met her at Ray Marsh Brydon's "Believe It or Not" dime museum in San Antonio, Texas, in 1946 where she was featured as the main blow-off attraction. Ward found her delightful and they became life-long friends until her death in 1994. Reagan was good with the media. During a run in Savannah, Ga., she was asked by a reporter about being exploited and exhibited on a sideshow stage. "I think the sideshow's a good business for people considered physical monstrosities," she said. "You're able to do your own living without being institutionalized."

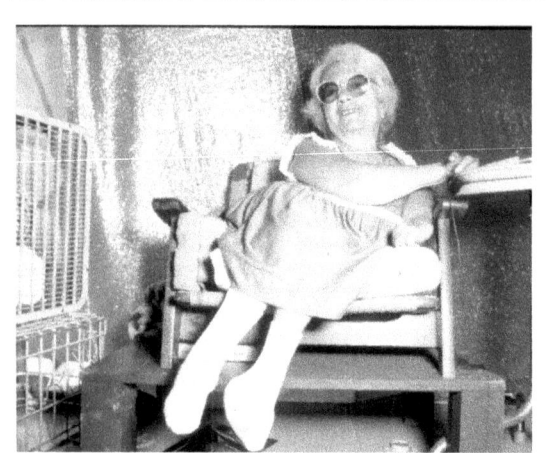

Dolly Reagan.

The 1973 season was bountiful, with four units on the road – the #1 unit run by Chris; the #2 unit appearing as the Congress of Oddities, run by Dick Johnson; the newly acquired Kortes show now run by Scotty McNeal; and Duke and Ethel Mayhood oversaw a fourth unit which consisted of several grind shows including a giant rat show, a freak baby show, a giant spider exhibit, and a new show featuring Carl Norwood as Carl the Frog Boy. Several times during the season, one or more of the single-o shows from Norwood's unit would join Chris for a week or so.

That fall, the Kortes unit was turned into a magic and illusion show; the banner line was completely revamped and a new tent was added. The bad news was that with all this renovation the shows could no longer fit into their trucks. The good news was that a new 45-foot trailer was built and especially fitted for their new equipment. Having seen that all projects were well underway at winter quarters, and with no shows on the road at the time, Ward and Chris headed to Europe for an extended trip during which time they purchased several illusions for the new magic show being built back home. While in Hamburg, Germany, they represented the IISA and were the honored guests at a banquet of the European Showmen's Congress, which was then the umbrella organization of European showmen's clubs.

Ringling is Calling:
Ward and Chris Build a Super Show

CHAPTER 22

Upon arrival back to the states in January 1974, they met with Irvin Feld, president of the Ringling Bros. and Barnum & Bailey Circus, who hired them to produce and operate a sideshow for a date at the National Armory in Washington, D.C. He wanted the biggest show possible that would not only intrigue circus goers but would dominate news coverage in the area. A competing circus was being created to play the newly-built Capital Center in Landover, Md., a suburb of Washington D.C., and Feld wanted to make sure his stood out above the other, which it did, thanks to Ward and Chris.

They went back to their winter quarters in Gibsonton and started to sign up acts for the new "super show" for Ringling. Included in that show were: Cliff and Mamie King, the world's smallest married couple; Freddie "Mephisto" Lulling, a fire manipulator; Betty MacGregor, as Stella the Bearded Lady; Emmett the Turtle Man; Lady Sandra Reed, an albino sword swallower; Pete as the dwarf clown; Bobo Francis Duggan, the rubber man; Johann Petursson, the Viking Giant; Jamal Tyrone Reeder, the Egyptian Giant; Big Jim (Harold Connors), a fat man; Jolly Dolly (Jo Ann Winters), a fat lady; and Chris as the knife thrower. Milt Robbins was the master of ceremonies.

Betty MacGregor as Stella the Bearded Lady.

"On stage now in the inside you will see the biggest, fattest, funniest, sweetest girl in the world. A little piece of sugar is sweet, but a big piece is much sweeter and our little Jolly Dolly is the sweetest girl you will ever meet. It takes four men to hug her ladies and gentlemen, because she measures 109 inches around the waist. That's over nine feet!"

Johann Petursson, The Viking Giant.

The show went off without a hitch and, thanks to Feld's publicist Sy Freedman, the sideshow received the lion's share of all publicity. Much of that attention was centered on Johann Petursson, the giant from Iceland. He had come over to the U.S. originally to work with Ringling and after a few years had gone out on his own. He was semi-retired but he was convinced to come out and play his last gig for Ward on that 1974 Ringling show. Feld had Ward bring the giant in a week ahead of time and Freedman had media lined up waiting to meet and interview Petursson.

Lady Sandra Reed also received a great deal of attention. Freedman promoted her in his publicity package thusly: *"Her ambition was to be more than just a showgirl, so with great courage, she learned to swallow swords."* His prose for Stella the Bearded Lady read: *"Admittedly, her beard hampers Stella's social life to some extent."*

With the strong start that the Ringling event in Washington D.C. provided, the 1974 season looked promising. Following the success of the first Boston Summerfest the year before, Ward and Chris had committed all of their equipment to the event this year. It had been a nice profit maker with just one unit and they had high hopes when they committed their entire arsenal of shows to the event's second showing.

The new illusion show went out before the rest that year to make sure it was operating at its finest by the time it pulled into Boston and it played several successful dates in upstate New York. When Ward arrived in Boston, he found that the new, larger location planned for the new and improved Summerfest had not been approved at the last minute due to the neighborhood's concern over noise and other potential problems.

A last-minute effort to find a new, suitable location failed and the organizers called off the entire event. By this time Chris and the rest of the units were well on their way to Boston. With no place to go, they sat quietly on an old fairground lot for several days while they searched for another event to fill the two weeks they now had free due to Summerfest's cancellation. They jumped to Derry, N.H., where they set up part of the show in a shopping center parking lot with the Billy Burr Carnival. As a gesture of his friendship, Burr tore down three of his own rides to make room for Ward and Chris.

The subsequent turn of events had everyone wondering what would happen next. All the units were set to play the always-successful Brocton (Mass.) Fair the week after the two-week Summerfest date. They arrived in Brockton only to learn the fair had moved from the Brocton fairgrounds to a dog track in Raynham. The week produced less than half the revenue than the previous year, even though it had appeared to have more potential, thanks to its expanded location. Following those frustrating few weeks, 1974 started looking better.

Earlier in 1974, ABC-TV network had called Ward asking him to pull together several sideshow acts for another *On Location* segment they wanted to air in late spring, playing off the success of the one they had aired from the Indiana State Fair the previous fall. Ward pulled together a stellar group of performers, one of whom was the famous Melvin Burkhart.

Best known for his human blockhead and anatomical wonder acts, Melvin Burkhart also ate fire, swallowed swords and was quite an accomplished magician. "To me, Melvin was one of the finest sideshow acts ever. He was an actor and was a marvelous performer," Ward said. "He was a very funny entertainer and had some great lines! He was very loyal to promoters Slim Kelly and Whitey Sutton but, when he wasn't working for them, he would sometimes come over with us for a couple dates." Burkhart spent 30 years, 1955 to 1985, with Kelly's storefront museum and Sutton's sideshow on the James E. Strates carnival.

Burkhart's anatomical wonder act was unique. He could suck his stomach back into his spine and distort his face to the point that one side of his face would be smiling, the other frowning, all while stretching out his neck and dislocating his shoulders so the blades would stick out of his back. The idea for his blockhead act came about while having a nose operation that fixed an injury from his earlier days as a competitive boxer. He was unimpressed with the small instrument the doctor shoved up his nose. "I

Melvin Burkhart performing the Blockhead.

can do better than that," he thought. And he did, typically using a 20-penny nail or an icepick to "get a good start before pounding like a devil," as he would often explain, basically while carrying on a comical monologue.

While Burkhart wasn't the first person to stick a nail up his nose, "he was the first to add amusing patter and truly transform a gruesome stunt into a very entertaining act," said fellow sideshow performer Todd Robbins. As a good friend of Burkhart, Robbins was given "the official permission" to replicate Burkhart's comical human blockhead act. "Even though my routine was different from his, he was very much the inspiration for my approach to the act," Robbins relates. "I asked and he gave me permission to use his exact routine. It was possibly the most generous gesture I have ever experienced."

When Robbins and his soon-to-be wife Krista were planning their Oct. 8, 2001 wedding, they created a show instead of a ceremony, held at the Sullivan Street Playhouse in Manhattan. They had puppetry, burlesque, a stripper, Wild West stunts and the "featured" entertainer was Melvin Burkhart, then 94 years old. "I didn't know how sick he was and exactly one month later he died in Florida." Several weeks later Robbins received a box of Burkhart's props and his costume. A couple weeks after that he received Burkhart's cremains which he, Krista and Coney Island USA's Dick Zigun sprinkled in the Atlantic Ocean off Coney Island's Steeplechase Pier.

In late 1974, Ward and Chris contracted with Crystal Beach Park, just across the border in Crystal Beach, Ont., Canada, to present Dr. Miracle's Wondercade, a new vaudeville-themed magic and illusion show for the entire 1975 season. Instead of sending their existing illusion show to the park for the summer they decided they would use extra illusions they already had, build a few more, and keep their existing show intact. No tent or banner line was needed because the show was to be inside in the ballroom building. What started out as a small venture turned into a large and elaborate illusion revue featuring live musicians, dancers, production numbers, sideshow acts, magic and illusions. Ward and Chris had never created a show of such scope and size.

The seats, stage and a semi-truck to haul everything were purchased from a show no longer being produced by Gooding's Million Dollar Midways. They bought the lighting, musical instruments, scenery and costumes once used in Leon Claxton's *Harlem in Havana* show from his widow, and bought costumes and lighting from Jack and Bonnie Normand's Broadway to Hollywood production. They also acquired a variety of stage sets from Jackie Gleason's Scenery, Inc.; illusions came from Bill Siros. Larry Crane choreographed the show and Marge Porter created special costumes, reworked the others and altered the staging drapery.

Marge Porter, whom Ward describes as "good as gold," spent eight years with him. During that time, she "did just about anything that needed to get done." She and her husband, Glen, had their own sideshow for a while and then had a monkey speedway they booked with Royal American Shows. When Glen died, Marge joined Ward and Chris. She handled the books, created costumes, built two four-legged illusion shows from scratch, lectured the various inside acts, and, when Chris got Toby the chimp, she ended up helping train both the chimp and Chris.

Cast auditions were held in New York City by Larry Crane, long-time friend and producer. They ended up with a stage 80 feet wide by 40 feet deep, with 12 major illusions and several production numbers. Needless to say, they had no room to spare in the Crystal Beach Park ballroom once it was transformed into an impressive theater. Ward stayed in Florida, keeping busy with his Showmen's Club duties and readying the sideshows for the road. Chris and Marge Porter took a crew to Crystal Beach and installed the show.

Within a few months the Crystal Beach operation, which turned out to be an expensive show to operate, was losing money and Chris went up to the park to close it down. But park management loved the production, as did park guests, and a deal was worked out to forego rent for the rest of the year if the show would continue to operate. The payroll was trimmed and the show stayed open. It didn't lose any more money, but there was little profit.

Circus World theme park, in Haines City, Fla., which opened in February 1974 and was owned and operated by the Feld/Ringling organization, was undergoing its first major expansion in early 1975 and

Irvin Feld and his team asked Ward and Chris to set up their sideshow at the park for six months. It proved to be very popular due to its circus midway allure. Thinking everything was fine, Ward planned to expand the show for the busy Florida tourism months. But the planning came to a quick halt, when, in a short, to-the-point letter from Mike Downs, the park's new general manager, Ward was told to "make no further commitments or contracts regarding any acts for Ringling Bros. and Barnum & Bailey Circus World." In other words, the contract was not going to be renewed for 1976.

In addition to Circus World and Crystal Beach activities, it was a busy start to the 1975 season. Ward and Chris, now part owners of Circus Vargas started preparing for the circus route while they played the Florida State Fair in Tampa in February. At the annual meeting of the IISA that year Ward advanced from second vice president to first vice president.

The arrangement with Cliff Vargas made during fall 1974 was a handshake partnership. Vargas had just come off a bad season and needed money. Chris and Ward had just come off a successful season with cash in their pockets and looking for an opportunity. In exchange for operating capital, Cliff Vargas sold part of the show to Chris and Ward with the stipulation that the two also create a sideshow for the circus. "His word proved to be 100%," Ward said. "We always got what we were supposed to get and we never felt like he would take advantage of us."

Shortly after opening with Circus Vargas in mid-February 1975 and spending three weeks on the circus with his sideshow, Ward was preparing to return to Florida when he received a call that his aunt Alda had died. He left immediately for Nebraska to attend the funeral and to assist in getting her estate in order. Upon returning to Florida, he received a call that his friend W.J. Hart, who was then the president of the IISA, had died. Ward was appointed acting president and ended up serving the remainder of Hart's term as well as his own the following year.

During summer 1975, Billy Sheets managed the travelling illusion show; Chris managed sideshow #1; the Johnsons continued to manage sideshow #2; and sideshow #3 was with Circus Vargas. Additionally, Freddie Lulling managed the baby show, the mummy show, the rat show and a snake show. Lulling, who was deaf, was "always one of my favorites," Ward recalls.

By 1975, Chris had stopped performing as much and started concentrating more on running the company, booking the routes and moving the shows. "It got to the point where I just didn't have time to devote to performing, which was never really a top priority for me anyway," Chris said. Previously, he would eat fire, throw knives and swallow swords, in addition to his administrative duties.

By the end of the season, the two realized it was impossible to keep up the quality and to field good attractions with so much going on, even with Chris concentrating more on the business side of the shows. Their contract had not been renewed with Circus World and they decided not to renew Crystal Beach. They sold back their share of the circus to Cliff Vargas, who also purchased from Chris and Ward the sideshow that had been travelling with him that year.

Ward had mixed feelings about not going back to Crystal Beach but he and Chris had too much on their plates. "We presented 73 performances in 15 weeks in the same location and I think it was a great artistic success," Ward recalls, noting that all his shows except one had profitable seasons in 1975.

Having ascended the offices, Ward was installed as the IISA President in February 1976. "When Bernie Mendelsohn handed me the gavel making me president, I was a very proud, happy man. It was a great year for both me and the Showmen's Club because I had the greatest officers, board of directors and committee people anyone could ask for. Heading up one of the largest showmen's clubs in the world was quite an honor for me and it was the first really big recognition I had ever received. I was very much interested in the club and its well-being, so I worked very hard those two years to be a great president."

Ward and his mother Opal Koske at his February 1976 IISA installation ceremony.

What might still be the most spectacular showmen's parties in history took place in early February 1977 at the Egypt Shrine Temple in Tampa for Ward's farewell banquet as his terms as IISA President expired. A circus calliope blared away outside as banquet guests arrived and a trio played in the lounge. As soon as everyone was seated, a 60-piece marching band burst through the rear doors. Dignitaries entered through an arch of running-lights and were escorted to the head table, where sat a representative of nearly every showman's group in the country.

Illusionist Roy Huston began to entertain, surrounded by 24 dancing girls. Then Huston displayed an empty drum to the audience, covered both ends and hoisted it into the air. He fired a pistol at it, and Ward burst through one of the ends. That entrance was designed by Huston at the last minute; the original idea had Ward coming in on an elephant but three days prior to the event the elephant dropped dead.

The girls danced and the 16-piece dance band of Dean Hudson performed, having come directly from the Presidential Inauguration Ball in Washington, D.C. Then for everyone's dancing pleasure, the Clyde McCoy Orchestra played until the wee hours of the morning. During one break, the musical comedy of the Conti Family took the stage. What a memorable way to end his time as president of the IISA. Tom Powell, then editor of *Amusement Business,* was there and recalls it was big and spectacular and "surprised us all evening long," as no one knew what was coming up next. "I have covered many banquets as a journalist in my day, but this was the greatest one ever!"

"It was the most important night of my life, marred only by a deep disappointment that Chris could not be there," Ward said. "Our sideshow was playing the Florida State Fair and there were difficulties there that needed his constant oversight."

As anyone who runs a business and at the same time serves as the head of a large volunteer organization knows, you can't do it alone. During the four years Ward was an officer and president of the association, Chris had to be prepared to pick up the slack on day-to-day operations, and it was something he gladly did. "I spent a lot of time during those years doing my job as well as his because he was off doing club business, but, you know, I was very proud of him and happy for him and I was happy to support him," said Chris. Ward adds: "Without his help and understanding, it would have been impossible for me to have done so well in club politics."

Trouble in Mexico:
Magic Show Goes South

CHAPTER 23

When Charlie Gutermuth offered to sell his portable wax museum, Ward was not interested but Chris saw great potential and wanted to buy it so Ward relented. It was purchased and underwent a complete overhaul with a new, dynamic front painted by Bill Browning. It turned out to be a good and profitable show. Ward said he learned to love wax displays that year. "Best of all, they are wax. They never get drunk. They're always on time, and on Tuesdays they don't line up to get paid."

The Dr. Miracle's Wondercade magic show Ward and Chris created for Crystal Beach Park the previous year, served as the basis of another show, Magic on Parade. It was developed to play for an 18-month tour of Mexico during summer of 1976, starting in Mexico City. Chris and Ward were to be paid a set weekly fee, and built a budget based on that revenue flow. It turned out to be an elegant show, with costumes purchased from the Ice Capades and a large portable stage grid built to hold lights and scenery. Julian Hilton, Anita Yulsman and Vince and Jackie Carmen, all of whom played in Dr. Miracle's Wondercade show in Canada, joined the new production and headed to Mexico City.

Arrangements were made guaranteeing that the truck carrying all the equipment and costumes could easily cross into Mexico. That wasn't the case. In fact, trouble began before they even got to the border. Due to the amount stuffed into their semi-trailer, they were fined twice in the U.S. for being overweight. The lion used in the "beautiful girl changing into a wild lion" act turned out to be the hardest to get across the border, taking them nearly a full day to get the proper permits. The miniature horse used in a "now you see it, now you don't" illusion was given away to a Texas veterinarian who lived nearby rather than attempting to get it permitted. Finally the show was on its way, with a driver sent to the border who knew where they were going and what groups along the way that needed to be paid off to secure a safe journey.

The original schedule allowed for three days of setting up the show and a full week of rehearsals prior to opening. When they arrived on the lot, Ward was not able to secure the promised crew that was supposed to be waiting. He was also surprised to see that the tent was still on the ground being fireproofed. Already short of rehearsal time, they moved into an old animal barn on the lot and began rehearsals there after relocating a camel and a few donkeys to an outside pen.

Opening night went off without a hitch and Ward, content that everything was under control, headed home to prepare the other units for season premieres, with a short stop in Chicago first to attend an OABA board meeting. While there, he received a call that a freak snowstorm hit the show in Mexico and collapsed the big top, causing considerable damage. Luckily no one was hurt. Ward flew back to Mexico to survey the damage and help the crew. This incident turned out to be only the beginning of a Mexican tragedy for the Hall and Christ Magic on Parade show.

By mid-summer, the word from the road was not good. All but one of their U.S. units was doing poorly and the news was not good from Mexico as things down there were going from bad to worse. The promoter started missing paydays and at the same time started hiring locals who would work much cheaper than the U.S. performers. Upon closing in Mexico City the show was torn down and headed out on the road tour visiting smaller cities throughout Mexico.

Leonard Simons, manager of the Magic on Parade show, who had previously managed the Rogers Bros. Circus, knew magic and illusions but didn't know how to tear down and set up nor did he want that responsibility. Instead, He wanted to come home to the states and he urged Ward to sell the show to the Mexican promoter. Ward didn't want to sell but the show was a losing proposition and he didn't have the cash to pay off the performers' 18-month contracts or to get the equipment home.

Ward and Chris agreed to sell the show for $100,000, payable in installments, and the promoter promised to honor all agreements with the performers and pay them what was owed, which he did. However, Ward received the first check for $1,000 and nothing more. A lawsuit was filed in the State of Florida and Ward was awarded judgment. He sent his friend Charlie Cox to Mexico to find the show and either get the rest of the money owed or to bring the show back. Cox found the show and reported that its condition had deteriorated extensively. Ward told Cox to forget about it and return home. More legal proceedings followed to get the money. On the day of the trial in September 1979 the promoter settled with Ward in the hallways of the courthouse for $10,000 cash. "The final chapter is that by the time all legal fees were paid, we ended up with only $5,400," Ward said, noting that much of the show was "irreplaceable."

The movie *Jaws*, premiered on June 20, 1975, and a young showman named Danny Walters, seeing a timely opportunity, created an exhibit showcasing a shark in dry ice, and booked it at the State Fair of Texas that fall. He did very well with it. Ward and Chris met Walters at the IAFE convention in December and partnered up. Walters would provide the shark and a truck to pull the trailer and would manage the show. Ward would book the route.

As the 1976 season approached, with the shark show booked at big fairs, Ward was unable to find Walters so he immediately cancelled their partnership. That left them with a route but no shark. In late February, Ward located an 11-foot tiger shark preserved in a tank in Pensacola, Fla. He bought it, and Chris framed a show that proved profitable for the five years he kept it, selling it after the 1980 season.

During the mid-1970s, a self-proclaimed carnival chaser, photographer Randal Levenson, befriended Ward and Chris and not only photographed the show but worked it as well. Levenson was creating a book of carnival and sideshow photos and Ward gave him free reign. Occasionally, Randal would be joined by his wife, Rusty, on the road and she would work the show while visiting him.

Rusty handled the snakes on the bally and Randal did a little of everything, including lecturing the blow-off for Artoria, the tattooed woman. In 1982, *In Search of the Monkey Girl,* the book on which Levenson was working was published by Aperture Books to great kudos. It included several individual portraits of Ward's performers, including Barbara and Ed Bennett, Bruce Snowden, and Emmett the Turtle Man, all from the 1976 show, as well as a group shot of the entire Hall and Christ 1977 sideshow team at the Ohio State Fair.

Jaws, at the 1977 State Fair of Texas.

Ward Hall – King of the Sideshow!

Ward considers the mid-1970s to the early 1980s the "Golden Years" of the shows he and Chris owned and operated. "We had multiple shows out and we were playing the biggest fairs and events in the country during those years," he said. "During that same time I was an officer of the IISA, and on the boards of OABA and Showmen's League of America. When I wasn't on the midway with one of our shows, I was in a plane heading off to a board meeting." Of all the years presenting shows, he singles out 1975/76 as his apex. "I had more than 300 on my payroll and we had many shows on the road. Those were good years for us."

The *Howdy Doody* children's television show ended its 13 year run on NBC-TV in 1960 but remained popular in reruns and in the hearts of those who grew up watching the redheaded marionette and his cast of characters. Chris negotiated the rights to license the character for a show to be called the New Howdy Doody Magic Show that would feature ventriloquism, magic and illusion. There were to be costumed characters, Clarabelle the clown, Howdy Doody himself and Simon the chimp. Acquiring the license took longer than he had expected and it was too late to book the show into amusement parks and fairs for the 1977 season. Not wanting to pay for the rights for a year with few bookings, he let the idea die.

Ward had wanted the Howdy Doody Magic Show to replace his #2 unit, operated by Dick Johnson that was not going out in 1977. Johnson, an important cog in the sideshow business of Ward and Chris, had decided he didn't want to take out the unit that year as he had the previous 10 years.

Instead, Johnson purchased a freak animal show and took it out for a successful run under his own ownership. Ward said that, even though he lost a great employee, he "was happy that it (the animal show) was a success" for Johnson. "Indeed, it was a success," Johnson said. "I paid $7,500 for it and by the end of the season, it was paid for, plus we lived off the revenues all season long."

Johnson, who is the same age as Ward, grew up in Erie, Pa., and two weeks after returning from the Korean War, joined Herb Walter's Famous Cole Circus. Johnson and his wife Mavis joined Chris and Ward in 1967. They brought along their parrot, a monkey, and a 14-dog act. When Chris and Ward purchased the Pete Kortes show, the Johnsons ended up running it through the 1976 season.

"Ward was very fair and our deal was very good," Johnson said. "He paid us a nice salary plus a percentage, plus I was in on the pitches as well." But most of all Dick was pleased that Ward let him run the show his way. "We did things differently, but we both were happy with the outcome. It was a hard relationship because we were good friends and he was my boss, but it worked out well because I always knew he trusted and respected me," Dick said. He, Ward and Chris are still good friends to this day.

During the spring of 1977, Ward recalled how much he liked a two-headed girl illusion he had seen in the 1960s and decided to build one. It became an enormous project but was completed in time to open at the Milwaukee Summerfest in late June.

> *"Today you are going to see Miss Atari from Egypt who has two normal, beautiful and functional heads. She's going to talk with you, first with one head, then the other and she will sing a duet with both of the heads singing for you. Yes, inside right now, a live girl with three breasts and two heads."*

It was a great idea but, in actuality it didn't work. Ward sent it back to winter quarters for a rework. During that off-season, it was "fixed" and it went out again in 1978, letter perfect. While it looked great and worked well, it didn't attract any business. It was sent home once again where it remains today in storage, having never again been set up. Meanwhile, a small illusion show featuring a girl's head on the body of a snake - put together at the last minute because there was extra room on the truck - was raking in the cash. "On that success, a second snake girl show was built and also did very well," Ward notes.

Ward Hall – King of the Sideshow!

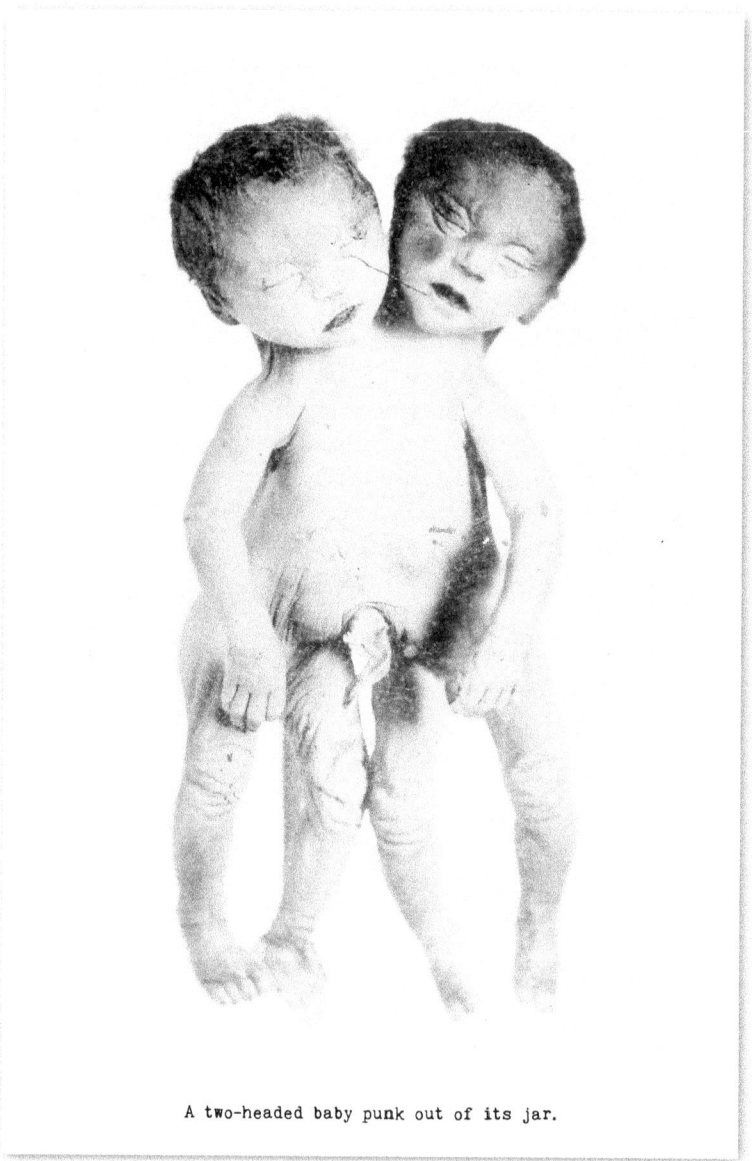

A two-headed baby punk out of its jar.

Punk Problems:
Dead Babies Vs. State of Illinois

CHAPTER 24

On July 29, 1977, at the Lake County (Illinois) Fair in Grayslake, Chris was arrested and the show's freak baby attraction, "Children of Forgotten Fathers," was confiscated by local authorities. Ward said it looked like a raid on mafia headquarters. Around 8 p.m. several police cars and a van pulled up to the baby show and off went Chris in a police cruiser and off went the contents of the show in a van.

"It was a cool summer's night and for some reason, I had decided to put on a suit and tie, something I rarely did," Chris recalls, noting that he looked like a respectable business man. The policeman walked up to Chris and said, "We have a warrant for your arrest." Chris read the warrant, looked at the officer and said, "Let's go." They wanted to handcuff him, but he convinced them that he would give them no problems and that it "wasn't necessary to parade me down the midway in cuffs." He was being charged with "illegal disposition of bodies and illegal possession of human remains." Chris was released upon posting a $2,000 bond and ordered to appear in court on Aug. 15. "I was out of there in 45 minutes and for the entire time, the policeman kept apologizing for having to do this," he recalled.

The bust came as a result of an anonymous call from a woman who complained that her daughter was emotionally upset by the exhibit. Neither Ward nor Chris believed that is the case. The real reason, Ward surmises, was right across the midway. The show faced into the big double roll-up door of an exhibition building where just inside the door was a booth for a right-to-life organization. The ladies running the booth could look out and see the freak babies' show, and all day long they had to listen to an endless taped bally proclaiming:

> "These children are of forgotten fathers. They did not ask to
> be born. Twenty strange freak babies, all different, all strange.
> They did not ask to be born. Is the pill right?
> Is abortion the answer? You be the judge, but first
> see these children of forgotten fathers."

All the babies were real fetuses, preserved in formaldehyde, and all were more than 100 years old, which an autopsy during the court proceedings proved. Ward and Chris had acquired them when they bought out the shows of Bill Chaulkas and Pete Kortes several years prior. Ward thinks the women in the right-to-life booth assumed they came from an abortion mill and that was why they had contacted authorities. "It was all about politics," Chris said. "The coroner who pressed the charges had been in that office for nearly 30 years but the state that year had abolished the position of coroner and replaced it with the position of medical examiner, who had to be a medical doctor. The coroner was a bartender by trade and was not qualified to run again." Instead, he was running for sheriff and "obviously was looking for a hook to hang his publicity on" for his campaign, Chris supposed.

Chris could have pleaded guilty, paid a small fine and gone on with his life, but he decided not to. "I had not done anything wrong, so I wanted to fight this to the end. At first I think they thought I was a transient bum who would blow bond and they would never hear from me again." Over the next few days, Chris called the other operators around the country who were running baby shows, told them what happened, and warned them that the media might be visiting them. That turned out to be very helpful advice because two days later the Associated Press ran a story that was carried in dozens of newspapers across the country. One operator with whom Chris had talked, "put his real babies away and put out rubber ones just hours before the local authorities and the press paid a visit."

Prior to the trial date, nearly 50 different publications ran stories on the bust. The Tampa Tribune published a story about the ordeal and called Chris "The Ghoul of Gibsonton." Chris was arraigned on Sept. 8, 1977 and on October 19, the trial began. More than 100 members of the press showed up and, while it was contentious at times, the spectacle ended two-and-a-half hours later with the judge dropping all charges. The outcome was based on the fact that the unborn baby fetuses were more than 100 years old, there were no birth or death certificates and, because of that, the fetuses could not be considered corpses. Chris was acquitted of all charges and his record expunged. The vindication was expected but the ruling went virtually unreported in the press. The case ended the era of major baby shows on the midway.

More than $6,000 was spent on the defense, but the real damage came as a result of all the press the case received. The sensational slant the wire services placed on the story was unflattering to the entire sideshow industry and caused most fairs going forward to request that the shows not be set up at their events. "That certainly cut into our income. This was a real popular show," Chris noted. The baby show was booked to open at the Ohio State Fair two weeks after the raid and was to premiere at the State Fair of Texas later in the fall. Ward and Chris didn't want to miss out on the popularity of a baby show at those two large fairs so they made a quick trip to the rubber factory to have duplicate exhibits manufactured.

This is where irony chimes in. In Ohio, every attraction must be inspected by official state regulators prior to opening at any fair. Having played the Ohio State Fair in Columbus for several years, Chris and Ward knew the inspectors well. About a month after the Grayslake, Ill., raid they were setting up in Columbus and the Ohio inspectors asked to see one of the babies outside its jar of formaldehyde. When he picked it up and realized it was a "bouncer," the term used to signify rubber babies, he shook his head, noting that "in Ohio, the law is very specific. You can't have any made-up freaks. They must be real. If you had the real babies as you have had in the past, I would be able to give you a license to operate, but I can't license these fakes."

Some of what you will see on the inside is really real.
Some of what you will see on the inside is really fake.
But everything you will see on the inside is really good.

While all this was going on, and unbeknownst to Ward or Chris, on August 11, Hillsborough County officials had raided their show's winter quarters in Gibsonton, found 13 additional jars of baby fetuses and confiscated them. They had been seized under a Florida law that gives police authority to confiscate to determine whether they were the result of illegal abortions. It was not until Ward and Chris returned home later that fall that they found the raid had taken place. A search warrant dated August 11 had been "served" to their kitchen screen door. A few weeks after they returned home, a letter arrived from the district attorney's office informing Ward that he had been charged in August and that he needed to turn himself in. Ward went to his attorney who informed him to go home and that he would take care of it, which he did. All charges were dropped on Jan. 5, 1978 and Ward's record was expunged.

On Nov. 17, 1977, 14 of the 20 fetuses seized in Grayslake were buried in Highland Park, Ill., in tiny plastic foam caskets. Clergy from three faiths offered prayers, with one addressing the fetuses as "God's unknown children." The remaining six were donated by the coroner's office to medical schools. While there were no official mourners there were plenty of newsmen and photographers, including an Associated Press photographer whose photo of the 14 little coffins lined up at graveside appeared in newspapers across the nation.

Ward holding a two-headed chicken, Bruce Snowden, the fatman, and Pete, the dwarf.

Adding Oddities:
A Small Woman and a Fat Man Sign Up

CHAPTER 25

Barbara Bennett, billed as the "World's Smallest Woman and the Mother of Four," joined Ward and Chris in late 1976 as part of the main sideshow but Ward felt she would do well in a show that only featured her. So for the 1977 season, Chris built what Ward claims to be "one of the best grind show fronts ever designed." Bill Browning artwork "gilded the lily," adds Ward. Bennett suffered from osteogenesis. Her torso and head were normal size but her limbs were shrunken and disfigured. In the smallest mother show, she brought along her daughter who was similarly disfigured. For the next six seasons, Bennett was the star of the single-o, but in 1983, wanting to slow down and work less she created her own show and booked it sparingly. She would join Ward again in 1985 for several spots. She retired in 1990 and died on Christmas Day 2000.

Also in 1977, Bruce Snowden, who would be billed as Howard Huge, got in touch with Ward after reading about a fat man while perusing a story in his hometown newspaper. Snowden felt that if the guy he had read about could make money being fat, so could he. He found a copy of *Amusement Business* and called its editor, Tom Powell, and asked for information on how to get into the business. "I talked with him and when I realized he was serious about it, I referred him to Ward," Powell said. "Anything sideshow related, Ward was my go-to man." A few weeks later, he joined Chris and Ward and, for the next 26 years, Snowden plied the sideshow stages. He died on Nov. 9, 2009, at the age of 63 and a weight of 607 pounds.

"He's so fat, it takes four girls to hug him and a boxcar to lug him. When he dances you'll swear he must be full of jelly, 'cause jam don't shake that way. And you know, girls, he is single and looking for a wife. He'll make some lucky girl a fine husband. Why, he's so big and fat, he'll provide you with a lot of shade in the summertime, keep you nice and warm in the wintertime, and give you lots of good, heavy loving all the time."

"While there is no shortage of fat men in America, only one over the past few decades called himself a professional," wrote Marc Hartzman for *AOL* (now *Huffington Post*) *Weird News*. In a story about Snowden's death, Buck Wolf, writing for About.com *Weird News,* noted that he was "the last of the professional circus sideshow fat men."

Joy Scott, a reporter with the *Shelby* (N.C.) *Star* newspaper had visited with Snowden at the Cleveland County Fair in October 2001. She asked him what it felt like being called a freak and being consistently stared at. "Freak will do quite nicely," he told her. "People are going to stare at me anyway. At least in here I get paid for it." Answers like that endeared him to Chris and Ward. "He was very articulate and usually said the right things at the right time," Chris added.

The last year Ward and Chris featured a number of human oddities on the World of Wonders sideshow was 1986. After that, Pete the dwarf and fat man Snowden were the only oddities on the World of Wonders. The "Freak Wanted" sign was out, but nobody came knocking. Ward reasons there are plenty of disfigured and handicapped individuals who would still prefer a job today as a "freak" on a sideshow making good money rather than sitting at home or in an institution collecting government assistance.

"We are just running out of them because we can't find them," Ward said. "People would come and see them if we had them." That lack of "real" freaks led to the need to create illusions of freaks that are so common on sideshows today. "Illusions are fun, but they don't satisfy the crowds like the real oddities." Ward believes the basic reason for the dearth of true, living, genuine freaks today is the fact that they don't know how to go about joining up.

Ward admits that with all the social programs available today, human oddities can usually live a comfortable life without having to join up with a sideshow. However, he feels there are plenty out there who would sign up if they knew about the opportunities that existed. "At its peak in the 1940s, there were at least 105, 10-in-one sideshows crisscrossing the country playing hundreds of dates in small communities," he pointed out. "The locals had the opportunity, at least once a year, to come out and see the show and ask for a job. Today, there are very few opportunities to do that," he said.

Billboard published a weekly list of job opportunities and openings in all sorts of entertainment genres and now that source is gone. "At one time we would advertise in *Billboard* for a fat man or a legless person or an armless person or whatever, and we would get immediate response," Ward said. The *Billboard* began publishing on Nov. 1, 1894, and served thousands of traveling showmen through the years. In January 1961, the publication split into two weekly magazines: *Amusement Business (AB)* became the new outdoor entertainment go-to publication and *Billboard*

Adding Oddities: A Small Woman and a Fat Man Sign Up

began to concentrate more on the indoor entertainment industry, specializing in music and the charts it is famous for today.

AB was an able substitute for the original for many years and provided most of the same services and editorial support that *Billboard* had, but in the early 2000s, the publication's advertising and subscriptions started to decline and, following a failed format change, it ceased publication following the May 2006 issue. But it was only a shadow of its former self from mid-2004 when many of its features that allowed direct communication with the showmen were dropped from the magazine. Take away that communication tool and add the fact that so few shows are playing the hinterland today, few anatomical anomalies are stepping forward looking for a career on the midway.

There are two stalwart acts that once were staples of sideshows that Ward will not book today – a fat person or a tattooed person. "Go to the mall on Saturday and you will see plenty of both. No one will pay to see a fat man anymore," he pointed out.

Today's landscape for "working acts" (the non-deformed individuals who choose to perform the sideshow arts) is vastly different than it has ever been. Ironically, there could possibly be more sword swallowers, blockheads, fire eaters, glass walkers and snake charmers than there have ever been thanks to the Coney Island Sideshow School and Harley Newman's Oddity U near Allentown, Pa. But the possibility for them to make a living doing such is very small indeed. In reality, most who know such skills will tell you they learned them because they were odd, offbeat, and somewhat dangerous "tricks" that they learned for fun and to impress their friends. Few learned them to be their livelihood.

With no circuses booking large sideshows and very few carnivals that will book any type of show, there is, probably for the first time, more supply of working acts than demand. Those who did learn the arts to perform professionally are struggling to make ends meet. Ask most and they will admit to having a "day job."

During January 1978 while playing the South Florida Fair & Exposition in West Palm Beach with the show's wax museum, Ward was approached by amusement park legend Ken Wynne who asked him to build a full-size wax museum on Casino Pier, on the boardwalk in Seaside Heights, N.J., which he owned and operated. Ward, Chris and Ken Wynne became partners in 20th Century Wax, an attraction filled with characters purchased from the Las Vegas Wax Museum, with additional celebrities added. Chris designed and installed it in a large building directly across the boardwalk from the pier amusement area, spending six weeks on location to get it ready to open on the Friday before Memorial Day 1978.

Further down the Seaside Heights boardwalk, Ward and Chris took over another building and created a pickled punks showcase. It didn't do well and they soon turned it into an Oddities Museum, which did great business during the summer tourist season. Both the wax museum and the oddities museum operated for three summers before closing down. The oddities then went back to Ward and Chris's storage in Florida while Cumberland Valley Shows and a wax museum in Sweden bought the majority of the wax figures.

Among the highlights of the 1978 sideshow operation was the single biggest day's gross, to date, in their sideshow history, in Columbus at the Ohio State Fair, and the second biggest day at the State Fair of Texas in Dallas, both topping the $10,000 single day mark. The #2 unit came out for the first time since Dick Johnson left, under the direction of Henry Valentine, and had a so-so season booked on with Gooding's Million Dollar Midway. However, at season's end, Ward and Chris decided to not take out a second unit the following year.

During the previous year, they had mothballed the illusion show because they couldn't get enough help to run it and getting quality help was starting to be a major concern. A combination of not being able to get that needed help and losing a few of their best managers caused Ward and Chris to think about their future. Add burn-out to that mix and the two were not very optimistic about their future going into 1979.

The Smithsonian:
Being Saluted as True Americana

CHAPTER 26

The National Museum of American History and the Division of Performing Arts of the Smithsonian Institution in Washington, D.C., as part of its Spring Celebration of American Popular Entertainment, brought Ward and Chris's entire show to the mall in front of the Museum of Science and Industry for three days during April 1979. It was the first time a sideshow was endorsed and sponsored by the Smithsonian, and it went over so well they were invited back for three more showings, in 1980, '81 and '82, with interest and attendance each year growing larger and larger.

Richard Flint of the Division of Performing Arts, also a circus and entertainment historian, had known Ward for several years before being asked by the Smithsonian to put such a show together. "I knew immediately who I wanted to represent the sideshow industry," Flint said. "Each year it got a bigger and better response. People in Washington, D.C., never got much of a chance to see a big show like what Ward and Chris had at the time."

"They asked us to be bigger and a little bit different each year and they moved us inside after the first year. Our last year there, we were set up next to the Old Glory Flag exhibit," Ward said, adding that he was especially proud of the shows he presented during those four years. "It was quite an honor to represent the sideshow industry as a true American art form in that celebration."

Sideshow banner painter Johnny Meah, was asked by Flint (separately from Ward and Chris) to be a part of the American Celebration in 1979. He was kept busy demonstrating the art of banner painting while lecturing on his style and technique. The first year of the Smithsonian series also featured a one-ring circus produced by Johnny Herriott. In the following years there was no circus, but Herriott was hired by Flint to be the announcer for the various performers booked for the event.

Herriott, Ward, Meah, and Flint enjoyed each other's company. "The only reason we got booked for four years in a row was because Dick (Flint) liked to talk about the circus, and each night after the show closed we all went to dinner and cut up jackpots until they closed the bars early in the morning," Meah said. When asked if that were true, Flint laughed. "Yes, that worked. Those were wonderful times with wonderful friends and by hanging out with me definitely guaranteed their booking for the following year."

Playing the Smithsonian gave the show prestige that stayed with them for more than a decade. On Aug. 26, 1987, while the show was playing the Missouri State Fair, reporter Ron Jennings of *The Sedalia Democrat* became quite enamored with Ward and the show. In the coverage of the fair, Jennings pointed out that the sideshow was "becoming a vanishing part of Americana" and that the Smithsonian obviously agreed with that point because, "It has booked him (Ward) four times in recent years."

Jennings continued. "Hall doesn't need the prestigious Smithsonian stamp of approval to confirm that what he has to offer is in keeping with a time-honored tradition of American entertainment. But he hopes it has clarified it in the public's eyes. He understands the increased reservations of many people regarding what are commonly perceived as freak shows, and what's more he agrees." He then notes that Ward thinks people are becoming more and more sensitive. "And I think that is a good thing," Ward was quoted.

Back in Gibsonton following that first year at the Smithsonian, Ward hired Meah to paint several new banners, which he did in Ward's backyard. "As we were talking, I asked him if I could join the show, doing whatever he needed me to do," Meah said. "He hired me and I was with him and Chris through 1985." While not working for Ward and Chris on a full time basis today, Meah continues to paint new banners for the World of Wonders sideshow. "Ward is one of the most considerate, kindest men I have ever known," Meah said. "That's why I have continued to be associated with him and Chris for more than 40 years. Sometimes, to his disadvantage, he was too generous to me."

Today, Meah continues to paint and to exhibit prints and original art of some of the 2,500 banners he has painted since his first one in 1957. His artwork and his writings have been featured in various worldwide publications and in the book he co-authored in 2004, *Freaks, Geeks & Strange Girls*. In a Feb. 14, 2003 article, the *Tampa Tribune* called Meah the "Sideshow Van Gogh."

Percilla the Monkey Girl and her husband, Emmitt the Alligator Skin Man, billed as the "Strangest Married Couple in the World," joined their friends Ward and Chris for the full season of 1979. "They spent most of their lives operating their own single-o show," said Ward. "They only spent that one year with us."

Being billed as the strangest married couple in the world, the two received a great many requests for interviews, many of which they gladly granted. Emmitt especially frowned on anyone using the term "freak" to describe him or Percilla. "We are not freaks," he would proclaim. "We're all God's creatures no matter how we look. When you are mixing 24 hours a day with people who look like freaks, you come to know they are not freaks after all. They can be beautiful people, despite their appearance."

Ward and Percilla Bejano, (a shaved Monkey Girl), ready to go dancing in 1991.

Born in Puerto Rico in 1918, Percilla had a condition known as hypertrichosis and had excessive hair over her entire body and face. Her parents brought her to the United States, where sideshow promoter Karl Lauther adopted her and immediately put her on display as the "Little Hairy Girl."

Lauther reportedly loved her as if she were his own and was quite protective of her on the midway. It was on his show where she met the love of her life, Emmitt the Alligator Skin Man. Emmitt was born in Florida in 1918 and was afflicted with ichthyosis, a condition that made the skin on his body both hard and scaly. Emmitt was also adopted into the sideshow business at a young age by promoter Johnny J. Bejano, with whom Emmitt stayed until he joined Lauther's show when he was 20. Emmitt and Percilla eloped and were married for 57 years. They used the name Bejano as their legal surname.

"Unlike Schlitzie the Monkey Girl, who was an imbecile, Percilla the Monkey Girl was a very charming and very well educated lady," said Ward, who kept in close contact with her until her death on Feb. 5, 2001. Emmitt had passed earlier, on May 14, 1995.

> "The featured attraction of the big sideshow this year is the world's strangest married couple. Emmitt the Alligator Skin Man, who has growing on his body, from head to toe, the same kind of rough, tough scaly hide that you would find growing on an alligator or crocodile. A skin so thick, so rough you could hardly penetrate it with a needle, so tough, so rough you could strike and light a kitchen match on it.
>
> "With Emmitt is his unusual wife, Percilla the Monkey Girl, who has a strange complexion and has long, silky black hair growing over her body and face from the top of her head to the soles of her feet. She has a second set of teeth, just like a monkey. Here, inside is the world's strangest married couple.
>
> "They are on stage now waiting for you to go in and see them."

Percilla the Monkey Girl, in her retirement years.

"She could speak several languages, was a marvelous cook and was an amazing dancer," according to Ward, who was quite the dancer himself in his days. Percilla couldn't get Emmitt to dance with her, so Ward was happy to fill in. "On most Fridays during the off season, the Showmen's Club (in Gibsonton) featured a live dance band and on many of those nights, Percilla and I danced until they turned off the lights," he recalls.

The Hall and Christ Shows nearly closed down for good in the fall of 1979. The sideshow had shown no profit for the year and the two gave serious thought to discontinuing the operation. "But it had been my life's work, and it wasn't something we really wanted to end," said Ward. "So we decided to try it for another year." It proved to be a wise decision.

While the shows owned by Ward and Chris played virtually every major state fair in the country, Ward never performed or presented his show on Coney Island until the early 1980s. The spot many call the sideshow capital of the United States never appealed to the King of the Sideshow. "I don't like Coney Island, though I like the idea of Coney Island," said Ward. The World of Wonders was playing the Westchester County Fair, in Yonkers, New York, and Ward and his friend Todd Robbins drove down to Coney Island one afternoon just to look around.

He was recognized, of course, and was asked to bally for the Sideshows by the Seashore, a permanent 10-in-one, which was located on the boardwalk at the time. He gladly accepted the invitation. Then he and Todd went off to ride the 150-foot tall historic Wonder Wheel located at Deno's Wonder Wheel Park, the first time for Ward. "I could only think of one thing while we were up there," Ward recalls. "I kept thinking how old that piece of equipment really is that I was riding on." They (and everyone else who has ridden the wheel since 1920) survived.

Carnival and circus historian Joe McKennon owned Carnival Publishers, a Sarasota company created to publish his own books on the industry. In the 1970s, he published three volumes of *A Pictorial History of the American Carnival*. Ward was accidently left out of volumes one and two, but his name was in the index. "I put his name in the index, intending to insert a page on him some place in one or both of the volumes. I just plain forgot it and Ward's name appears in the index, with no page number beside it," McKennon wrote. Ward adds that, "I was just honored to be in the index. Joe's account of the carnival history is the most accurate that has ever been published."

One day in the late 1970s, McKennon called Ward and said he wanted to rectify his forgetfulness and put him in the next one, volume three. He asked Ward to write up an eight-page biography to be included in that third volume. Shortly thereafter, Ward presented those pages to McKennon and, within a few days, he got back to Ward and told him that he would only publish a small part of the story in the third volume but asked if Ward would be willing to expand the story a bit and, if Ward agreed, McKennon would publish a separate book, just on Ward. The only restriction was that Ward could not dwell on "freaks" or submit any photos of freaks for the book.

Playing on the title of P.T. Barnum's biography published in 1872, *Struggles and Triumphs,* McKennon titled Ward's autobiography, *Struggles and Triumphs of a Modern Day Showman.* The 112-page book was published on Sept. 10, 1981 the same day McKennon's third volume of *A Pictorial History of the American Carnival* was published. McKennon did not edit the copy Ward provided; he was quick to point out, because he wanted it to remain Ward's personal story, told totally in Ward's words. The story he tells "is the foundation of a great show business historical work," noted McKennon. In addition, Ward still ended up with four full pages in McKennon's tome and the *Struggles and Triumphs of a Modern Day Showman* was graciously plugged.

McKennon wrote: "Just reading about Ward Hall's exploits in the manuscript of his upcoming biography leaves a person bewildered. A circus and carnival trouper, tab show and night club entertainer, magician, lecturer, performer, director of the OABA (Outdoor Amusement Business Assoc.) and the Showmen's Club president. How does he do it all?" McKennon concluded: "If all should go sour on the midways, Ward Hall still would have a career in television and the movies."

The fact that Ward's book did not have photos or accounts of freaks did not get by everyone. "Several people asked why, and I told them the truth. Joe did not want that part of our business in any of the books he published," Ward added. In 1991, Ward gathered up information and nearly 200 photos of the people he knew over the years and self-published *My Very Unusual Friends*. Today, it remains one of the most comprehensive photo essays of the unusual humans who worked the sideshows during the golden years.

Following the 1980 IISA Trade Show and Extravaganza in Gibsonton in February, Ward and Chris visited Carnivale in Rio De Janeiro, Brazil, in hopes of getting some new show and promotional ideas. They also trekked to Argentina to visit with their friend Vince Carmen who ran the Aqua-Rama show. As they visited, Carmen suggested they also visit Circus Tihany which featured a huge variety show including illusion, sideshow arts, a live musical revue, and theatrical production elements.

As soon as Ward saw what was going on, and how he had been caught up in the excitement, he turned to Chris and said, "This is what we have to have." He immediately saw how it could all work under the big top. While it was a spectacular idea and while the partners were able to create a similar large variety show in 1981, it would ultimately lead to their financial downfall.

Once back in the states from their South American adventure, Chris and Ward headed to Wildwood, N.J., where they purchased the World of Wax Museum on the boardwalk from the Nickels family and began an intensive renovation of both the interior and exterior of the building. They changed the name to World of Wax and the new artwork was executed by Johnny Meah and Jack Synrex. Marge Porter created new costumes for the many new figures, and stayed on as resident manager of the attraction. "The efforts of everyone who helped out on the wax museum really paid off," Ward said. "Business was far beyond our expectations."

Ward wasn't able to stick around for the grand opening of the World of Wax, having to catch up again in Hawaii with Kane Fernandez, son of E.K., who now owned a large carnival, for a seven-week run across the islands. Fernandez had most of the equipment needed so Ward only took along banners, sound equipment and of course, Pete and a selection of performers.

The sideshow had another rough summer in 1980. Several of the larger spots, in Chicago and the big Ionia Free Fair in Michigan, were busts. Revenue at the Ohio State Fair in August was good, and business picked up throughout the fall at smaller dates, but it was not nearly enough to make up for the early season losses. After much conversation Ward and Chris made the tough decision to shut down their big 10-in-one sideshow. Increasing costs, specifically in travel, and having to pay higher rents and percentages at fairs, was starting to make it economically unachievable to continue producing big shows and spectaculars. An announcement was made in the Dec. 20, 1980 issue of *Amusement Business*.

"Rather than compromise to a version reduced in quality or size, we have decided to phase out this branch of our company," Ward said in a statement, while noting that he and Chris "will continue to present other midway shows for fairs and carnivals." The statement went on to explain that, while the big show was now history, the company would "be operating at least 10 (smaller) shows in 1981, including a new illusion show, an incredible oddities museum and a new half-lady/half-baby show." The article added that "what 1981 will bring is speculative, what with interest rates and the stock market acting like a yo-yo. All efforts will be made to consolidate routes of touring units to control costs, and promotional efforts and advertising will be increased at all permanent locations." Needless to say, both Ward and Chris were heading into the New Year a bit uncertain and a bit disheartened.

During the Las Vegas IAFE fairs convention in early December 1980, it was announced that the Ohio State Fair in Columbus would not only be changing carnivals, they would take a daring leap for their August 14-30

Ward in front of the Hall and Christ Show's 1988 banner line in Brocton, Mass.

run the following summer by introducing an all-inclusive pay-one-price policy. By reported attendance, it was the largest fair in the U.S. and the stakes were high for them to try something this radical.

Traditionally, fairs charged a small gate price and then inside there are additional charges for each of the rides and shows. With the new pricing policy, patrons would come to the front gate, pay one price, and enjoy all the rides, grandstand entertainment, and shows for no additional cost. The price was $4 on weekdays, $5 on weekends. The gate fees were increased over the previous year by only $1 to accommodate the pay-one-price ticketing.

The new pricing policy received a lot of attention at the convention. Ward and Chris, Bobby Pugh of Pugh Shows, and several others were having dinner together when Ward mentioned that it looked like he and Chris were going to lose the Ohio State Fair because it was going with a new carnival and the whole new ticketing system. Bobby Pugh leaned over and whispered to Ward, "Pugh Shows just got the contract for the Ohio State Fair, and you are going to play it."

Ward and Chris had played the Ohio State Fair the previous nine years and it was always a lucrative spot for them. Once Pugh Shows landed the midway contract, the Pugh family started working with Ward and Chris to develop a package of 12 separate shows that would be offered free of charge to fair goers. Pugh would pay for the dozen shows on a flat-fee basis and Ward would know going into the fair how much he would be paid, making it possible to create a budget and build accordingly.

Among the 12 shows fielded that year at the fair were a 10-in-one sideshow; the Aquarama, booked through Bob Maxwell, featuring three Olympic gold medal divers who also provided a comedy diving routine; The Sky High Circus featuring Johnny Rivers' diving mules and April Fossett's sway pole act; Douglas MacValley's Globe of Death; alligator-wrestling Seminole Indians; a laser light show; a girl-to-gorilla illusion; and Harry and Bea Fee's Monkey Speedway, in which trained monkeys raced little cars around an oval track.

Ward said he was proud of the showing he and Chris made that year. "We pulled together a very good lineup of shows," he said, noting that he felt if the shows were excellent and helped both the carnival and fair attract a larger number of guests, then the Hall and Christ shows would be in great demand to play more pay-one-price fairs across the country in the future. Before and during the fair, Ward told anyone who would listen that the pay-one-price ticketing concept would revolutionize the industry because "it is the greatest entertainment bargain ever offered" to the American public.

"We anticipated that all the major fairs would soon go to the pay-one-price system and that carnivals looking for an edge to get a booking would look to our shows to create the difference." Chris said at the time that the new pricing concept "has changed (the scene) for backend pieces. Now (fair and carnival) buyers are looking for what will make the people happy. It's the biggest thing to happen to this business in 20 years."

"Any carnival with enough money can basically get any ride," said Ward. "So a lack of any particular ride probably wouldn't keep a carnival from getting a lucrative fair date. They could either buy the requested ride or book an independent operator who owned that ride." To compete, he emphasized, "carnivals are going to have to have quality shows." If a carnival could offer, along with a stellar ride arsenal, quality shows from Hall and Christ, it would give them bargaining power and it would set them apart from their competitors, Ward reasoned. With that in mind, Chris and Ward put high-quality shows together for the Ohio State Fair, investing more than their original business plan and budget allotted, in order to build a quality reputation.

That concept didn't work, Ward notes, because he "over-estimated the intelligence of carnival owners." Instead of offering a fair more for its money by offering shows, carnivals took less for their contracts and beefed up their rides and concessions and didn't bother with shows.

Wondercade 1981:
The Big and Costly Show Premieres

CHAPTER 27

In preparation for their big showing at the 1981 Ohio State Fair in Columbus, all show fronts were refurbished and new banners were painted by Johnny Meah. However, most of the work that year centered on the biggest show ever for Ward and Chris, the Wondercade, patterned after Circus Tihany, the show they had seen and loved in Argentina. They used the same familiar name for their new show as they had used several times in the past, but it was a vastly different show than any before it.

Planning went well and, with all the excitement, they seemed to have forgotten their claim of just a few months prior that they were finished with large shows. Wondercade was a huge show and the version they would tour the following year was even larger – and costlier. The 1981 Wondercade was performed under an 80 by 200 foot tent with seating for 700. At the Ohio State Fair, the show was performed three times a day during the entire 17-day run of the fair. Reports indicate that the free-admission variety show, with something for everyone, was packed to near capacity for every show.

The 55-minute show featured a live orchestra, show girls, production musical numbers, juggling, unicycles, a comedy musical act, an elephant, a Roy Huston magic presentation and a European illusion show. But the Wondercade was just one of the 12 shows Chris and Ward presented at the fair. It wasn't easy pulling everything together in such a short time, but the shows went on. During spring, Ward had gone to Atlantic City to see the Globe of Death act of Douglas MacValley who at the time had one of the few globes in operation in the U.S.

Ward made a contract for the Globe of Death for the Ohio State Fair, but two weeks prior to the fair MacValley contacted Ward and said he couldn't make it because his contract had been extended in Atlantic City. Ward had already signed a contract with the Ohio fair to feature the globe of death act, so MacValley helped Ward find another globe, one that had been dismantled and had not been used for years. It was in such bad condition that it had to be totally refurbished before it could be used. Chris secured it with less than a week to go before it was to open, had it painted and ready to go on time. The hardest part, according to Ward, was "figuring out how to put the damn thing together."

WARD HALL and C.M. CHRIST

Wish To Thank

**GOVERNOR JAMES RHODES — JOHN EVANS
BOBBY, TOM & JEFF PUGH**

For Selecting

WORLD ATTRACTIONS, INC.

To Exclusively Provide the Midway Shows for the "Pay-One-Price"

1981 OHIO STATE FAIR

COLUMBUS — AUGUST 14-30

Including

WONDERCADE

The World's Largest Illusion Revue!

This Family Show Will Continue Tour in Principal Cities,
Theatres and Auditoriums Following Columbus.

AQUA SENSATIONS **SEMINOLE INDIAN VILLAGE**
A Water Wondershow   Featuring the Alligator Wrestlers

THREE STAR THEATRE **CIRCUS UNIQUE**
An Illusion Spectacular The Most Unusual Show on Earth

Also:
**GIRL TO GORILLA ILLUSION • MONKEY SPEEDWAY
LORD'S LAST SUPPER LIFE SIZE WAX ANIMATION • DANCING WATERS — THE CLASSIC FOUNTAINS**

CAN PLACE: Motordrome, Globe of Death, Lasarium, Cinema Dome and other shows of quality for a flat fee.
NEED: Stage Managers, Showgirls, Musicians (all chairs), Boy and Girl Swimmers, High Divers, Comedy Divers, Log Rollers, Boy and Girl Dancers, Novelty Acts.
WANT TO BUY: Circus Big Top, Elephants, Modern Railroad Cars.

CONTACT:
WARD HALL or C.M. CHRIST
P.O. Box 907, Gibsonton, Fla. 33534
(813) 677-9480 - (813) 677-2987
(800) 824-7888, Ext. 3462

Wondercade 1981: The Big and Costly Show Premieres

The toughest task completed, all that remained was to go to the airport and pick up the Colombian riders that MacValley had lined up for the show. They showed up on time, WITHOUT motorcycles! They had to be purchased locally, at great expense. All that said, Ward liked the riders and felt the show was a highlight of the fair. Several times, Ward would be a part of the act. "I would stand in the middle with my top hat on and they would ride around me, take off my hat, pass it back and forth between them, and then put it back on me. It was quite a thrill being in there!"

Other than a verbal showdown with Bob Maxwell, from whom Ward booked the highly publicized divers and clowns for the Aquarama, everything went relatively smooth for those 17 days in Columbus. Because of the great expense of the divers, Ward felt he needed to have pitchmen working the Aquarama show in order to bring in more revenue. Joe Fairchild, in addition to serving as master of ceremonies was asked by Ward to create a candy pitch, of which he would earn a percentage of sales. Johnny Meah had built an attractive 120-foot front for the Aquarama stadium and the bleachers seating 1,200 patrons around the large tank in which the high divers performed.

However, when Maxwell visited early in the fair, he told Ward he couldn't allow any pitches at the Aquarama because it "belittles what we do." He said he was going to pull his people out of the show unless it was stopped. The show was very popular with the fairgoers, fair officials and the local media and had already received a great deal of media attention. Ward called Maxwell's bluff.

"I told him if he pulled his divers, I would bring a contortionist in from the sideshow, dress him in a frog suit and float him on the water of the dive tank. Then I would bring in a couple girls from the Wondercade and sprinkle water on them and have them dance and perform Singing in the Rain. I pointed out to him that we had not promised a diving show, but a water show. It was called Aquarama." Then Ward pulled out the zinger. "I told him that I was not going to tell the crowds one way or another that they were or were not watching Maxwell's famous show and that most would never know the difference." Maxwell backed down from his threat and left quickly. "However I thought at one point he might slug me," Ward laughs.

Ward and Pete on the bally at the Meadowlands Fair.

So Few:
Why Have the Sideshows Disappeared?

CHAPTER 28

The most frequently offered answer to the question of why there aren't as many sideshows and freak shows in operation today as there were 30 years ago is that they are not "politically correct" in a modern society. The pundits say that it's not proper to show off people with deformities; it runs against current family values to show a legless man, a bearded lady, or a half-naked person swallowing a sword.

That's mostly crap, Ward strongly responds. He contends the real reason there are so few sideshows out today are the economics that have been created on carnival midways. It is getting tougher and tougher for a sideshow to make money, according to Ward, and if you accept the fact that it all has to do with economics, you'll understand a big piece of sideshow history. Here are several examples:

It's Hard to Make Money with a Show Anymore – Reason #1

The carnivals on which sideshows flourished for decades are now spending their money on bigger and more expensive amusement rides, and they are less willing to give up their allotted midway space to any sort of a show. It all changed with the proliferation of what the industry calls "spectaculars," large, expensive, flashy, trailer-mounted rides. The tradeshows that the IAAPA and the IISA hold each year helped introduce the U.S. showmen to the big rides that are being produced in Europe. "For years, the big rides remained in Europe and most U.S. carnival operators didn't know about them," Ward said. "American carnivals were happy with their American built rides and to showcase many different shows on the midway. It was a good mix that had served the public well for decades."

Once the big European ride manufacturers started exhibiting at the American trade shows however, the landscape changed forever. Fair managers saw the big, beautiful rides and started pressuring their contracted carnivals to buy them, which they did in order to keep the fair's midway contract. "What new rides can you bring us this year?" became the first question many fair managers asked of their carnival operators.

Many, if not most, fair boards each year contract with the carnival on the basis of what rides they can offer that they, the fairs, can then use to create colorful and enticing promotional and advertising material. Carnivals today need a big showing to win the contracts for the best spots in the country. On some rides, it will take five to 10 years to pay them off, but the carnivals continue to buy them "because the fairs want and require them."

As rides got more expensive to purchase, the smaller independent ride operators were at a disadvantage by not being able to afford them. The bigger carnivals could buy them, often nudging the smaller guys out of the game. Once having purchased high-cost equipment, the carnival owners were forced to get the most money they could out of every square foot of space they were allotted. Paying a percentage to an independent ride operator, or subsidizing sideshows that would contribute less to their midway gross than a large ride would did not make good business sense. As a result, fewer independent operators were booked and shows on carnival midways nearly vanished entirely.

World of Pleasure Show owner Rod Link and Ward were walking through Link's midway during a spring date in the parking lot of a large shopping center when Ward asked him why carnivals were having such difficulty in making ends meet. "It's because we don't entertain the people anymore. Their average stay on the lot has come down to 20 to 25 minutes. They come in, ride the rides they want to ride, maybe play a game or two, and leave," Link replied. "We are not in the entertainment business anymore, we are in the amusement business and people's attention span to be amused is very short."

Ward sternly points out that today's generation of carnival owners are not "show" people; they are "amusement" people. And he takes umbrage with modern carnivals that have "show" in their name. "They have no business with show as part of their name. They are anything but show; they are an amusement concern selling rides, foods and games. There is no show to it!"

In the days when most carnivals presented various types of shows, people had a tendency to stick around longer. "They would come up to the bally stage and listen and spend some time being entertained, even if they didn't go into the show," Ward said. "They had more to do than just ride."

In addition to sideshows, carnivals also offered free acts as a promotion to get people onto the lot and to spend more time which, of course, meant they would spend more money. High wire acts and various circus acts were popular, at one time, to attract and hold people on the midway. People would come early, ride rides, listen to a sideshow bally or two and maybe go into one of the several shows being offered. Then they would wait around for the free act to perform.

So Few: Why Have the Sideshows Disappeared?

It's Hard to Make Money with a Show Anymore – Reason #2

"I love the coupon system at fairs and carnivals if it is done right, but so few of them get it right and, when they don't, it negatively affects our business," Ward said. Today, the great majority of fairs and carnival midways have gone to a universal coupon system. That is, guests buy tickets at a series of ticket boxes and then use those tickets for all of the various attractions, including rides, games and shows. The individual attractions do not and cannot take cash, just a certain number of coupons, which differs from one attraction to another. Patrons buy them individually or at a discount in strips and booklets. The more you buy, the less expensive each is. The big problem arises when a person wants to visit a show or ride a ride and they don't have the correct number of tickets in hand. They have to physically leave that ride or show area in pursuit of a ticket booth to purchase the additional ticket(s) they need.

"Once a person is interested in coming into the show and is standing right there ready to do so, you just can't let them turn their back and go away to find a ticket box. Many, of course, will buy what is needed and come back, but others may go off with the intent of coming back but never do, for one reason or another," Ward noted.

Chris and long-time employee Jimmy Long.

A lack of tickets in the hands of a patron can be a real bally-killer. The bally is intriguing and if done right can turn the watchers into buyers. The speaker gets the crowd involved and gets them to participate in many different ways, but one thing you will always hear is, "just come in a bit closer, step right up to the stage, because you don't want to miss a thing," or "come up close and I'll show you how this trick is done." Then when everyone in the crowd is up close and personal, the talker makes the sales pitch.

> "The show is about to begin; Just step right over to our ticket box, and come on in to see the show you will be talking about for years. Come right in, right now. The show is about to begin."

The talker has their undivided attention, he has made the pitch, and they are ready to spend their money. "Our rule is to never turn a customer away or let them turn their back on you, but that's exactly what you are doing if they have to go and find a ticket booth," Ward said. When the coupon system first began, people got confused, plus carnivals didn't have enough ticket booths and skilled people in the booths to take money, sell tickets and give out change quickly. Ward thinks that is still the case today. "Most (fairs) don't get it right." Ward says a slow cashier can take people away from money-spending opportunities. He gets frustrated with ticket box backups. He remembers telling show owner Hal Eifort one day that the cashier in front of the sideshow "seems like a nice lady, but she has to take off her bra to count to two!"

The Minnesota State Fair and the Wisconsin State Fair are singled out by Ward as "getting it right" because they make an effort to have ticket boxes close by the bally stage. Ward said it helps if you can point out the ticket box while you bally and say, "Buy your tickets right there and come right back." It keeps many from walking away in search of a ticket location. "There is nothing wrong with the coupon system if it is done right and the fair and carnival cooperate," according to Ward. "I love it, because we don't have to handle money and we don't have to stay up half the night counting it. We bundle up the coupons and take them to the office."

It's Hard to Make Money with a Show Anymore – Reason #3

Jumping, with long jumps in particular, has always been an obstacle for showmen, whether it is a large circus, a large carnival, or an independent traveling with only one or two trailers. Road conditions, weather, Department of Transportation (DOT) rules and regulations: and more recently, finding qualified and dependable drivers who have their Commercial Driver's License (CDL) are all true obstacles that need to be overcome.

The cost to maintain a fleet of vehicles and to pay the high fuel costs, along with stringent state and federal regulations costs more today than ever. "The DOT regulations we live with today, that we didn't have to deal with 30 years ago, are not bad things because the new rules make it safer and, in the end, probably have saved lives and injuries," Ward said, adding the anticipated "but."

"But, it was so much easier, and cheaper, when we had big shows on the road. There was a time when you could sit down with a state trooper in the cookhouse and pay him $60 for the state permit. You could even get them over the phone, but now, the red tape and bureaucracy sometimes is insurmountable."

Ward Hall is undeniably the undisputable King of the Sideshow. Even those who consider themselves to be his competitors have no problem calling him the king. But is Chris and Ward's World of Wonders sideshow really the "Last American Sideshow," as it is promoted? That can be debated but, in the long run it doesn't really matter because it's all hyperbole anyway.

Jim Zajicek, owner of the Big Circus Sideshow, operated at the 2014 Florida State Fair exhibiting only his live and stuffed freak animals. At this spot he downsized his tent and removed the inside stage where working acts such as sword swallowers and blockheads usually appear. He went without that part of his show at this year's fair taking into consideration that Ward and Chris had their World of Wonders set up nearby with working acts.

"Nobody will ever be in a position to call themselves the King of the Sideshow after Ward is gone," Zajicek said. "When Ward joined the industry, there were literally hundreds of sideshows and, over the years, most have come and gone. But Ward is still here. That says something about Ward right there." Zajicek, who handled circus elephants before getting into the sideshow business in 2003 said he isn't in it to compete. "It doesn't bother me that he claims to be the last," Zajicek said. "We all kind of do that." Walk by the Big Circus Sideshow and you will hear what Zajicek is talking about.

> "The Big Circus Sideshow is the last and the largest.
> See it now or miss it forever. Here we go, there they go.
> They are going in to see the freaks right now."

John Strong has been around circus and carnival sideshows his entire life. He was raised on his father's show, the Big John Strong Circus, and comes from a long line of performers and circus entrepreneurs. Today, year-round, he operates a 10-in-one sideshow, a live freak animal show with 19 creatures, and several smaller single-o shows. "If you count the years I operated the sideshow for my father's circus, I have been promoting sideshows for nearly 40 years," Strong said. Over the years he has purchased many items from Chris and Ward, including illusions and ticket boxes that he still uses.

"Ward is kind-hearted and enthusiastic with everyone and I learn something from him every time I talk with him. It doesn't bother me that his show is often called the last and the biggest, because he always does a good job and is very good at getting press for all of us," Strong said.

Ohio-based Tim Deremer has operated sideshows since the mid-1970s. He first fielded the Palace of Illusion, his 10-in-one, with a combination of working acts and illusions, in 1978 and created his first single-o show, Gabora the Gorilla, a girl-to-gorilla illusion, in 1973. "I had heard of Ward and Chris but had never met them for the first several years that I operated the gorilla show. Ward is certainly to be lauded as the grand ole man of our business because of his longevity. To be operating for 70 years, he has to be doing something right, for sure," Deremer said.

Deremer agrees with both Zajicek and Strong in not caring if the World of Wonders gets media attention as the biggest and last sideshow in America. "It doesn't bother me because I have always tried to stay low key and don't really promote myself very much," Deremer said. "He's good at it and he helps us all when he talks about the sideshow industry."

In addition to Zajicek, Strong and Deremer, several other shows in operation travel and work the fair and carnival circuit. Dennis York has freak animal single-o shows as well as a larger Amazing Animals Show which touts live oddities such as a six-legged cow and a giant rat. Jack Constantine has had shows on the road since the early 1970s and specializes in single-o illusion and freak animal attractions.

While they don't play fairs or travel a regular circuit, preferring to play in clubs and special events, the 999 Eyes Freakshow & Surreal Sideshow is different than the rest. It is a vaudeville-style celebration of real genetic diversity by showcasing performances of living human oddities only. In addition, there are dozens of other troupes who travel and perform mostly in clubs and theaters.

Two large, permanent sideshows that do not travel focus on the beach crowds. The Coney Island Circus Sideshow performs in the Sideshows by the Seashore theater on Coney Island, Brooklyn, N.Y., and on the other coast you'll find Todd Ray's Venice Beach (Calif.) Freakshow. The Coney

So Few: Why Have the Sideshows Disappeared?

Island operation is run by Dick Zigun's Coney Island USA and features continuous live working acts during the summer months. On Venice Beach, the year-round sideshow is a combination of live freak animals and working acts. AMC cable television network airs a weekly reality offering, Freakshow, using the Venice Beach attraction as a backdrop and features its acts, as well as those of other sideshows.

It is obvious that, depending on definition and on how much buncombe is put behind the statement that Ward and Chris do not have the last sideshow in existence. There are many ways to enjoy the sideshow arts in the United States.

One place you won't find a sideshow today is at its once traditional home – a circus. As recently as the early 1950s nearly every American circus had at least one sideshow. The shows included the traditional 10-in-one live performance shows, jig shows (African-American musicals), menageries, girl shows, freak animal shows, and oddity museums.

The shows were set along the side of the path from the main box office to the big top entrance. Some, such as menageries, were free to walk through but the rest usually cost extra. All would stop operation when the whistle blew starting the big top show. The smaller shows were there to keep circus patrons entertained and, of course, to bring in extra revenue prior to the circus performance.

The bally stage for the biggest sideshow would usually be set up across from the main ticket wagon, which did not open for business until after at least one or two turns of the sideshow. The concept was simple. At that time there were few advance sale tickets and, when the people arrived at the circus before the ticket box opened, they had nothing to do to fill the time, so they would be drawn to the bally and, in most cases, pay to get into the sideshow even before buying their big top ticket.

The bally would always assure the waiting patrons that it was still too early to buy a circus ticket and that "you will have plenty of time" to enjoy the acts in the sideshow tent before the circus begins. It was essential that the doors to the big top not open until the bally had a shot at everyone in the crowd. "With the circus ticket wagon not open, we usually had the undivided attention of everyone there, and once the doors to the big top opened, we closed down for the evening. It was a model that worked," Ward said.

Then it all changed. In the early 1950s, local circus sponsors started hiring phone salesmen to hawk advance tickets, sometimes at a discount if they purchased early. Knowing they had a ticket in hand, families had no need to come out early to the circus. When they did get there, they headed right to the entrance.

Ward saw the slow decline of the circus sideshow first hand over a 30-year period. "It's really quite simple. We can't make a living if there are no people in front of us to buy tickets. At one time I would guess 70% of those coming to the circus were there at least 30 minutes before show time. The last time I watched, that number had dropped down to 20%, with 60% showing up within 15 minutes of show time, with 20% entering after the show had begun."

Focus for 1982:
An Even Bigger Wondercade

CHAPTER 29

Based on the success of its first run at the Ohio State Fair the previous year, the Wondercade show was to be the focus of the 1982 season. It was also a transition year for many long-time managers who had run the smaller shows for Ward. A couple left for other shows and one bought their own show. That left Chris and Ward without the talent needed to field as many attractions as they wanted in 1982. As a result, they cut back on sideshow presentations and put their money and their existing personnel on the Wondercade project. It was their single focus.

The 1982 Wondercade production was huge. A larger tent, one measuring 90-feet by 210-feet was acquired; this one seating 2,700, and new "gorgeous" wardrobes for the girls were purchased from the Royal American Shows. That carnival on rails had dropped girl shows and revues from its midway, creating an opportunity for the Wondercade operators. "I loved picking through those railroad cars full of costumes the girls had worn through the years," Ward recalls.

The new and larger spectacular consisted of many returning acts from the 1981 edition but the production value increased tremendously. There was a full, live orchestra, a line of high-kicking chorus girls, five musical productions, an elephant, wire and aerial acts, trained tropical birds, and Roy Huston whose magic show was once again the featured act with 17 illusions. Moving the show required 20 trucks, along with all the personal house trailers and prop wagons. It was quite the entourage for one show.

"There was nothing outside of Vegas that could have touched that show for quality," Ward said. In each town, on the first night, as the Wondercade was being assembled, a wrestling match would be held in the big tent, serving two purposes: immediate revenue and a promotional tool that would advertise the upcoming performance.

With great expectations, Wondercade opened in Florida, playing three-day runs in Palatka, Tallahassee, and Panama City. The Memorial Day weekend run at Ft. Walton Beach was its last. "We simply started running out of money. We had too many people in the show, the acts were too expensive and everything was over-produced. Our daily costs were around $4,500 and we just couldn't make the nut. The tent could

seat 2,700, but the average attendance for the short run was 175 per show," Ward noted.

In circus terms, a "nut" is the amount of money needed to pay the bills. The term was coined in the 19th century when a circus would pull into town and set up. The local authorities would come and take the nuts off their wagon wheels, making a quick, middle-of-the-night exit nearly impossible. When the authorities were assured that all local bills were paid, the nuts would be returned and the circus was free to leave town.

During the last weekend, the Friday and Saturday shows were performed at Ft. Walton Beach but after the Saturday shows, Ward

Focus for 1982: An Even Bigger Wondercade

called the cast together and told them he couldn't pay them beyond the show they had just performed but said if everyone was willing, they could finish up their schedule for Sunday performances and split the gate amongst themselves. They voted not to do that, so the run was over, no Sunday shows were performed and the show was sent back to Gibsonton. Wondercade had failed.

Meah, who was on the short-lived spectacle as a lot man and a drummer in the pit band, said Ward overestimated the show's potential. "Ward based his budget on the perfect scenario – totally sold out houses for every performance and, unfortunately, it didn't work out that way." Based on the profitable venture of the previous year at the Ohio State Fair, Ward assumed that success would follow the show wherever it went. "Of course it was a success at the Ohio State Fair. It was a big, beautiful show with free admission," Meah noted.

In retrospect, Ward thinks that advertising wrestling in conjunction with the show confused the public and was one of the major contributing factors in its failure. "I made a thousand mistakes with it that I know of and probably a thousand that I don't know of. I look back and have mixed emotions about the show. Chris and I both loved it and were very proud of its beauty and its acts, but seeing the problems it set in motion, I can't help but regret we ever took it out."

Prior to taking the show on the road that spring, Ward had told Carol Neef, a reporter for the *South Hillsborough Tribune,* that with the right marketing and the right bookings the show should be successful because "we have a good product and we're appealing to a wide range of people." In that April 15, 1982 story, Ward opened up to the reporter and admitted that "if it's not successful, I won't have anything to return to Gibsonton in. I'm up to here in debt." It was a devastating loss for Ward and Chris and it put them in a dire financial situation. "Considering the amount of money we had to borrow in 1981 to create the show and what we lost producing it, we were more than $1.5 million in debt at that point," Ward said.

Ten years later, in the early 1990s, Tihany, from whose show Wondercade was based, brought his big show to the U.S. and played Houston, New Orleans and Miami and then shut down, due to a lack of business and the lack of interest for such a show. While it sounds somewhat narcissistic, Tihany's failure made Ward feel better about his own failure with the same type of grand show. Tihany demonstrated that even though his ventures in Argentina had been successful, this type of spectacular show didn't translate to the U.S. market.

Upon arriving back in Florida shortly after they closed Wondercade, the two put their 10-in-one sideshow back together, made a few calls for

> **Complimentary Invitation**
>
> It is our pleasure to invite the bearer to be our guest to see
>
> # 20th Century WAX MUSEUM
> AT
> Casino Pier • Seaside Heights, N.J.

talent and headed north in an attempt to save the season. Good dates were slim as most good spots had already been booked and the two had to settle for what they could get. They were able to close out the season at the State Fair of Texas in Dallas where they made a small profit. After a devastating start, "we did better than we thought we would in 1982, but all the money we made went directly to the bank to help make our note," Ward explains. "We were short of the payment we had to make so, instead of defaulting, we borrowed the difference so we could make the payment."

While the sideshow was out, their permanent locations including the 20th Century Wax Museum in Seaside Heights, N.J., a snake girl illusion show in Wildwood, N.J., and a museum of oddities and a headless girl show at Shaheen's Fun-O-Rama in Salisbury Beach, Mass., all were hurt by rainy weekend weather for most of the season.

The two were adamant that they would not declare bankruptcy and that they would pay back everyone they owed, including the bank. With limited capital for the 1983 season, they took the 10-in-one back out. This time they headed to Canada where they had a season-long deal worked out to travel with the Conklin Shows. Money was good and it was one of their best years, but all profits went to pay off their bills.

> "It's a big show for little money. If you are in line, you're in time!"

For 1984, with little money to work with, Ward and Chris booked onto Circus Vargas and opened on January 6 in Yuma, Ariz. Because of tight lot sizes that didn't allow room for a separate sideshow tent, Vargas

Focus for 1982: An Even Bigger Wondercade

had them create an after-the-big-top show. It featured a wrestling show and several sideshow acts. These after-shows charged an additional admission fee, but the revenue didn't follow and in March they went back to Gibsonton not knowing exactly what they were going to do next. "It was a novel attempt at something new, but it didn't work well enough for us to stick with it," Ward said.

James Roller, one of their long-time friends, was taking a newly formed Roller Bros. Circus on the road that summer and Chris booked a lizard show, a shark show, their 10-in-one sideshow, and a moon bounce on the circus midway. Business was okay, according to Ward, but the circus was too small to draw enough people to create the revenue he

Attending a confab in Las Vegas, from left: Ward, Jack Kaplan, sideshow operator Bobby Reynolds, and Chris, 1984.

needed. They stayed with the circus until fair season in Ohio began and then jumped to play their traditional spots in the Buckeye state – Carthage, Fremont and Canfield, followed by the Kansas and Oklahoma state fairs. They closed at the State Fair of Texas. It was a good season, but once again they tried to buy more time with the banks and paid all they could, while nearly living in abject poverty.

1985: The Bankruptcy

CHAPTER 30

After fighting what proved to be the inevitable for three years, Ward and Chris declared bankruptcy in early 1985. "We tried to keep it going, but finally, after a big confrontation with the bank, I just threw in the towel and gave up," said Chris. "We should have filed immediately when we knew we were in serious trouble but we tried to work our way out of it. A smart businessman would have pulled the plug a lot sooner than we did." They still owed well over $100,000, were broke, and were paying 18% interest on the note. As could be expected, both Chris and Ward felt they were under extraordinary pressure. It was emotionally very stressful for them before, during and especially after the official proceedings.

Bunny Fitzgerald, a money-man, friend and a partner in their Seaside Heights, N.J. wax museum, offered to help guide Chris and Ward out of the bankruptcy. The attorney Chris and Ward hired was a "bad one who gave us bad information," said Ward. "He told us we had to give up everything – our house, our life insurance, our jewelry, our cars – everything, which we found afterward was not necessary."

Immediately prior to the March 1985 bankruptcy auction, showmen from across the country offered help in various ways. Among them, long-time friend Rod Link, who had helped the boys before, came forward and provided advice as well as cash. Link told the pair that he would "see to it that you have enough money" to buy things back at the auction. Jack Libbert, Billy Burr and Leonard Simons, among others, also provided cash advances.

"When an item came up for bid, our friends would look at us to see if we were going to bid on it. If we were, they backed down so they wouldn't run up the price," said Ward, choking up a bit as he recalls how quickly his friends stepped up to help. "Several others were also buying for us, so we got most back except for our trucks, but Ed Murphy of Modern Motors had told us he would sell us the trucks we needed for no money down." Murphy also delivered the trucks, at no additional cost, to Ward and Chris in Florida.

No one lost any money on this bankruptcy, except himself and Chris, adds Ward. "It took us five years to do so, but every person we owed got their money back. Although we didn't have to, we paid off everything, including the hardware store, our friends, our doctors and everyone else."

Following the auction, Ward's mother told him: "I have never seen anyone recover so quickly after a bankruptcy." Ward adds that "while we were bankrupt, we were never out of business."

Using words such as "devastating" and "terribly humbling," the two said the entire bankruptcy process took its toll and "mentally goofed us both up," said Chris. Ward said he was "embarrassed by the bankruptcy," especially after having fought it for so hard and long.

Even though they were able to buy their equipment back, they did not plan to go on the road in 1985. Each followed separate pursuits, but it was a difficult year for both. "We knew we weren't out of business forever and that we would be back. It was just that we didn't have the energy or the money to immediately get back out there," said Ward.

Chris went to work for Alan Hill, owner of the Great American Circus, and built a new smaller unit, Circus USA, from scratch, in 32 days - an unheard of accomplishment. "I was in such a depressed state of mind following all the bankruptcy stuff, I had to get busy and prove to myself that I could do something," Chris said, noting that he was always "project driven" and needed a large challenge at that time. "Once I got started I began feeling better. I didn't have time to dwell on the bankruptcy because we worked from six in the morning to nearly midnight every day until it was ready."

When Circus USA hit the road, Chris stayed on as operations manager and Johnny Meah was hired as ringmaster. Ward was contracted as general manager but his heart wasn't it, said Chris. "Ward's state of mind was really making him self-destruct. I never saw someone try so hard to get fired." Alan Hill sacked Ward on June 20; the show had been on the road only a month and a half. Chris was promoted to the GM position when Ward departed. "I was practicing to be the world's biggest asshole and I almost had it perfected," Ward said. "I would argue about anything to anybody. I was unhappy and depressed about the bankruptcy, and Chris started drinking heavily and that made me unhappy and we weren't getting along. I was a mess."

Chris looks back at that summer's experience with Circus USA as one of his greatest accomplishments, from building the circus from scratch to running it through its season of one-nighters. "I started feeling better as the season went on." And, according to media reports, he had created something in which he should be proud. Circus historian and author Joe McKennon was impressed in his assessment of Circus USA under the eyes of Chris. "Shining like a jewel when it went out, the circus looked better when it came in."

Gordon Taylor visited the circus in its first week on the road and wrote in the June 17, 1985 edition of the *Circus Report,* that the show featured "a cast that is a Who's Who of circus names and skills." Taylor's

1985: The Bankruptcy

review drew this conclusion: "It's a fine equation. Great circus names, plus great circus skills, plus great salesmanship equals great crowds for a great show. Circus USA makes it work." Paul Horsman wrote in the July 22, 1985 issue of *Circus Report* that the circus "makes a beautiful appearance on the lot." He added. "This circus has an excellent performance, is well put together and all personnel are friendly and exhibit high morale."

With no route booked, Ward framed a show featuring Barbara Bennett, billed as the "Smallest Mother in the World." He loaded everything into an old station wagon and headed north. He booked Bennett with the Reithoffer Shows in Brocton, Mass., followed by several other New England spots with Billy Burr. Along the way, he added a small oddities museum. At one small date where business was bad and Ward and Barbara didn't bring in much revenue, Burr refused to charge Ward a cent for his midway privilege.

Ward booked both shows into the West Virginia State Fair, which the George Carden Circus had booked as well. As his two shows, both with a taped bally, easily took care of themselves, Ward sold snow-cones at the circus to make a few extra bucks. Did selling snow-cones hurt the sideshow king's ego? "Not at all, in fact it was fun," he said. "My years of bullshitting from the bally stage paid off and I really sold a lot." By this time in mid-July, Ward had started losing some of his anger and was becoming more of himself again.

Ward snapped the rest of the way back to reality the day he received a surprise call from Ringling's Kenneth Feld who wanted a 10-in-one sideshow for several Midwestern circus dates. Ward drove to Dallas where the equipment he bought back at the bankruptcy auction was being stored, quickly got it in shape, hired a few acts and joined Ringling's Blue Unit in Kansas City around Labor Day. That Ward Hall-produced sideshow in 1985 was the last time Ringling had a touring sideshow under a tent, and it was the first time Ringling booked a sideshow and let it be under the sideshow owner's complete control. Ward was paid a flat weekly rate and was required to do a bally twice each day. It was an enjoyable tour, Ward recalled.

Immediately following the final date in St. Louis, the show jumped to the State Fair of Texas in Dallas. The season for Circus USA ended about the same time and Chris and his crew joined Ward in Dallas. Fresh from a successful and ego-building season with the circus he framed from the ground up, Chris was also feeling much better and was ready to get on with the rest of his life. "I was so depressed that summer that I self-medicated myself with beer, lots of beer," said Chris. He sought professional help after the season and had his last drink of alcohol on Feb. 4, 1986. It took him longer to kick the smoking habit but he smoked his last cigarette on New Year's Eve 2006.

Ward Hall - King of the Sideshow!

Once Ward was fired from Circus USA and left for New England he and Chris did not see each other for nearly three months, the longest they had been apart. But the separation did not dent or alter their relationship as business or life partners and they picked up in October in Dallas without missing a beat. That's not to say, however, that they were consistently amicable with each other.

Right from the beginning, it was Ward out front getting accolades while Chris worked hard in the background to make it all happen. For nearly 50 years, Chris has created the spotlight in which Ward takes the bow. Chris has become the ever-important producer and director, while Ward, looking spiffy in a spangled suit and a fresh flower in his lapel, regales in the love and applause of an audience. "Chris has always done most of the work," admits Ward. "He has a solid, steady hand and mind and enjoys being a back line guy who negotiates contracts and works the business deals. He's good at that."

Ward and Chris goofing around with Connie Kelly, a knife thrower, in the show office, 1980.

Luckily for both, it's a role that Chris enjoys. "From day one it has been like that. It has been by design, and we each do what each excels at. I have never had any jealousy. Our personal relationship and our partnership has worked for all these years because you couldn't find two people more different than we are," Chris said. "Our personalities, our talents, and our drive – they are totally different and in our case, that has been a great asset and has helped us create a strong unit. We have mostly played good cop/bad cop, and you know who the bad cop is."

If you ignore a few fist fights between the two and the time Ward pointed an unloaded gun at Chris, the two have "never had a serious argument over anything serious" during the years they have been together, Chris avers. Their business partnership would not have lasted as long as it has if they didn't have that strong personal commitment. Without one the other would not have been possible. However, anyone who has ever worked for the pair will readily note that while the two get along and work well together, they are "constantly bickering." Chris smiles and admits, "That assessment would not be totally wrong."

Ward's relationship with Harry Leonard was a bit different in that they seldom argued. "We were more concerned about making a living and working hard enough to keep from going broke," Ward said.

Ward's only true partners, both in business and in passion, have been Chris and Harry. "I have worked closely with others over the years and have split percentages with several others, but I have never until recently, shared the business with anyone but Chris and Harry."

As Ward and Chris mended their personal and professional relationship that winter after closing at the State Fair of Texas, Chris booked their sideshow on the Toby Tyler Circus, a large tented show fielded by Richard Garden, for the entire 1986 season. Except for a highway wreck that demolished their tractor it was a good season and, as the circus closed in early October, Ward and Chris jumped back to Dallas to play the State Fair of Texas.

Both wanted to get back to the carnival and fair circuit for 1987. But since most of their acts and help had scattered and joined other shows, they decided to operate with a lower overhead for the season and re-framed the sideshow into an oddities museum. In the show were a few wax figures from the two permanent wax museums they had owned (and closed) on the Jersey shore. The presentation consisted of figures of "famous" human and animal freaks, and a copy of the famous and fictitious Cardiff Giant. The bally was taped, but a ticket seller was always out front.

The show wasn't all static. Ward and Chris added a small live freak menagerie including a four-winged duck; a four-horned sheep; and a Peruvian Hairless dog named Pinky. Also at various locations, they added Vivian Wheeler as Melinda Maxie the bearded lady, and Lorett Fulkerson as the tattooed lady. As usual, little Pete was there as the fire-eating pygmy.

> "You are going to be entertained by Lorett, the world's most completely tattooed woman. Covering her body from her neck to her ankles are 287 famous works of art. You will see reproduced on her flesh the works of art by da Vinci, Michelangelo, Picasso, Rembrandt, Renoir and Rubens, making her truly a walking, talking human art gallery."

Pinky would join Lorett on the bally stage and would sit quietly until Lorett would stand, and Pinky would do the same. Lorett would turn, and

Pinky would do the same. Lorett would sit, and Pinky would sit. It was a peculiar sight, a lady with tattoos all over her body and a strange looking dog with no hair and wrinkly pink skin. When not eating fire, Pete would sit on the stage with a snake as the endless taped bally played over and over again. Occasionally Ward would perform a live bally, but for most of the time only his voice could be heard up and down the midway.

Once the decision was made on what show to tour that summer, Ward approached John Hiner, a one-legged banner painter of Gibsonton who painted a 15-banner front for the show - on credit. "We were broke and we didn't have much time," Ward recalls. "We hired John because he is a very talented artist and he is very fast. He gave us credit and we paid him off by mid-summer. He saved our butts that year."

They broke even on their first stop at the Spring Festival in Birmingham, Ala., and quickly found that live animals caused more problems than they created more revenue. One day, several ladies from the local animal welfare organization came by and asked him the condition of the animals. Ward, being Ward, commented on the stuffed freak animals in the show. "I am having a few problems. The baboon is losing its stuffing and the two-headed cow is falling apart. Would you like to see?" They declined but said they had a report that the dog on the show had mange and they were here to check it out.

The live animals on the show were well cared for and Ward had health papers on every one of them. The dog in question was Pinky, the Peruvian Hairless, a rather odd looking dog with its origins in Peruvian pre-Inca cultures. The ladies had never seen such a dog, didn't believe Ward when he explained what it was, and gave him a citation. The show left town, but a few days later, an inspector visited their new location saying she had received a report from the earlier inspectors that he had a dog with mange and she was there to check it out. He showed Pinky to the inspector and she gushed, "What a beautiful Peruvian Hairless. You don't see too many of these around here." They laughed and she tore up the citation.

Following a couple less-than-stellar weeks in the south, they didn't have enough money to get to their next spot, which was to be with Reithoffer Shows at the new Pennsylvania Fair, in Bensalem, Pa. They used Lorett's credit card to get on the road. Then, following a truck breakdown in Richmond, Va., they had to call Chris's father for an emergency loan of $1,500 to get the truck out of the garage and get on their way to Pennsylvania.

All the live animals were retired in late 1987, and the show focused mainly on static exhibits that Chris and Ward created during the winter. "We had a pleasing exhibit of figures we took from our wax museum to create famous sideshow stars." In other words, they took wax figures of Hollywood stars and turned them into sideshow personalities. For example, singer Sammy Davis Jr. became Willie "Popeye" Ingram, the man with elastic eyeballs; Actor Bert Lahr, who played the Cowardly Lion in the Wizard of Oz became Lionel the Lion-Faced Man; and the beautiful actress Kim Novak (originally posed in her Planet of the Apes role), became Percilla the Monkey Girl.

Spring 1988 started out slow, but it was profitable. "We found that it was good to not have so many shows on the road and, of course, it was easier to make money with less overhead," Ward said. However, the best was yet to come that spring, specifically, on May 28.

Plagued with a rainy start of the Pennsylvania Fair in Bensalem, the fair got a huge boost when it contracted to have Colonel Oliver North give his first public address since going under indictment for conspiracy and covering up illegal activities stemming from the Iran-Contra scandal. His speech, entitled "Commitment, Trust and Family," packed the crowds onto the grounds. The speech was free with the $5 fair admission. "It was very high profile and controversial, so huge crowds came out to listen, and many came out to the Reithoffer Shows midway, on which we were booked," Ward recalls, noting that "we saw big revenues; lots of money that afternoon and evening."

Chris went to work promoting events for World Championship Wrestling in early 1988 and did not travel with the show full time that year or in 1989. He would be gone for a couple weeks at a time and then catch up with the show for several days. When the show wasn't on the road, Ward would drive to the Tampa International Airport to pick him up. Virtually every time Ward offered to pick him up, he had to wait for Chris to show as he would be the last one off the plane. "That guy would work so hard and long that when he got in the air he would fall asleep and the flight attendants would have to come back to his seat and wake him up to get off the plane," Ward laughed. "He loved that job and was very, very good at it."

After 17 years playing the lucrative State Fair of Texas the 1988 fair would be the last for World of Wonders as they got caught up in the fair's programming and management changes at the top. "We did well that year with our live acts and museum show, but a management change at the top changed things for us quite drastically," Ward said. Longtime fair manager Wayne Gallagher left in February 1989 to become manager of the New York State Fair and was replaced about six months later by Errol McKoy, who had been manager of nearby Six Flags Over Texas. McKoy said that when he was hired, "They told me my number one priority was to reprogram all of the entertainment, which involved a lot of changes. I eliminated high school football games on Friday nights, big beer company stages on every street corner, the ice skating show on the Esplanade, and sideshows, to name a few. So (there was) nothing personal (against Chris, Ward or the sideshow industry), it was just business."

In 1989, with Chris still working as a wrestling promoter, Ward decided to not go on the road either, preferring to stay at home and concentrate on his literary work. Bob and Lorett Fulkerson took a tattooed lady/snake show and a fat man show on the road for the entire season for Ward and Chris and had a break-even year. Pete was on the show as was sword swallower Red Stuart. Lorett Fulkerson's own bally always received a great deal of attention:

> "Ladies, gentlemen and children. I am Lorett, the Tattooed Lady. Upon my arms I have 106 roses. On my chest, there is an American eagle. On my stomach is a three-masted schooner. And on my legs, I have snakes of various sizes and shapes. On my left knee, I have the face of Genghis Khan, and on the right knee a Chinese pirate girl. Below her is a peacock and below him, from India, the hooded cobra."

Lorett Fulkerson was 75 years old in 1989 and had just had a knee operation. The scar from that surgery cut through the face of Genghis Khan.

Ward decided to take a vacation in fall 1989 and while Chris continued promoting wrestling, Ward visited the Oktoberfest in Munich, Germany on a tour organized for carnival people by Monsignor Robert J. McCarthy, a Catholic priest. In 1971 Father Mac, as he was called, had been appointed by the Vatican's Pontifical Commission for the pastoral care of itinerant people as the official chaplain of the carnivals in the United States. In other words, he was the Carny Priest, a moniker he relished.

Father Mac was a well-traveled priest. Carnival owners would fly him to their larger locations to say Mass, baptize the newborns and marry the lovebirds. He normally said Mass in the show's bingo tent or cookhouse or, if the weather was good, he would often hold Mass outdoors, using the platform of a ride as an altar. Although neither is Catholic, Ward and Chris witnessed several of Father Mac's midway missions.

"I remember, in Munich at the Oktoberfest, he said Mass for those of us who went on the tour with him, in the showground's hippodrome," Ward recalls, noting that the Carny Priest was a good and knowledgeable tour guide, taking the group on special tours of cathedrals, castles and cemeteries in Germany, Belgium and Austria. His reservations had been made and deposits paid earlier in the year for the trip and Ward was looking forward to the time on the road in Europe with fellow showmen. However, when Ward contacted Legionnaires Disease and was hospitalized during

1985: The Bankruptcy

Father Mac, the carny priest, and Ward in Germany in 1989.

late summer the trip looked doubtful. "We almost cancelled the trip, but once I turned the corner, I started getting a little bit stronger every day and by the time we left, I was still a bit weak, but I was okay," he said.

Ward and Chris had effectively swallowed up most of their competition by 1990, including sideshows owned by Pete Kortes, Whitey Sutton, Slim Kelly, and Dick Best, some of the best operators of all time. "As those owners and operators got older and wanted to retire, we bought them out," Ward said, noting that later he realized that eliminating that competition was not good for the industry for two reasons.

"The more shows that are out there, even though the competition is greater, allows more people to appreciate the sideshow arts and create the desire to see more and different shows," he said. "Also, we soon found it hard to get good performers or good help because there was now no place for people to learn the business and get experience." Sideshow historian James Taylor agrees with Ward that in the long run, buying up everything available was not good for the industry. "Sadly, Ward's acquisitiveness was fed by the wave of old showmen leaving the business and a near cascade of shows changing hands, to two people – Ward and Chris. It turned out to be a pretty fateful business model, pulling the outdoor show biz into what seemed a final vortex," said Taylor. "I'd say the business was already collapsing for an assortment of cultural and economic reasons following World War II; Ward's buy-up was really just a final shovelful of dirt into what everyone thought would be the sideshow's grave."

Taylor sees how it happened and how easy it was for Ward to get caught up in the buying frenzy. "Certainly, the path of least resistance, the easiest path, was for the retiring showmen to sell to someone they knew, someone in the business, someone like Ward, rather than seeking out other buyers or younger show folk to help enter the business," notes Taylor. As he was buying up his competition, Ward was asked by one carnival operator if he "wanted to own all the shows." Ward replied. "No, I want to own the only one."

In early 1990, Ward was asked by Dick Garden, who had purchased Sterling Bros. Circus and was reframing it as a new indoor circus out of Sarasota to be the ringmaster and announcer for its spring dates. Ward liked the idea and accepted the offer thinking it "would be an enjoyable show to be around." There was a live band and a great lineup of acts and the best part for Ward was the fact that during the time they wanted him, the circus was playing close enough that he could come home every night. He planned to bow out when it got too far from home.

As part of the arrangement, Ward had a deal with the concessions department to pitch a lighted plastic sword in return for 10% of the sales. At the start of the show, he made the initial pitch, telling the kids that later in the show, there would be something special for everyone who had purchased a sword. During a two-minute break later in the show, Ward would have the lights shut off in the arena and have everyone with swords light them up and hold them high in the air, making a big deal out of it and making everyone holding a sword feel special.

That action with the lights out was a great deal more than making anyone feel special. While the lights were out and everyone was holding up the swords, he would look through the crowds and make a quick estimate of how many swords there were; thus he could figure out approximately how much the concessions department owed him. "I was being treated very badly, to the tune of at least $100 a week," he said of the concessions department.

Ward's interpretation of a ringmaster is that he should announce the act, then be quiet and let the act do its thing. But many performers want some kind of a narration or special announcement to take place during their performance. Ward has always refused all such requests. One act on this show repeatedly asked Ward to do it and Ward kept refusing, even when a bottle of good whiskey was used as a bribe. The act told Ward, "I don't know why you refuse; they give it to me on the Ringling Bros. and Barnum & Bailey Circus." Ward retorted: "Take a look around. Isn't it obvious that we are not on Ringling? I don't do it."

The Musical is Alive:
Saigon Doll Premieres in Florida

CHAPTER 31

Ward was content staying home for most of the 1990 season and was busy spending Chris's money dusting off *Million Dollar Doll*, the musical he wrote in 1962 and 1963. This time around he changed the beginning, reworked a couple characters, changed a few lyrics in the songs and renamed it *Saigon Doll*. He had read an article in *Variety* about a new musical to open in London called *Miss Saigon*. He was impressed with its big advance billing and the promise of a huge box office. He thought if he "could take advantage and in some way capitalize on that show's success" and get his own show on the road before the Broadway debut of *Miss Saigon* in late 1991, he would have an advantage. He had the soundtrack music re-recorded with the changes, expecting to use the recorded music instead of a live orchestra when he presented the show.

He cast the production with local talent, gathered costumes from various organizations, including his own stock of wardrobe, rented out the Lakeland (Fla.) Civic Center and filmed footage for the television commercials. The show opened in Ormond Beach and went on to play six different Florida cities, the last being in Melbourne. He felt the show was good enough by the Melbourne date to capture it on video tape and arranged with the theater tech staff to do the taping. On the way out that night, they handed him the tape. Alas, several days later when he got time to view it he discovered

Chris and Ward, all dressed up.

the tape was blank. He was quite disappointed, especially since the show never saw the stage again.

It failed miserably, according to Ward, losing $35,000, some of which was regained by selling some of the props and the wardrobe. Looking back, Ward regrets not handling his stage shows better. "I was very egotistical, thinking that I could do it all. I took way too much on myself. I was the writer, director, designer, scenic designer, lighting designer, costume designer and the casting director."

He understands why he did it the way he did. "Hiring people to do all those things would have been very, very expensive and I was working on a shoestring budget." He thinks his biggest mistake was doing his own casting. "I put my friends into the roles. I loved them, but they weren't capable of doing these parts." He tries to justify everything today by noting that even had he been able to afford help, "the shows would have probably flopped anyway, but I should have done a better job."

A Hallowed Venue:
Ward Sings in Carnegie Hall

CHAPTER 32

With the life that Ward Hall has led, it seems impossible that one single event would stand out to him as the best. What's even more improbable is that event had nothing to do with a sideshow.

On April 22, 1994, Ward was the singing master of ceremonies at the hallowed music hall for *Circus Blues,* a show that was part of The Carnegie Hall Folk Festival. Stephen Holden, a reviewer with the *New York Times,* attended the show and wrote of Ward. "Wearing a sequined top hat and tails, Ward Hall, a former lion tamer and pitchman, presided over the program of old-time circus musicians, like Ralph Edwards leading a big-top version of *This is Your Life.*

Ward sang three numbers with the orchestra to get the show under way. "Hi, Neighbor!," "There'll Be Some Changes Made," and "When You're Smiling." Among the musical guests on the same bill were Blind Willy, Guitar Gabriel (Robert Lewis Jones), Diamond Tooth Mary and Willa Mae Buckner. When it was time for intermission, Ward stepped forward and gave a pitch:

> *"Ladies and gentlemen, several boxes of Cracker Jacks that our friends are now selling throughout the theater have diamond rings and gold watches buried deep inside. You buy a box and you just may be buying a real diamond ring or a genuine gold watch."*

But before it got too far, he assured them that he was just kidding, explaining that's the way it would have been done in the olden days of the circus, an historical anecdote as it were.

> *"Of course we really don't have a candy sale with prizes; however for the next 15 minutes there will be for sale in the lobby books, photos and music from tonight's entertainers. I will be there to sign them for you because now it is intermission time."*

"I have said it many, many times that singing at Carnegie Hall in New York City was the highlight of my life," said Ward. "It's the one singular thing that I have enjoyed most, and being a part of that program is one of my proudest moments." Surprisingly, not too many people who know of Ward and his sideshow prowess know that the Carnegie Hall event took place, said Ward. "I don't usually tell people that I sang at Carnegie Hall. It is so unbelievable that this sideshow bum would have been top billed in a program at Carnegie – with great reviews the following day." Chris, who attended the event, was quite proud of Ward and quite happy for him. "That night gave him the warm fuzzies, and I was so happy for him," Chris said.

Ward and Chris decided to call it quits, once again, in late 1994 and this time decided to cash in on it, appealing to the circus fans and historians who read Bandwagon, the journal of the Circus Historical Society. In the November/December issue they purchased a full page ad with the headline declaring – "The Final Sideshow."

The copy-heavy ad started off. "Ward Hall and C.M. Christ announce the closing of their sideshow at the end of the 1994 season, after 46 years. To commemorate the passing of this indigenous American art form, they gathered for the final performance, sideshow performers who you will see perform and personal interviews of each." *The Final Sideshow* was an hour-long limited edition video tape selling for $29.95. Ward had filmed much of the video on that tape during the previous year's fall season, which also was captured by the British Broadcasting Company and appeared in the television documentary, *The Last American Freak Show*.

A Hallowed Venue: Ward Sings in Carnegie Hall

That video was soon out of date as a last reminder of the American art form because their retirement plans were foiled again and the art form survived another year.

A headline in the Feb. 27, 1995 edition of *Amusement Business* revealed: "For the 18th Last Time, Hall to Take 'Wonders' Sideshow on the Road." It seems even the press had noticed that Ward and Chris just couldn't stay away from the midway. "I keep saying I'm going to retire from the road, but it always seems I'm talked into going out again for just one more season," Hall told the publication during the IISA Trade Show & Extravaganza in Gibsonton in early February.

It was Pat Reithoffer who talked him back on the road this time. "I had played many dates with the Reithoffer Shows and

Chris and Ward prior to Ward's Carnegie Hall debut, 1994.

had been playing the Pennsylvania Fair in Bensalem with him since its beginning in 1986," Ward recalls. "When he heard we weren't planning on going out, he called and asked if I would just play his dates in the Northeast and in a few days, Dominic Vivona of Amusements of America called asking me if I would play his Northeast dates as well, so I agreed and out we went."

> "Welcome to the World of Wonders Museum, where on the inside you will experience strange cultures from distant lands. You will see the giraffe-necked girl with the world's longest neck. She came from Burma. Here you will see the reptilian girl, the girl who had the head of a human but the body of a Python snake."

In addition to fat man Howard Huge (Snowden) and Pete, the fire-eating dwarf, the show was billed as a "freak museum" featuring 250 artifacts behind glass, plus the wax figures of sideshow celebrities that Ward and Chris had created in 1987.

Essentially 1995 was a season of easy jumps. From Bensalem in May to its last date in September the sideshow never went outside a 150-mile radius of Philadelphia. "That made it real nice for us and sure cut down on a lot of headaches."

But being a relatively large show with only a couple working acts created another problem. "When you work for us as a performer, you also help set up and tear down everything. We are a non-discriminatory employer," said Ward. "We found out during the Meadowlands Fair the previous year, that not having live performers on one hand made for an easier season, but on the other hand, we created a major problem for ourselves. We never had enough help to tear down and move and then set up again. We opened late in a couple spots because we just couldn't do it in time, so we knew we were going to have to do something differently for the 1995 season."

By coincidence, Keith Nelson of the Bindlestiff Family Cirkus and his wife, Stephanie Monseu, visited Ward and Chris during that spring in Gibtown, and Ward asked them if they were available to play the 1995 Meadowlands Fair in East Rutherford, N.J., Keith Nelson as a sword swallower and Stephanie in the girl-to-gorilla act. The couple jumped at the offer. "We accepted because we wanted the opportunity to work with the pope of our art form," Keith Nelson said. Ward made it clear that part of the deal was they were going to have to be part of the set-up and tear down crew as well. Keith and Stephanie had no problem with that, luckily, because they were put to work immediately upon joining the show. "We were greeted by Jimmy Long, Ward's lot man, holding two sledge hammers," Keith laughed.

Ward went out with the sideshow in 1996 while Chris went to work promoting the E.L. Barnes Circus. To make it easier, now that Chris was unavailable to help, it was decided to paint the side of two semi-trailers and let them serve, instead of a canvas banner line, as the front end to the illusion show that they had booked for the season. "It was a good idea and was certainly a great deal easier than putting up and taking down a banner line at each spot, but it didn't really work and that was the only year we did it," Ward said.

From the late 1990s, Chris and Ward's kingdom would ebb one year and flow the next. Nothing new or revolutionary would take place and most of the effort was made maintaining a quality show and quality bookings, not reinventing the artform. "It was pretty much the way we wanted it," Ward said. "Lots of things happened, of course, but none of it seemed as important or as drastic as it did when we were younger. There has been a lot less drama in our everyday lives, that's for sure." Succinctly put, the past 15 years for the show have been "the same old shit," according to Ward. But they have been very good years for Ward, as most of his big kudos, awards, and acknowledgements have been during these same years.

9/11/2001:
"We Were Way Too Close"

CHAPTER 33

As most of us can, Ward remembers exactly where he was on the morning of Sept. 11, 2001. "I was doing what I usually do, sleeping late," he said. "We were setting up at the Great Frederick (Md.) Fair and Chris was laying out the lot. He came in and woke me up yelling that we were in terrible trouble. I thought we were having a problem with the lot or the fair. But then he turned on the television just in time for me to watch the second plane go into the second tower of the World Trade Center."

Ward remembers that he was "very worried, very concerned and a bit scared" of what was going to happen, especially after another plane hit the Pentagon, less than 50 miles away. Fair management told everyone to stop setting up for the fair because they weren't sure it would open. Two days later, Ward and Chris got the go-ahead to open and, surprisingly, "we did very well that week." They also did well at the next two fairs they played in South Carolina, even one that had been on the decline for the past several years. "I can't figure it out but, strangely, we were up when most everyone else struggled."

James Taylor, sideshow historian and publisher of the *Shocked and Amazed!* series of journals dedicated to the sideshow industry, and his partner Dick Horne opened the storefront American Dime Museum in Baltimore on Nov. 1, 1999 and on May 13, 2002, they sponsored a talk by Ward at that city's Port Discovery. Ward, with little Pete beside him, was asked by a member of the audience how he felt about making a living exploiting deformed and handicapped individuals.

"I feel fine about it," he answered. "Yes, I do exploit them and they make a lot of money because I do exploit them. The more I promote and exploit, the more money they make." He added that "90% of them are ham actors to start with, so this is a good livelihood for them." He pointed out that this was the only way many could make their own money and stay off welfare and government aid, pointing out that many of them were living comfortably in retirement on the money they made on the sideshow.

Johnny Meah, who had his own sideshow before joining up with Ward, said that he always found that the deformed acts were a reasonably happy, well-adjusted group. "For the time slot they occupied in history, they were self-sufficient and were better off than their counterparts who were often hidden away in the family attic," Meah said. "Titles (freaks, oddities) did not offend them and were, in fact, their passports to a better than average income."

No matter what they say to your face, people are willing to pay to see those less fortunate. In his book *Very Special People,* Frederick Drimmer writes that people are "morbidly fascinated" by any human being who is different than them. "Although people have disowned or depreciated the human oddity, they've usually flocked to see him. They may shudder with horror and cover their eyes with their fingers, but they always peek through them."

Ward was tired and not feeling well by the time they wrapped up their successful 2002 season. Noting that he was in "pretty bad" shape, he assembled his own team of specialists; six doctors to look after all that ailed him. After a couple months, Chris confided in long-time friend and employee Dick Johnson that Ward was in no shape to go on the road in 2003 and that he was going to suggest it to Ward. Johnson laughed and added, "Good luck doing that Chris."

Surprisingly, Ward had no problem with the suggestion and stayed home in Gibsonton during 2003, only joining the show one time, in late August at the Allentown (Pa.) Fair. Ward had been invited to be the guest of honor at the first Sideshow Gathering, to be held in Wilkes-Barre, Pa., over Labor Day weekend. The dates corresponded with the fair's run, so Ward flew in, rented a car and drove out to Allentown before heading to the Wilkes-Barre event.

Chris and the show were jumping from Maine and they were running late. Chris called Ward to see if he could round up a crew to help set up when they arrived because everyone was exhausted. Ward did so and Chris went right to bed when he arrived and Ward oversaw the set-up and got the show up in time for opening that night. Just as the show was ramping up to good business, sideshow entertainer Harley Newman, billed as the Professional Lunatic, stopped by on his way to the Sideshow Gathering in Wilkes-Barre, to see Ward. The show had no sword swallower, so Newman went back to his car, retrieved his equipment, and started performing.

He had just taken the stage when showman Todd Robbins, also on his way to Wilkes-Barre, showed up with his bag of show implements. Ward put them both to work and he talked the front that night for the first time in more than a year. Ward wished he had that night's lineup on his show permanently. "I had two of the most capable and popular sideshow performers in the world, right up there on my stage. If our customers only had known what they were seeing." Both Robbins and Newman

9/11/2001: "We Were Way Too Close"

Four BFF, from left: Dick Johnson, Ward Hall, Chris Christ, and Johnny Meah in February 2014.

swallowed swords and performed a blockhead act. In addition, Newman lay on a bed of barbed wire and Robbins ate one of the 5,000 light bulbs he has consumed during his career.

Not having time to hang around for long, Ward headed to Wilkes-Barre the next morning and Chris took over the show. Obviously, the audience realized something special was going on because word of mouth spread about the magnificent sideshow at the fair. Chris reported that every night for the rest of the run, people came up and wondered where the guys were who ate light bulbs and laid on barbed wire.

The Sideshow Gathering was organized in an attempt to gather all those practicing the sideshow arts. "Most of us who perform, don't get a chance to see each other work because we are always out there trying to make a living of our own," said Dan Meyer, a professional sword swallower who founded the Sword Swallowers Assoc. International. "This was a weekend we could all enjoy together, watch each other's acts and jackpot all night long. It was great fun while it lasted." The Gathering ran through 2012 and closed down, but Meyer is optimistic that it will return in all its glory.

In late 2003, both Chris and Ward made the decision to retire once again after their run in late October at Ybor City's Guavaween celebration in Tampa. Ward was not his old self, Chris was tired, and their number one operations manager, Jimmy Long, passed out while tearing down the show at Guavaween and fell off a ladder. While at the hospital, it was discovered that Long had diabetes and was told to take it easy.

Ward Hall – King of the Sideshow!

Long had been an essential boss canvas man and truck driver with Ward since 1967 and when he had his leg amputated due to the diabetes in 2004, he had to leave the show for good. With Ward's help, Long found an apartment at the Showfolks Retirement Village in Gibsonton, run by the IISA. Long remained there until his death in July 2011. Ironically, Pete who had travelled with Ward for 55 years, died a week later.

"That was a very bad couple of weeks for me, losing two of my long-time friends," Ward recalled.

Following Guavaween, Chris and Ward sold their trucks and tractors, expecting to totally retire, which they did for a year. Neither Chris, Ward nor a show owned by them went out in 2004. They enjoyed their time at home and found the time to take a long cruise, along with Pete.

Ward on the bally at the Bloomsburg (Pa.) Fair.

This time, the news of impending retirement garnered Ward and Chris a bit of local publicity. In a Jan. 22, 2004, article in the *Tampa Tribune,* Ward told reporter Liz Bleau that everything was for sale, from the sideshow equipment down to the pickled punks and the two large Burmese pythons.

"There's nothing wrong with the business," Ward told Bleau. "It's just that I'm too old to follow the trucks down the road." This is significant, because this is the first time that Ward, 74 at the time, admitted openly that he was quitting because he was getting too old and too tired. He also gave another reason. "The last couple of years, Chris has worked the sideshow mostly. We used to take turns, but I found I was making excuses not to go. I guess I just got tired of the noise and the crowds," he said.

Gary Syres approached the two late in 2004 and asked if they would design and build him a large sideshow. He told them that he had the money, the time, and the desire to get into the sideshow business. By now both Chris and Ward were somewhat bored staying at home and needed a project to keep them busy, so they agreed and created the deal.

He visited Gibsonton and it was obvious he wanted only the best. Banner painter Bill Browning drew up a colorful design, which Syres readily approved, and construction began. New banners, a new tent and a state of the art sound system would nearly guarantee success for the new show.

Chris took the plans to Fred Brown, operations director at the Florida State Fair, who immediately upon seeing them told Chris that, "This show is beautiful; I want to be the first to have it." Pulling out a map of the fairgrounds, Brown showed Chris a prime location where the new sideshow would be placed. But when Brown discovered that the show did not belong to Ward and Chris he balked at the booking, insisting that he would not contract with an operator he did not know. To save the date, Chris took the responsibility and promised that he would be there every day overseeing the action. The contract was put in Chris' name.

The Florida State Fair, which opens in early February, is important because it is the first major expo of the year and is known to be a showcase in which to show off a new product to other showmen. Fair managers and carnival owners from all over the world come to the fair each year to see what's new and will often book a ride or show on the spot for their own event. The fair takes place during the IISA Trade Show & Extravaganza, held nearby in Gibsonton, and while the OABA and other industry groups meet for their annual meetings in Tampa. The area is a virtual Who's Who in the outdoor entertainment industry for those first couple weeks in February every year.

In December 2004, two months before the fair, Syres reported that he was out of money and couldn't finish the show. "We had to finish it

Ward takes a closer look at Bambi the Mermaid
at the Allentown (Pa.) Fair, 2003.

because we had the contract with the fair," said Chris. "So we put in our own money, finished building it and ran the show for those 13 days." As expected, visiting fair managers loved it, business was good, and the 2005 route card was mostly filled by the end of the fair.

Syres worked the show for the entire run, expecting to get enough additional financing to take over full ownership. He played the electric keyboard on the bally, which created a nice change of pace. Once he saw the work needed to put on a show of this size, he offered to sell out to

9/11/2001: "We Were Way Too Close"

Ward and Chris. Now with a new show, a new tractor and trailer had to be purchased to move it. The boys were back in business.

"The dollar you spend to come inside, you will never remember; but what you see in here today, you will never forget!"

Syres also wanted to be a part of the Minnesota State Fair that August, in St. Paul, where he once again played the electric keyboard on the bally. Ward joined him on most days, playing the drums. It drew so much attention and brought the show such good business that the following year they also provided live music on the bally stage, although neither Syres nor Ward contributed their own musical talent to the show.

Coney Island girls Bambi the Mermaid and Bunny Love created excitement and beauty on the World of Wonders bally stage in Minnesota as well as at various other large fairs for four years, 2003 - 2006. The two New Yorkers "begged" Ward to allow them to perform on the show and, according to Bambi, it didn't take much convincing. Both had careers and obligations in New York so they couldn't go out full time but they hit the show when they could during those years.

"We loved it," said Bambi, who is the official Mermaid Queen of Coney Island. "It was kind of like a sideshow fantasy camp for us because we were so excited to be there and to learn the sideshow arts." Ward loved when they showed up. "They added a lot of class to the show because they brought their own costumes and they looked gorgeous." With the intention of only performing on the bally, Bambi said they were surprised when they were asked if they would like to learn a few new things. They ended up as snake charmers, glass walkers, sword ladder walkers, and they learned to stretch out on a bed of nails. "It was everything we thought it would be," Bambi added.

Lane Talburt recalls witnessing a "wonderful" example of how Ward can work a crowd at the 2007 Circus Fans of America convention in Hershey, Pa. Ward told the gathering that he brought only 10 copies of his novel, *Gypsy Hot Bloods,* to sell and that he would use the proceeds to pay for his travel expenses incurred while in Hershey. He started selling the books and it sounded something like this: "That's number 10, thank you, 9 more left and here you are, thank you, here's another, only 8 left, thank you. Here's number 7, thank you, only 7 left, OK, thanks, only 7 left, thank you sir, OK folks, only 7 left. Here you are ma'am, now only 7 left, thank you, only 6 left now." Talburt laughs and says it was magic to watch and that to no one's surprise Ward had sold more than 20 copies by the time he ended his pitch.

Magic was the first skill Ward taught himself, back in his father's apartment in Denver. He attended live magic shows and saw many of the masters of magic work first hand and he read everything he could find on magic. When he joined Dailey Bros. Circus in 1946, he was taught more magic by Milt Robbins. Through the years, Ward's love for magic was evident in the types of shows he and his partners produced.

It was without a moment's hesitation that Ward accepted an invitation to be a guest speaker at the 11th Los Angeles Conference on Magic History on Nov. 5 - 7, 2009. He was to be interviewed on stage by fellow magician and sideshow performer Todd Robbins. In a post-conference account in *Circus Report,* Chuck Burnes noted that "the final talk on opening night was supposed to be an interview; however, the interviewer didn't need to do much with the legendary circus, carnival and sideshow impresario. He regaled the audience with his background for a solid 15 minutes with interviewer Todd Robbins never speaking one word." When Ward slowed, Robbins was finally able to ask him a question. But Ward, in his revered manner and without skipping a beat, jokingly replied, "Do you always have to dominate the conversation?" The crowd laughed, Robbins laughed and Ward continued his monologue.

Burnes went on to report that in their coverage of the event, both *Magic Magazine* and *Genii Magazine* proclaimed that Ward was the "biggest star" of that year's event. Burnes closed his story with similar praise. "Ward really was, without question, the highlight attraction of the entire three-day symposium!"

New York 2011:
To Lincoln Center and Beyond

CHAPTER 34

Ward received a phone call in mid-June 2011 from his long-time friend Spike Barkin, the person who had been responsible for booking him into Carnegie Hall in 1994. Barkin was now the consulting producer for Lincoln Center's Out of Doors festival in New York City and he wanted Ward to be the talker for a special event to be held on various plaza areas around Lincoln Center on Aug. 10. Entitled "Spike's Sideshow," it was widely promoted throughout the region.

"Honoring the King of the Sideshow Ward Hall, who will do the 'call for the bally,' a dozen different artists, including a cornucopia of conjurers, marvels and freaks, take over Lincoln Center's plazas," read the promotional material. Among the performers that day were Adam Cardone, Magic Brian, Heather Knight and Keith Nelson of the Bindlestiff Family Cirkus.

It was a date that Ward came close to missing.

A week before he was to leave for New York City, Ward came down with a severe case of gout and was admitted to the hospital. He told Chris to cancel the Lincoln Center gig but his doctor told him to wait and not to cancel at that time. That advice was a good thing because three days later he was released from the hospital. "Whatever the doctor gave me certainly worked in a hurry," Ward recalls. Two days later he flew to New York and made the date while renewing old friendships with many of the performers. He was still weak and wobbly on his feet, but he made it. *The Show Must Go On.*

Ward was invited by Jennifer Miller, the director of Circus Amok, to perform his vent act and be interviewed in front of a live audience at the Sideshows by the Seashore in Coney Island, in Brooklyn, N.Y., on Oct. 17, 2013. The show was co-sponsored by Coney Island USA and the Pop-Up Museum of Queer History.

Ward was asked to perform with his favorite dummy, Homo the Brave – The Queer Indian Boy, an act that went over very well with the assembled capacity crowd of approximately 120. He then sat and answered questions from Miller for about an hour. "The main topic we discussed was gay life on the midway, a subject I have not talked much about through the years, but in a nutshell, I told them if you removed the gays from the circus, sideshow and club circuits, you would eliminate about half the entertainers," Ward laughed. "It is an important topic that should be discussed."

Ward, Pete, and Chris.

Taboo Talk:
Sexuality on the Midway

CHAPTER 35

Ward was bullied as a high school student in Denver. Slight in build and with absolutely no desire (and no talent) to play any sports, Ward spent his time reading, listening to music and attending any form of live entertainment that came to town. He was different from the other boys.

"You're a queer aren't you?" he was tormented. "At that time, I didn't even know what that word meant. But I knew they were making fun of me and bullying me. That's one of the main reasons I didn't go back to high school after summer break." Ward said.

During his long career, he has seldom talked much about his sexual orientation and when asked if were gay, he would normally say no. He once said that his sex life, on the whole, has been about as exciting as "reading a Bible to a three-year-old."

At the Coney Island event in 2013 with Jennifer Miller, Ward called himself a "puritanical, narrow-minded Christian homosexual." The crowd laughed. Ward was serious as he added, "Actually I'm not gay, I'm not straight, I am asexual. I had major cancer surgery nearly 25 years ago that made me a eunuch, so physically I am not gay; mentally I am gay."

In the 2005 video documentary *Showman – The Life and Times of Ward Hall,* showman Todd Robbins noted that "Harry allowed Ward to find out who he was. He appeared at a very important time in Ward's life and he was loving and supportive. That relationship helped their business because trust and love were there and everyone saw it."

Robbins continued: "Ward and Chris also connected at a very important time in both of their lives." Robbins laughs when he calls Ward and Chris "an old married couple" who bicker all the time. "But underneath it all is a lot of love and respect. They have amazing and complete trust in each other on all levels."

Ward loves his family of misfits and in return, that family of misfits loves Ward. They found each other at the right moment in their lives. They found community, they found love and they found trust in each other, many of them for the first time in their lives. In the same 2005 video, Ward laughs that, on occasion, he is asked if he ever married. "Yes," he always answered. "I am married to the sideshow business and to my sideshow family. The good Lord made me of the orientation that I have

Ward Hall – King of the Sideshow!

Chris and Ward, standing inside the sideshow tent, ready for the crowds.

not been burdened with children. If you have children, they grow up and they leave you. My children never left. They are growing old with me."

"I don't approve of a homosexual who goes flitting around like a butterfly," Ward said. "I don't think swishiness is particularly attractive." Ward never flaunted his sexuality, but he never hid it. The industry knew, the fair managers knew, his acts knew, but it never made a difference. Being different never was an issue on carnivals and circus midways. There, being gay has always been an open lifestyle. Ward was with Harry for 19 years and has been with Chris for nearly 50. To the general public, they are business partners first. To those who know them, they are a dedicated and loving couple.

Diversity on the midway has always been accepted. Fat ladies, bearded ladies, three-legged men, no-legged men, fat men, tattooed people, armless ladies, being Russian, being American, being French, being white, being black, being Asian. None of that mattered. "We all worked, lived, ate and partied together. We were family," Ward said. "Everyone knew each other and everyone had to get along so we did." The midway has served as a magnet for the misfits, the rebels, the nonconformists, the odd, and the lonely. It serves not only as a haven but as a support group and everyone respects everyone else's itinerant lifestyle.

Diane De Elgar/George Searles, the half-and-half on Ward's shows for many years, was once asked by carnival owner Rod Link if he thought there were any gays on his show. "Rod, there are so many gay people in your concessions department alone that they are dripping off your canvas awnings," Searles answered. Ward said Link was genuinely surprised.

In the earlier days when most of the circus or carnival workers and acts lived on trains and in communal housing there was very little hanky panky in those areas, Ward said. "Today, everyone can go back to their trailer and interact as they wish."

When Ward joined the circus in 1946 there were virtually no performances on Sunday. It was a day when everyone relaxed, went to church if they were inclined, and pursued other interests. On one of those Sundays, when Ward was 16, he washed up, walked into town from the railroad yard where the Dailey Bros. circus train was parked, and enjoyed a nice dinner alone. Following his meal, he went outside and with the small town's two movie houses a block apart, he stood in the middle trying to figure out which movie he wanted to see.

One of the workers on the circus, Carl, came by and they started talking. That's when Carl asked Ward if he would like to spend the night with him in the local hotel where he had taken a room. That's when Ward learned about circus Sundays in hotels. That night, he discovered that hotel rooms were for more than taking one's weekly bath and sleeping on a comfortable mattress.

He spent the night and admits that he learned many new things in that small room in that Midwestern town on that hot summer's evening. It was all pleasurable, he recalls. It was on those Sundays in hotels when many of the performers and workers on a circus would discover the sexual orientation of all the others. There were gay trysts, there were illegal dalliances, there were threesomes, there were husbands cheating on wives and wives cheating on husbands. It was all accepted. Sundays in hotels gave everyone an opportunity to get away from the noise and the dirt of the train. No one seemed to care who was sleeping with whom.

Ward and Harry spent a circus Sunday in a hotel the second week after Harry joined Dailey Bros. in 1946. That night, in Springfield, Mo., a beautiful relationship of 19 years began. Harry asked. Ward accepted. The rest is history.

Here Come the Kids:
New Generation Makes Its Move

CHAPTER 36

In the mid-1980s, Chris and Ward had taken all the working acts and human oddities out of the show and travelled a wax and oddities museum instead. They did it to decrease payroll and make life easier on the road.

In the late 1990s, they thought about doing it again. This time it wasn't in an attempt to save money or make life easier; it was all about not being able to find enough workers willing to swallow swords, eat fire, and walk on glass, among other acts. Today, that isn't a problem.

"There has been a resurgence of young performers, with these skills that want to work on our sideshow," Ward said. "The skills we have been practicing for decades now have an official name. It is now being called sideshow performance art, and the kids want to learn."

Jim Rose is commonly credited for bringing the sideshow arts to the attention of a new generation of performers and a youthful audience. He took his circus of shock artists, which included sword swallowing and other traditional sideshow arts, along with extreme acts such as lifting heavy objects from pierced body parts and stomach pumping, on the rock and roll circuit, including tours with the Nine Inch Nails and Marilyn Manson. Rose brought the sideshow to prominence for a genre of American audiences as a second stage act on the 1992 Lollapalooza tour. "Ward was my inspiration," Rose said.

Another young performer who was inspired by Ward is Todd Ray, who owns the Venice Beach (Calif.) Freakshow. "When I was thinking about opening the show, Ward Hall was the first showman I called for advice," Ray said. "He was nice and wished me all the luck in the world and reminded me to 'have all the fun you can, but when it comes down to it, get the money, because without it, there is no show.'"

Tommy Breen followed his dream of being a sideshow artist with the help of Ward and Chris. He graduated in Cinema Studies from Rutgers University and was always fascinated with the sideshow arts. When he saw an ad in *Amusement Business* looking for sideshow help, he responded, and it wasn't long before he was travelling with the World of Wonders. Tommy joined the show in 2006 as a sword swallower. He soon learned to talk the front and in 2010, Ward made him manager of the show. Today he is a partner and officer, along with Chris and Ward,

Talker Tommy Breen on the bally with Bambi the Mermaid and Bunny Love, adding a new twist to the bally.

in Family American Magical Entertainment Inc. (FAME). He appears to be the heir apparent to Ward and Chris.

When asked about his partners, Breen laughs. "That's easy. Ward is the flash and Chris is the beef. Both of them have many talents and have done incredible things with their respective lives." Breen adds that Ward's "crazy drive and 24/7 persona" is unstoppable. "It's an all-consuming thing in life for Ward, and that's why he has had such a positive influence on the carny lifestyle. Ward is the last of his kind."

Though he has lived for decades amongst them, Ward is adamant about not being called a carny. "I am not a carny, I am a showman." He answered the phone one day when this journalist was sitting next to him. "Hello, is this Ward Hall the carny?" queried a female voice on the phone. "No ma'am, this is Ward Hall, the showman. A carny is one who has rides and sells greasy food."

Circus historian Lane Talburt adds that one reason Ward has succeeded on so many levels is that he was never threatening to his employees, employers, or to his peers. "One reason he fit in right from the very beginning was his gregarious personality," Talburt pointed out. "He got a good start because at the time he joined the circus most people of that era didn't have much of an education other than the circus and Ward walked on to his first circus lot with a voracious appetite to learn."

Here Come the Kids: New Generation Makes Its Move

Ward's influence goes beyond sideshow performers. Mikee Plastik, known for his cutting edge scoring and soundtrack work within the film and gaming industries said that Ward helped him realize that he could do things against the norm, with a unique perspective, and still be successful. "He helped me see through the fine line that separates the art of human oddities and the art of audible oddities, not just in the production of performance art, but in my painting portraits of uniqueness with sound."

Sunshine English joined the World of Wonders cast in 2006. She remembers the piece of advice Ward gave her on the first day on the job. "Always be on because you never know who is watching," he told her. That's one of the reasons one never sees Ward out in public not looking his best, often dressed in a flashy suit with a carnation in the lapel. "It's frightening how good he is," English adds. "He can talk anyone into anything. He is very grand and has a great way with everyone. He performs the same perfect bally out front whether it's in front of 300 people or a single, potential customer."

Working on and off with Ward and Chris since 1989, John "Red" Stuart is one of the few sword swallowers who swallows a car axle as part of his show. He is also a human pin cushion, a blockhead, and is

Red Stuart, Sunshine English and Tommy Breen on the World of Wonders bally stage at the Wisconsin State Fair, 2013

happy to have a customer staple paper money anywhere on his body with the condition he gets to keep it. He enjoys working for Chris and Ward because of their honest and upright reputation in the business. Stuart said it appears that Ward knows just about everybody and is a true gentleman. "He will communicate with you, no matter who you are. Backstage, he is always one of the boys, but once he walks out onto the stage that man turns into a star, a first class showman."

Doing All Right, Thanks:
Enjoying Life; Working a Little

CHAPTER 37

Over the eight-year period of 2006-2013, the Hall and Christ sideshow was booked at the major fairs, including Minnesota State Fair, Wisconsin State Fair, Westchester County Fair, and the Meadowlands Fair. The format stayed basically the same, and each season the show made money. A solid, steady route, a good talent lineup, good management and good business, especially at fairs in the Northeast, followed for several years. Nobody was getting rich, but the World of Wonders, billed as the Last American Sideshow, continues to exist.

Ward and Chris have started going out with the show less and less, leaving their young protégé, Tommy Breen, to oversee the operation. Chris still does the bookings but rarely goes on the road. The last time Ward went out with the show for more than a day here or a day there, was in 2012, when he stayed out for the three consecutive state fairs of Wisconsin, Minnesota and Kansas.

Financially, physically and personally, it has been a roller coaster life for both Chris and Ward. Today they live comfortably on a couple acres in Gibsonton, in a house they purchased in 1999. Their workshop and winter quarters are located there as well, and they both get out often to local showmen's events, when the circus comes to town, and when old friends invite them out to dinner.

Ward notes that while they aren't "rolling in the dough," they are doing okay. "Chris and I made a lot of money over the years," Ward said.

Chris makes a point!

"Of course there were big years that were really big and thin years that were very thin. We took in a lot of money, but didn't end up with much each year because we would always invest in new shows. We were way too ambitious in our re-investing." After most seasons they would come back home with a wad of cash, but by spring not much of it was left, due to that re-investing. "Many years we didn't have enough left to pull out of winter quarters in the spring without financial help," Ward said.

Following their bankruptcy in 1985, neither Ward nor Chris was as aggressive in fielding big shows with large casts of characters as they had been. "Prior to bankruptcy we had years in which we employed up to 350 people," Ward said, adding that, after bankruptcy, they scaled back and were able to start saving money by sending out what he calls "mummy and dummy" shows, which included wax and freak animal museums that didn't need a large cast of employees to move or to operate.

Following more than a dozen "farewell tours," it appears that Ward's hustle and bustle days on a carnival or a circus back lot are over. Although he doesn't travel with the show, he knows what is going on through daily reports from Chris and from the road. Chris doesn't do much traveling either but talks with Breen at least once every day during the season. How would Ward appraise the business to which he dedicated his life and his

Ward Hall - King of the Sideshow!

state of mind? "There were times I hated it. There were times I loved it. But most of the time, I tolerated it."

Today, while still active, Ward has several health issues, but certainly no more than most 84-year-old men who have led the lifestyle that 70 years on the road requires. He has had heart problems which are now being controlled by a team of heart specialists, had kidney stones, and has had broken bones from falling off and running into equipment. "Most of the time I feel good," Ward reported in early 2014. Hard physical work has also given Chris some mobility problems and he has a hard time getting around.

Anyone who knows Ward also knows that the man is full of stories, backed up by his impressive memory of dates and details. He is a living history book. He loves talking about his career and the history of the circus and sideshow. Today, one does not get the sense that Ward is bitter that it is all coming to an end. In fact, there is only one thing about growing old that bothers him. "I miss being able to dance," Ward said. "I was quite the ballroom dancer and for much of my life I would have rather danced than eaten. Unfortunately, I am not steady on my feet anymore and can't dance. That's what I miss most."

Many of the regulars who frequented the Showmen's Club dinner dances in Gibsonton recall Ward and his long-time dancing partner, Percilla Bejano the Monkey Girl. But Ward doesn't want to be remembered for his dancing, or even the endless hours he spent at the club working for the benefit of showmen everywhere. "I want to be remembered as a good performer and a kind person who worked hard through the years providing good family entertainment that made thousands laugh and smile."

He also would like to be mentioned when people in the future talk about sideshows and how they were able to survive as an American art form for so long. "I hope they remember that, along with some fantastic help through the years, it was Ward Hall who was instrumental in keeping the sideshow alive in America." He told a reporter from the *Southwest Times Record* in Fort Smith, Ark., in 1987 that he planned to work forever and then made a prediction. "I imagine my name will always be attached to the sideshow business."

In the 2005 film, *Showman – The Life and Times of Ward Hall*, he was asked the basic question that one asks of those who have achieved great things. "If you had your life to live over, would you change anything?" His answer may surprise many. "Yes," he quickly said. "I would change my entire life and not do anything the same. I have lived a great life and had a great adventure. But I've lived this life. I would like to try something new."

In the same documentary, Ward said he would like to make an arrangement with the Smithsonian Museum for them to take his body when he dies, put it in a big bottle of formaldehyde and put him on display in perpetuity. "I just don't want to ever get out of show business." Richard Flint, who booked Ward into the Smithsonian from 1979-83, smiled when he recalls Ward saying that. "More power to him; hope it works out! He would certainly be history's biggest pickled punk."

Network News, in writing about Ward while his show was at the Smithsonian, closed its story with the following. "And here he is, take one last look. Yes, he's the greatest talker of our time, of the century. The telephone companies want to hire him to replace 100 operators. He can talk a blue streak red. And you're looking at him, Ward Hall, an endangered species, a Smithsonian exhibit."

Chris and Ward visiting the IISA Trade Show & Extravaganza in 2005.

WORLD FAIR FREAKS
Circus Side Shows

GRIND SHOWS

WARD HALL
C. M. CHRIST

SUITE 600
155 W. 46TH STREET
NEW YORK, N.Y.

WARD HALL
Third Vice President

813—677-1109
POST OFFICE BOX 188
GIBSONTON, FLORIDA 33534

No. 2398
Expires May 1, 1983

MEMBER
CIRCUS HISTORICAL SOCIETY
Ward Hall

Edward L. Jones
Secretary-Treasurer

The Blow-off:
Additional Stories for only a Quarter

Told by Ward Hall, the King of the Sideshow himself.

- "My mother told me that when I was four years old she came into the kitchen and saw that I had pulled a blanket over several chairs and that I was playing underneath them. She asked me what I was doing, and I told her I was playing in my circus tent. I had never been to the circus and to her knowledge I had never heard the word circus before. She was quite baffled."

- "Of course I want to retire; I have had at least 26 Farewell Tours, figuring each would be my last. I wanted to retire but, unfortunately, the man who delivers the bills to my house every day didn't."

- "I had very few altercations during all these years on the midway. Maybe the largest was the afternoon I was on my way to the carnival office with a bag of money and I stopped off at the cookhouse for a cup of coffee. One of my employees came and started getting smart with some of the others and I got up and suggested he cool off a bit and then he smarted off to me. My first instinct was to hit him upside the head with the bag of money, which I did, knocking him down. On his way down, he broke his glasses and that was bad because he had to drive one of our trucks that night. So I had to take him downtown, and it cost me $100 to get him a new pair of glasses."

- "Harry and I never displayed our private and personal life. Others around us, including family, knew of our true relationship and it was never discussed or was there anything ever made of it."

- "I don't think I brought anything new or different to the industry. There was not as much innovation in my life as there should have been."

- "I never meant to live in Gibtown; it just happened. We would stop on the way to Miami and liked it. I always wanted to be in Houston."

- "You have no right to judge or criticize (he said to a reporter) until you've sat up all night with the fat lady in a hospital room or consoled a brokenhearted dwarf or helped an armless girl change a flat tire at the side of a muddy road. Only then will you begin to understand."

- "When this book becomes a movie, my life should be played by Leonardo DiCaprio and Clint Eastwood would make a great Chris."

- "I once asked Obert Miller, who with his family owned the Al G. Kelly & Miller Bros. Circus, what his method of success was. He told me he believed in the 3 P's – Paint, Paper and Ponies. Paint it up to look like a circus, put up lots of paper so they know it's coming and fill it full of ponies."

- "You hear funny things almost every day. A woman came up to me after she exited the baby show and asked me if we put them in bigger bottles as they grow."

- "Another woman, after visiting the baby show, said to me that it was so sad and wondered how their little souls got out of those bottles and got to heaven."

- "My friend Johnny Meah always said that the worst two weeks any showman can experience were Christmas week and any week you played Cincinnati."

- "For a short time, while we were on the Steven's Brothers Circus (1950), I did the tight wire act with Alfredo and Cha Cha Sanchez."

- "When we had both sword swallower Patricia Zurm and the Viking Giant Johann Petursson on the show, it was a lot of fun. Patricia kept teasing him by grabbing his kilt to 'see what was under it.' Johann would run away with Patricia chasing him. It was a game they loved to play."

- "Most of all, people love a circus and they should."

- "Here is a photo of me with President Bill Clinton. I'm a Republican, but I didn't admit that to Mr. Clinton."

- "You only need two things to do this trick. First, you need a midget who's willing to let you take his head off."

- "Freaks are fascinating people to work with. They are inspiring people because they have overcome the handicaps which they were born with. In fact, 99% of them who worked for us were well adjusted and happy people because they felt they were on their own and doing something meaningful."

- "One time I went to Saudi Arabia in search of a giant said to be 10 feet tall. When I found the giant, he was about the size of a high school basketball player in the states. But to the villagers, who were small in stature, he was a giant."

- "We're the old ones now, the dinosaurs if you will."

- "We always said that the best location for a dime museum is as close to a Woolworth's as you could get."

Say What?
Jargon, Lingo, Definitions and Acronyms

This book contains many strange and somewhat mysterious words and phrases, not commonly known outside of the circus, carnival and sideshow industries. Many of them are totally strange words. Some of them are just strange uses of words we already know.

One must go way back to discover why there was a need for this strange language. In the Feb. 24, 1884 edition of New York City's *The Sun*, a reporter revealed the mystery. "In some inexplicable way the men of the sawdust arena have made unto themselves a language peculiar and to a very great degree unintelligible to the uninitiated. Those who habitually use this speech not infrequently find a serious value in the power it gives them of exchanging ideas, purposes, and warnings in [the] presence of 'outsiders' who may be hostile to them."

We suggest you dog-ear this page so you can easily refer to it as you take this journey with Ward and his fellow showmen. Here is a sampling of some of the colorful vernacular you will find in this book:

10-in-one – A sideshow that has 10 different attractions in one show under the tent. The attractions are often a combination of illusions, working acts, human oddities and freak attractions.

Annex – The area in which the blow-off takes place.

Baby Show – An attraction dedicated to exhibiting pickled punks of real baby fetuses and/or bouncers.

Backend Piece – A show or one-sided attraction used to line the back end of a carnival midway.

Bally – The spiel the talker gives is known as a bally. Often a free show takes place on the bally stage next to the talker.

Bally Stage – The platform in front of the attraction on which the bally takes place.

Banner – Pictorials on canvas or vinyl hung in front of circus and carnival sideshows depicting the wonders to be found inside.

Banner Line – The lineup of banners hung in front of the sideshow.

Blockhead – A person who shoves, pushes and hammers objects into his nose.

Blow-off – An extra attraction in a separate, closed-off area of the sideshow tent where those finished with the "regular" show can go to see an extreme act of some sort. It requires additional money.

Bouncers – Rubber babies made to substitute real babies as pickled punks. Used when displaying the real thing was outlawed or when the showman could not afford to purchase the real human punk.

Candy Butcher – A concessions salesman who vends items to those already seated at a circus.

CFA – Circus Fans of America

CHS – Circus Historical Society

Concert – An extra-admission event after the main show in a circus. In earlier days, motion pictures were big concert draws in rural areas where there were no theaters. Wrestling and big band musical shows were also popular concerts.

Dime Museum – A sideshow set up in an indoor store front containing live acts, freaks and wax museum figures or displays of oddities. Most were open year-round, such as Hubert's in New York City.

Fixer – A person on the carnival or circus who adjusts complaints and claims in a manner satisfactory to the show. He also works with and pays off local authorities so that unlawful games and exhibitions may be operated. Also known as a patch.

Freak – A human oddity, anomaly or disfigured person on exhibition in a circus or carnival sideshow. Most sideshow freaks who worked on sideshows over the years did not mind being called a freak.

Grind Tape – A pre-recorded sales pitch on an endless tape. It replaces a live bally. Sometimes used when business is slow, saving the live bally for busier times. It is usually the only type of bally on a grind show or a single-o.

Grind Show – A show or an attraction that regardless of what it exhibits grinds away hour after hour without a break. It never ceases operation and does not have a live bally. Instead, the pre-recorded tape promotes the show while the ticket sellers and the workers grind away all day long.

Half-and-Half – A human attraction claiming to be of both sexes – a hermaphrodite. Some were real, most weren't. Also called the half-man/half-woman attraction.

IAAPA – The International Association of Amusement Parks & Attractions is the world's largest trade association for the amusement park and attractions industry.

IAFE – The International Assoc. of Fairs & Expositions is the trade association for the fairs and festivals industry.

IISA – The International Independent Showmen's Association was founded in 1966 and is the largest showmen's association in the United States.

Jackpots (Jackpotting) – Showmen's stories of their former escapades, most often exaggerated. "Cuttin' up jackpots" is the expression given to swapping these stories.

Jig Show – A minstrel or a musical show featuring African-American musicians and performers. While today the term is politically incorrect, the shows were among the most popular and most attended on the midway by fairgoers of all races.

Joint – A concessions stand or booth selling food, drinks or merchandise at a circus, fair or carnival.

Jump – Moving a carnival or a show from one location to another is known as jumping. If the spot you leave is 150 miles from where you are headed, you have a "jump" of 150 miles.

Lecturer – A person who talks inside the tent about the various acts and tries to build the tip for the blow-off attraction.

OABA – The Outdoor Amusement Business Assoc. is the trade association for the North American carnival industry.

Patch – Another name for the show's fixer.

Pickled Punk – A carnival term describing human fetuses that are displayed in jars of formaldehyde. Originally they were real human fetuses, either deformed or normal specimens. Through the years, due to tougher laws, more and more pickled punks were fakes, but were usually presented as real.

Pitch – A sales concession where merchandise is sold after the salesman has given a demonstration.

Punch & Judy – A classic puppet show starring a harsh and violent Punch and his wife Judy.

Single-o – A sideshow consisting of a single attraction, such as a giant rat, the world's smallest woman, or a six-legged horse.

SLA – The Showman's League of America is a community of showmen dedicated to promoting the mutual welfare of all show people. It is the oldest showmen's association in America. Buffalo Bill Cody was its first president.

Store Show – An Indoor storefront location for live acts, oddity museums and wax museums. Often set up in busy metropolitan areas during the winter when the acts have no place else to work. Come spring, they go back on the road and the store front closes.

Talker – The person who makes a spiel from the bally stage trying to convince patrons to buy a ticket. Ward Hall is considered the best talker in the business.

Tip – The crowd that the talker attracts in front of the bally stage.

Turning the Tip – Selling tickets to the patrons gathered in front of the bally stage.

Vent Act – A performance by a ventriloquist.

Working acts – Performers who display a specific talent, such as sword swallowing and fire eating. The term is used to separate them from those born as human oddities, or freaks.

Bibliography:
Where it all Came From

Most of what appears in this book has been gleaned from multiple interviews with Ward Hall and C.M. "Chris" Christ. The sources of additional inspirations, quotes, facts, general information and background on the industry are noted below.

Albrecht, Brian E., "Blockheads and Backyard Elephants," *Cleveland Plain Dealer,* Feb. 26, 1995

Amusement Business, various news reports, May 12, 1973; Aug. 13, 1977; Dec. 20, 1980; Sept. 7, 1981

Associated Press, stories in multiple newspapers, July 31, 1977; Oct. 19, 1977; Nov. 19, 1977

Bambi the Mermaid, telephone interview, Jan. 21, 2014

Bandwagon, advertisement, "The Last Sideshow," November/December 1994

Bleau, Liz, "Taking a Bow," *Tampa Tribune,* Jan. 22, 2004

Breen, Tommy, interview at Wisconsin State Fair, July 9, 2013; interview in Tampa, Feb. 2, 2014

Bridgman, Mary, "At 128, State Fair will Become Pioneer," *Columbus Dispatch,* July 19, 1981

Burnes, Chuck, *Circus Report,* September 2009

Carlson, Raymond M., Attorney, letters to C.M. Christ, Sept. 3, 1977 and Sept. 28, 1977

Colavecchio - Van Sickler, Shannon, *St. Petersburg Times,* Feb. 6, 2004

Dallas News, "Philosophical Differences Led Fair Chief to Quit," Feb. 1988

Dallas News, "Gallagher to Manage New York State Fair," Oct. 4, 1988

Dallas News, "State Fair Appoints McKoy its President," Nov. 17, 1988

Downs, Mike, letter to Ward Hall, Sept. 15, 1975

Drimmer, Frederick, *Very Special People,* Citadel Press Book, 1991

Dufour, Lou, *Fabulous Years,* Vantage Press, New York, 1977

Edmunds, Lavinia, "Step Right Up Folks and Meet the World's Greatest Talker," *Network News,* April, 1980

English, Sunshine, interview at Wisconsin State Fair, July 9, 2013; interview in Tampa, Feb. 2, 2014

Flint, Richard, telephone interview, Jan. 23, 2014

Florida (State of), Trial Brief Case No. CA-80-000826/60-102

Gibtown, Decoy Films, 2000

Grossman, Ron, "Here's the Pitch," *Chicago Tribune,* March 3, 1994

Habeck, Larry, telephone interview, Feb, 28, 2014

Hall, Ward, video interview by Lane Talburt, July 4, 2011

Hall, Ward, *Backyard Magazine* transcript of audio interview from the 1991 CFA Convention in Natick, Mass., June, July and August, 2002

Hall, Ward, lecture, Showfolks of Sarasota Tent of the Circus Fans of America, Jan. 8, 1997

Hall, Ward, video by Lane Talburt at Circus Historical Society, June 11, 2011

Hall, Ward, "From Big Shot to Big Top to Big Flop," *Bandwagon,* January/February 1991

Hartzman, Marc, *American Sideshow,* Jeremy P. Tarcher/Penguin, New York, 2006

Holden, Stephen, *New York Times,* April 22, 1994

Horsman, Paul, *Circus Report,* July 22, 1985

Hudson, Walt, *Circus Report,* March 7, 2008

Jennings, Ron, *Sedalia Democrat,* Aug. 26, 1987

Johnson, Dick, interview in Riverview, Fla., Dec. 3, 2013; interview in Tampa, Fla., Feb. 2, 2014

Kirby, Irwin, editorial, *Amusement Business,* Aug. 20, 1977

Lake County, Ill., Circuit Court Papers, filed Aug. 16, 1977

Leagle.com, Gardner v. Johnson, No. 63665, May 31, 1984

Levenson, Randal, telephone interview, Jan. 21, 2014

Life magazine, "Carnival Town," June 1983

Lincoln Center, promotional flyer for Lincoln Center Out of Doors, July 2011

MacVicar, Jamie, *The Advance Man,* Bear Manor Media, Athens, Ga., 2010

McKennon, Joe, *A Pictorial History of the American Carnival,* (Volume three), Carnival Publishers of Sarasota, Sarasota, Fla., 1981

McKoy, Errol, email, Jan. 3, 2014

Meah, Johnny, interview in Safety Harbor, Fla., Dec. 4, 2013; interview in Tampa, Feb. 2. 2014; telephone interview, March 21, 2014

Mikell, Gary, *Savannah Morning News,* Nov. 6, 1982

Nelson, Keith, telephone interview, Nov. 2, 2013

O'Brien, Tim, "For the 18th Last Time, Hall to Take Wonders Sideshow on the Road," *Amusement Business,* Feb. 27, 1995

Osterud, Amelia Klem, *The Tattooed Lady,* Speck Press, Golden, Colo., 2009

Parkinson, Robert L., Directory of American Circuses, Circus World Museum, 2002

Pepke, Pete, "Ward Hall Begins 50th Season," *Carnival News,* June 30, 1998

Philadelphia Enquirer, May 28, 1988

Philips, Diana, interview at Showtown Lounge, Gibsonton, Fla., Feb. 3, 2014

Plastik, Mikee, email interview, Nov. 2, 2013

Polacsek, John, *Freaks, Geeks & Strange Girls,* Last Gasp Publications, San Francisco, 2004

Powell, Tom, telephone interview, March 5, 2014

Powell, Tom, *The Carnival Priest,* self-published, Nashville, Tenn., 1998

Ray, Fred Olden, *Grind Show,* American-Independent Press, 1993

Ray, Todd, email interview, March 5, 2014

Reynolds, Bobby, *The Talker – The Life and Times of the World's Greatest Carnival Sideshow Man* as told to Roy Hassett, Kindle Edition, 2011

Robbins, Todd, interview in New York City, May 2013; email interview, Jan. 31, 2014

Rose, Jim, email message, July 18, 2013

Sarasota Herald-Tribune, Jan. 26. 1978

Scott, Joy, *Shelby* (N.C.) *Star,* Oct. 2, 2001

Seattle Times, "Curtain Falling on Freak Shows," Nov. 1, 2004

Showman – The Life and Times of Ward Hall, Flood City Pictures, 2005

Slusser, Dale, *Freaks, Geeks & Strange Girls,* Last Gasp Publications, San Francisco, 2004

St. Petersburg Times, "Sideshow King revels in Heyday of Circus," Dec. 25, 2011

Stencell, A.W., *Seeing is Believing,* ECW Press, Toronto, Ont., Can., 2002

Stencell, A.W., *Circus and Carnival Ballyhoo,* ECW Press, Toronto, Ont., Can., 2010

Stuart, Red, interview at Wisconsin State Fair, July 9, 2013; interview at Florida State Fair, Feb. 3, 2014

Tampa Tribune, Aug. 3, 1977; Aug. 12, 1977

Talburt, Lane, interview in Stamford, Conn., Dec. 17, 2013

Taylor, Gordon, *Circus Report,* June 17, 1985

Taylor, James, email interview, Feb. 26, 2014; telephone interview, March 20, 2014

Taylor, James, *Shocked and Amazed! – On and Off the Midway,* Lyons Press, Guilford, Conn., 2002

Uyttebrouck, Olivier, "Show Manager not a Stereotype," *Southwest Times Record,* Fort Smith, Ark., Sept. 27, 1987

Waddell, Lynn, *Fringe Florida,* University Press of Florida, Gainesville, 2013

West, Rick, *Pickled Punks & Girlie Shows,* Schiffer Publishing, Atglen, Pa., 2011

Wolf, Buck, ABCNews.com, Nov. 18, 2000

Zajicek, Jim, interview at Florida State Fair, Feb. 3, 2014; email, Feb. 26, 2014

Acknowledgements:
Credits, Thanks and Kudos

This biography would not have happened had it not been for Ward Hall's unbounded enthusiasm for his peculiar calling and his eagerness to share his journey with the rest of us. He, along with Chris, spent countless hours answering myriad questions and teaching me about this amazing entertainment genre known as the sideshow. They opened up their hearts, souls, memories and archives to make this book possible.

A big "Thank You" goes out to:

- Sideshow operators, performers, scholars and aficionados who stepped forward to provide additional facts, stories and guidance to me through this long project. Those include: Johnny Meah, Todd Robbins, James Taylor, Harley Newman, Diana Philips, Dick Johnson, and Buck Wolf.

- The great team that edited, fact checked, and fine-tuned the manuscript: David Austin, Lane Talburt, Ralph Pierce, James Taylor, and Harley Newman.

- To the sideshow community as a whole for supporting this project by posting and reposting it on their social networks.

- Deborah Walk of the Circus Museum at the John & Mable Ringling Museum of Art in Sarasota and to Ralph Pierce and Pete Shrake at the Robert L. Parkinson Library & Research Center, Circus World Museum in Baraboo, for opening up their vast archives to me.

- To my understanding and loving wife, Kathleen O'Brien, who understood why I kept myself locked in my office for more than a year.

The front and back cover photos were taken by Andrew Brusso. He also designed the front cover and shot and edited a remarkable video of Ward and I for our Kickstarter program.

Through the years, literally thousands of photographs have been taken of Ward Hall, his shows and his performers. Most of the photos I found in the various archives and that appear in this book did not have the photographer's name attached. I tried many different ways to find the photographer of each photo in order to provide full credit, however, I was not able to credit most. Ward provided most photos to me with the assumption that they were given to him with all rights. Photographers I could identify are: Paul G. Gutheil, Diana Philips, Susan Nichols, Robert Moran, Bill Carter, R.C. Gray, Henry Rod, Robert Houston, Johnny Wise, Lawrence Victor, Ed Sullivan, and Liz Steger. To the rest of you, I apologize for not giving you proper and deserving credit. Thanks to D.B. Denholtz; Bonnie Wilpon; and John Robinson of Sideshow World, for providing additional photos and illustrations.

With the use of crowdfunding through Kickstarter, we were able to get the initial financial assistance needed to get this project off the ground. A huge thank you goes out to those who had faith in me to follow through and get this book written. Those who provided the financial help through Kickstarter are listed below:

Our All-Star team is: Jeremy Weiss, Bob Childress, the Outdoor Amusement Business Assoc., Todd Robbins, and Ivan Kotcher.

Additional participation through Kickstarter came from: Joe Burum, David Miro, D.B. Denholtz, David Kiser, Stewart Wagner, Ira West, Fred Kahl, Dennis Carollo, John Trumbower, Buck Wolf, Rachel Wayt, Meren Edna Marie King, Toni-Lee Sangastiano, Richard Vymlatil, Frank Lynch, Debra Darden-Munsell, Michael Joseph Cuneo, Adele Simons, Ian E. Rygiel, James Taylor, Leonard Martinez, Mesha Provo, James Stilianos, Michael Getlan, Gavin Mahan, David Tetrault, Steven Malloy, Dr. Brian Spencer, Red Stuart, and Johnny Meah.

Further Kickstarter help came from: Cat A. Strophoea, Reinoud van Assendelft de Coningh, David Hemsath, Vic Brisban, Jack T. Painter, Tommy Breen, Lynn Waddell, Sally Cinch, MabjustMab, Michael Kattner, Pete Genovese, Jan Gregor, Christopher Scarborough, J. Kurt Spence, Keith Nelson, Josh Sickinger, John Spitzer, Ross Greenwalt, Al D'Alfonso, Marc Hartzman, Benjamin Nemser, Don Spiro, and Eddie Garland.

It takes a village! Thanks.

Author Tim O'Brien with Ward during photo shoot, 2013.

About the Author

Tim O'Brien is a veteran photo-journalist who has chronicled the outdoor amusement business industry for more than 30 years during which time he has had more than 5,000 articles and 3,000 photos published. As senior editor of *Amusement Business* magazine for 18 years and then 10 years as a writer and public relations executive for Ripley's Believe it or Not!, Tim has traveled the world meeting and interviewing showmen of all ilk. He has written 13 books, including *The Wave Maker – The Story of Theme Park Pioneer George Millay* and *Legends – Pioneers of the Amusement Park Industry*. He is now CEO of Casa Flamingo Literary Arts, LLC, a small specialty book publisher in Nashville, Tenn. Tim is a proud graduate of The Ohio State University.

To my Readers:
Success for a writer depends on word of mouth and networking.
If you liked this book, please leave a review on Amazon.
It makes a great difference and I deeply appreciate it.
Thank you.

That's it ladies and gentlemen. You are finished.
Please close the book covers gently.
Thanks for your attention and your support.
Tell your friends about it if you liked it.
If you didn't like it, tell your friends you can't read.

Index

10-in-ones 7
20th Century Wax 169, 196
999 Eyes Freakshow & Surreal Sideshow 190

A

Adams, Alda 12
Al Dobritch Circus 121
Alexander, Sam 85-86, 118-119
Al G. Kelly & Miller Bros. Circus 4, 15, 78, 239
All American Indoor Circus 71, 75
Allen, Sandy 104
Allentown (Pa.) Fair 216
American Midway Shows 51-53
American Pickers 107
Amusements of America 213
anthropomorphic 29
Arbus, Diane 81
Arizona State Fair 113
Arkansas State Fair 106
Arnold, Floyd 20
Arnold, Tex 78, 89
Artoria 159

B

baby show 19, 49-51, 57, 74-75, 85, 112, 118, 125, 154, 163-165, 178, 239
Ballard, Dave 89, 119, 121-122
Ballentine, Carl 14
Bambi the Mermaid 220-221, 230, 243
bankruptcy 199
banner line 38-40, 57, 78, 89, 114, 141, 148, 153, 178, 214
Barent, Stanley 8, 138
Barkin, Spike 223
Barnett Bros. Circus 12
Barnum, P.T. 5, 29-30, 95-96, 101, 176
bearded lady 58, 94, 185, 203
Bejano, Emmitt 173-175
Bejano, Johnny J. 174

Bejano, Percilla 8, 104, 173-175, 205, 235
Belmont Amusement Park 85
Bennett, Barbara 159, 167, 201
Benny Fox Star Spangled Circus 46
Bergen, Edgar 21
Best, Dick 84, 90, 138, 207
Big Circus Sideshow 140, 189
Big John Strong Circus 189
Billy Burr Carnival 151
Bindlestiff Family Cirkus 214, 223
Blackwelder, Emmett 122
Breen, Tommy 106, 108, 229-231, 233, 247
Brest, Martin 103
Brisben, Dick 82, 85, 104
British Broadcast Corporation (BBC) 104
Broadway Sensations Revue 76
Broadway Theater 43
Brocton (Mass.) Fair 151
Brown, Buster 113
Brown, Fred 219
Browning, Bill 133, 157, 167, 219
Brydon, Ray Marsh 23, 147
Bunny Love 221, 230
Burkhart, Melvin 132, 151-152
burlesque 3, 7, 22, 45-46, 95, 152

C

Canadian National Exhibition (CNE) 85
Carmel, Eddie 81, 109
Carmen, Vince and Jackie 157, 177
Carnegie Hall 4, 211-213, 223
Carol, Jean 81
Casino Pier 169
Cavalcade of Amusements 56, 59, 61
Chaulkas, Bill 78, 164
Children of Forgotten Fathers 163
Christ, C.M. "Chris" 1-4, 19-22, 64-67, 97-246
Circus Ring of Fame 4, 127, 129
Circus Tihany 177, 181

Circus USA 200-202
Circus Vargas 4, 154, 196
Circus World 19, 153
Claxton, Leon 153
Clifford, Butch 109
Clyde Beatty Circus 88, 141
Clyde Beatty-Cole Bros. 4
Cole Bros. Circus 14-15
Collins, Bill 78, 91
Coney Island 5, 8, 152, 169, 175, 190-191, 221, 223, 225
Coney Island Circus Sideshow 190
Coney Island Sideshow School 169
Coney Island USA 152, 191, 223
Conklin Shows 86, 196
Connors, Harold 149
Constantine, Jack 190
Copa City Night Club 83
Cox, Charlie 141-142, 158
Crane, Larry 101, 153
Crystal Beach Park 152-153, 157
Curtis, Dave 20
Curtis, Millie 20

D

Dailey Bros. Circus 3, 15, 17-20, 23-24, 32, 40-41, 43, 53, 123, 128, 222, 227-228
David B. Endy Amusements 126
Deggeller Magic Midways 126
Deggeller Shows 116
Deno's Wonder Wheel Park 176
Deremer, Tim 190
Doran, Francis 26
Dr. Miracle's Wondercade 152, 157
DuFour, Lou 85
Duggan, Bobo Francis 149
Durks, William 125

E

Eagle, Nate 79, 93-94, 109
Eastern States Exposition 123
Eddie's Hut 133
Edwards, Mannie 90
Eifort, Hal 116, 119, 142, 188
E.K. Fernandez Circus/Carnival 4, 79, 80, 86, 177
Elitch Gardens 15

Elite Exposition 11
English, Sunshine 106, 108, 231

F

Fairchild, Joe 183
Family American Magical Entertainment Inc. (FAME) 230
Farley, Leonard 118
Feld, Irvin 104, 149, 154
Feld, Kenneth 201
Fernandez, Kane 177
Fitzgerald, Bunny 199
flat joints 52
Flint, Richard 171, 236
Florida State Fair 36, 45, 84, 90, 139, 140, 154, 156, 189, 219, 245
Florida Supreme Court 137-138
Fort Worth Fat Stock Show 114
Fossett, April 179
Frear's United Shows 25, 31, 33
Freedman, Sy 150
Fringe Florida 31, 36, 136, 140, 245
Frisco Follies 43, 45-46
Fritz, Frank 107
Froman Bros. Society Circus 70-72, 79
Fulkerson, Lorett 203, 206

G

Gallagher, Wayne 205
Garden, Dick 208
Gem City Shows 59, 62
Gene Ledel Shows 114
George Carden Circus 201
George Val George 27
Georgia National Fair 105
Giant's Camp 133
Gibsonton/Gibtown 56, 80, 102, 106-108, 121, 125, 127, 130-135, 146, 149, 164-165, 173, 175, 177, 195, 197, 204, 213, 216, 218-219, 233, 235, 244
girl shows 7, 31-32, 52-56, 59, 74-76, 161, 191, 193
girl-to-gorilla 179, 190, 214
Gladstone Exposition Shows 55
Gooding's Million Dollar Midways 59, 73, 116, 118-119, 121, 123, 142, 145, 153, 170

Gosh, Byron 71, 76
Great American Circus 200
Greater Rainbow Shows 51
Great Frederick (Md.) Fair 215
Groves, Ed 53
Groves Greater Shows 53-54, 56
Guavaween 217-218
Gypsy Hot Bloods 54, 85, 221

H

Habeck, Larry 134
half-and-half/hermaphrodite shows 26-27, 57, 227
Hall, Glen 11-13, 15-17, 20, 23, 86-88
Hall, Opal 9, 11, 155
Hall, Ward 1-246
Hames Show 113
Hankins, Doc 143-144
Harlem in Havana 153
Harley Newman's Oddity U 169
Harry and Bea Fee's Monkey Speedway 179
Harry Beck's Indoor Circus 117
Hartzman, Marc 82, 168, 247
Herriott, Johnny 171
Hicks, Tiny 81, 111
Homo the Brave – The Queer Indian Boy 22, 223
Hottle, Buff 54-55
Howard Huge – *see* Snowden, Bruce
Howdy Doody 160
Hubert's Museum 83, 125, 241
Huffington Post 168
Hunter, Charlie 27
Huston, Roy 156, 181, 193

I

Indiana State Fair 102, 119, 151
International Fair & Expositions Assoc. (IAFE) 103, 158, 178, 241
International Independent Showmen's Association (IISA) 103, 107-108, 125-128, 130, 134, 148, 154-156, 160, 177, 185, 213, 218-219, 241
Ionia (Mich.) Free Fair 177
Isis Theater 14

J

Jensen, Dean 96
Johnson, Dick 39, 102, 119, 123, 139, 141, 148, 160, 170, 216-217, 246
Jonas, Royal Flagg 137
Joy Theater 46
Judd, Billy 111-112

K

Kelly, Slim 125, 147, 151, 207
Kenn-Penn Show 142
Key City Shows 118
King, Alan 102-103
King, Jeff 103
King, Mamie and Cliff 122
King Reid Shows 123
Knight, Sunny 45
Kortes, Pete 86, 138, 142, 147, 160, 164, 207
Kotcher, Kathleen 54

L

Lakeside Amusement Park 15
LaMay, Grace 133
Larry Sunbrock's Super Colossal Wild West Show and Hollywood Thrill Show 15
Lauther, Karl 174
Lawrence Welk Show 101
Gypsy Rose Lee 45
legerdemain 29
Lentini, Frank 92, 133
Leonard, Harry 3, 23-109, 132, 203, 225, 227-228, 238
LeRoy, Doc 35
Levenson, Randal 159
Lewis Bros. Circus 9
Libbert, Jack 199
Lincoln Center 4, 223, 244
Link, Rod 73, 116, 186, 199, 227
Lone Star Shows 56
Long, Jimmy 187, 214, 217
Loyal-Repensky European Circus 60
Lulling, Freddie 154
Lupage, Bertie 27

M

MacGregor, Betty 93-94, 149-150
MacValley, Douglas 179, 181
MacVicar, Jamie 30
Madison Square Garden 4, 65, 79, 81, 84, 93, 99, 101, 109, 111, 117-118
Magic on Parade 4, 157-158
Manzini, Mario 81
Maxwell, Bob 179, 183
Mayhood, Duke 145
McCarthy, Monsignor Robert J. 206
McKennon, Joe 104, 176, 200
McKoy, Errol 205
McNeal, Scotty 147-148
Meadowlands Fair 5, 214, 233
Meah, Johnny 31, 39, 96, 135, 171, 177, 181, 183, 200, 215, 217, 239, 246, 247
Megerle Shows 112
Mendelsohn, Bernie 155
Merchants Free Circus 76
Meyer, Dan 217
Miller, Jennifer 223, 225
Miller, Obert 78, 239
Million Dollar Doll 67, 85, 86, 90, 94, 209
Minnesota State Fair 188, 220-221, 233
Missouri State Fair 173
Monseu, Stephanie 214
Moody, Al and Barbara 121
Murphy, Ed 199
Murray, Ken 90, 93, 97, 99, 102
Museum of the American Carnival 107-108, 134-135

N

Nebraska State Fair 91
Nelson, Keith 214, 223, 247
Nerveless Nocks 88
Newman, Glen and Billy 113-114
Newman, Harley 35, 169, 216, 246
New York World's Fair 110
Nolan Amusements 94, 111

O

Ohio State Fair 144, 159, 165, 170, 177-181, 193, 195
Orpheum Theater 13
Outdoor Amusement Business Assoc. (OABA) 4, 127, 138, 177, 247
Owens, Frances Lee 58

P

Penniman, Richard 18
Pennsylvania Fair 204-205, 213
Percilla the Monkey Girl – *see* Bejano, Percilla
Perky Perkins 21-22, 52, 79
Petursson, Johann 8, 104, 149-150, 239
Philips, Diana 132, 134, 152, 175, 246, 247
pickled punks 7, 30, 170, 219, 240, 242
Pike, Estelline 81
Plastik, Mikee 231
Polacsek, John 39
Poobah – *see* Terhurne, Norbert "Pete"
Porter, Marge 153, 177
Powell, Tom 156, 167
Pugh, Bobby 179
Pugh Shows 179
Punch and Judy 24-25, 52, 71, 79, 89
Pygmy Village 4, 65, 90-92, 94-95, 102, 111, 113-114

Q

Queen, Joe 83

R

Rand, Sally 45-46, 95, 102
Ray, Todd 37, 108, 190, 229
Reagan, Dolly 104, 147-148
Reed, Doreen 122
Reeder, Jamal Tyrone 149
Reithoffer Shows 201, 204-205, 213
Reynolds, Bobby 35, 81, 197
Ringling Bros. and Barnum & Bailey Circus 4, 19, 30, 60-61, 65, 79-81, 85, 87-88, 93, 99, 101, 104, 109, 117, 123, 130, 149-150, 153-154, 201, 208, 246

Rio Theater 43
Ripley, Robert 95
Rivera, Doc 107
Rivers, Johnny 179
Rivoli Burlesque 92
Robbins, Milt 16-20, 35, 111, 122, 149, 222
Robbins, Todd 5-6, 36, 152, 175, 216, 222, 225, 246-247
Rogers, Bernie 93-94
Rogers Bros. Circus 25, 90, 158
Roller Bros. Circus 197
Rose, Jim 229
Royal American Shows 45, 61, 84, 153, 193
Rush, Bud 122
Russell Bros. Circus 14

S

Saigon Doll 67, 85, 209
Sarasota, Fla. 4, 127, 244
Schlitzie 118-119, 174
Seal Bros. Circus 46-47, 50
Searles, George 26, 32, 57, 61, 227
Sedlmayr, Carl 45
Seminar of the Sideshow Arts 22
Sensations of 1958 78
Sensations of 1959 78
Shaheen's Fun-O-Rama 196
Sheets, Billy 154
Shepherd, Sam 111-112
Shocked and Amazed! 3, 54, 215, 245
Short, Albert 122
Showmen's League of America (SLA) 116, 242
Showtown Restaurant and Lounge 133
Sideshow Gathering 130, 216-217
Sideshows by the Seashore 176, 190, 223
Simons, Leonard 90, 158, 199
Slusser, Dale 39
Smithsonian Institution 35, 95, 128, 171, 173, 236
Smith Wonder Shows 118
Snowden, Bruce 105, 159, 166-167, 213
South Carolina State Fair 145
Southern Valley Shows 56
South Florida Fair & Exposition 169

Stapf, Lowell 145
State Fair of Texas 145-146, 158-159, 165, 170, 196, 198, 201, 203, 205
Steinmetz, Duke 116-117
Steven's Bros. Circus 48-49, 53
Strates, James E. 151
Strong, John 189
Stuart, John "Red" 106, 108, 129, 206, 231, 247
Stump, Gladia 122
Sugar Brown family 19
Summerfest, Boston 150-151
Summerfest, Milwaukee 121, 161
Surtees, George 119
Sutton, Whitey 151, 207
Sword Swallowers Assoc. International 217
Synrex, Jack 119, 123, 177
Syres, Gary 219-221

T

Tabor Theater 14
Talburt, Lane 37, 127, 143, 221, 230, 243-244, 246
Talburt, Martha 69
Tassel, Barney 54, 56
Tate's Curiosity Shop 107, 114
Taylor, James 3, 7-8, 96, 105, 207, 215, 246-247
Tennessee State Fair 59
Tennessee Valley Amusements 76
Terhurne, Norbert "Pete" 4, 27, 36, 62-69, 73-123, 138, 149, 166, 168, 177, 184, 203-207, 213, 218, 224
Thorne, Spain 90
Three-card Monte 52-53
Tihany 177, 181, 195
Toby Tyler Circus 4, 203
Tomaini, Jeanie 8, 133
Tomaini, Al 125, 133
Tom Packs Circus 77
Trower, John 104

V

Valentine, Henry 75, 144, 170
Vargas, Cliff 154-155

vaudeville 3, 8, 14, 21, 152, 190
Venice Beach (Calif.) Freakshow
    37, 108, 190, 229
ventriloquism/ventriloquist 3, 21-23,
    25, 79, 81, 89, 92, 160, 223, 242
Verelli, Natalie 106
Vitka, Mike 107

W

Waddell, Lynn 31, 36, 136, 140, 247
Wallace and Clark Circus 50
Westchester County Fair 175, 233
Western Fair (Ont.) 86
West Virginia State Fair 201
W.G. Wade Shows 71, 73
William T. Collins Show 78, 83,
    88, 91
Winters, Jo Ann 149
Wisconsin State Fair 188, 231, 233,
    243, 245
Wolf, Buck 135, 168, 246-247
Wolfe, Mike 107
Wondercade 4, 152, 157, 181, 183,
    193, 195
Wonder, Mush 35
Woods Famous Show 25
World Championship Wrestling 205
World of Mirth Shows 116
World of Pleasure Shows 73-75, 116
World of Today Shows 62
World of Wax 177
World of Wonders 4-5, 36, 38, 64,
    104, 106, 108, 136, 168, 173,
    175, 189-190, 205, 213, 221,
    229, 231, 233
World's Fair Freaks &
    Attractions Inc. 117
Wynne, Ken 169

Y

York, Dennis 190

Z

Zajicek, Jim 139-140, 189-190, 245
Zigun, Dick 152, 191
Zurm, Patricia 122, 123

www.ingramcontent.com/pod-product-compliance
Ingram Content Group UK Ltd.
Pitfield, Milton Keynes, MK11 3LW, UK
UKHW021314180426
11947UKWH00015B/1213